Letters to Mary

A Missionary Writes Home
from New Guinea, 1959–1963

PAMELA
SHAFFER

outskirts
press

DEDICATION

To my husband and children, Warren, Zachary, and Leah, the best and dearest in my life, and to my parents, Felix and Angela Beilman Schmidt, with my love and gratitude.

ACKNOWLEDGMENTS

I am greatly indebted to Doris Wellbrock Schmidt, without whose work of organizing and preserving the letters this project would not have been possible and to Fr. Blaine Burkey, O.F.M. Cap., for his important history of the beginnings of the Capuchin Franciscan Mission in Papua New Guinea. Also, my thanks go to Sandra Werth, for her skill in digitizing the letters and photos, to Sandra G. Ruelas, for her typing skills, and to Chris Hadley, at Northwestern Printers, for all her help and encouragement.

TABLE OF CONTENTS

INTRODUCTION

MONSIGNOR AND, EVENTUALLY, Bishop Firmin Martin Schmidt grew up in the village of Catharine, Kansas. The youngest of eight children, Martin was born on October 12, 1918, to Raymond and Sophia Karlin Schmidt. Raymond made a living as a farmer and owner of a general store in Catharine. Raymond and Sophia instilled in their children a deep religious faith and a strong work ethic. Like his other siblings, Martin worked hard, in Catharine and on the farm, which was eight miles northeast of the little town. Unlike some of his older brothers, Martin completed school beyond the eighth grade. He graduated from St. Joseph's Military Academy and St. Joseph's College, a private Catholic secondary school and junior college for boys, in Hays, Kansas. This school was co-administered by the Capuchin Franciscan priests and U.S. Army officers, who offered a junior Reserve Officer Training Corps (ROTC) program. In high school, Martin showed a strong intelligence and an aptitude for learning. An article published in June 1971, in the *Hays Daily News*, tells of the celebration of the 25th anniversary of Bishop Firmin Martin Schmidt's ordination as a priest. Fr. Blaine Burkey, O.F.M., Capuchin, writes that from 1932-36, Martin attended high school, excelling in academics and athletics. In fact, Martin Schmidt "won his class's medal for scholarship all six years of high school and junior college, and had been a three-year letterman in football, basketball and track. In addition, he won the school's highest award, The Citizenship Medal and was lieutenant colonel of the cadet battalion."[1]

After he graduated from St Joseph College, in 1936, he entered the seminary of the Capuchin Fathers in Cumberland, Maryland, the same order of Franciscan Friars Minor that served the Catholic parishes in Ellis County, Kansas. He added the name Firmin to his given name and was ordained a Priest of the Order of Friars Minor Capuchin, on June 2, 1946. He earned a doctorate in sacred theology from Catholic University of America, in 1951. The title of his dissertation was "The Resurrection of the Body according to Tertullian," an early Christian apologist that lived in the second and third centuries C.E.[2] In 1953, Fr. Firmin was appointed President of Capuchin College, and three years later, he became a member of the board of governors of the Capuchin Province of St. Augustine. In 1959, he was appointed Prefect Apostolic of the Capuchin Mission in the Southern Highlands of Papua New Guinea.[3] Theological scholar though he was, he would leave the U.S. to serve as the chief administrator of the Capuchin mission in Papua New Guinea.

The trajectory of Martin's life was very much shaped by his community, a German-speaking immigrant group known as the Volga Germans, who began arriving from Russia in 1876, on the plains of Western Kansas. The area had been chosen for settlement because the groups of immigrants were farmers, and the land of western Kansas resembled that near the Volga River, in Russia, from which they had come. After arriving, the different groups of Volga Germans established villages in Ellis County, one of which was Catharine. Deeply

---

1   Blaine Burkey, O.F.M. Cap., "Bishop to Celebrate 25th Anniversary of Ordination," *Hays Daily News.* June 3, 1971.

2   Blaine Burkey, *Only the Beginnings: Commemorating the coming of the Capuchins and Their Co-Workers to the Southern Highlands of Papua New Guinea.* (Denver: St. Conrad Archives Center, 2016), 124.

3   Burkey, "Bishop to Celebrate 25th Anniversary of Ordination," *Hays Daily News,* June 3, 1971.

religious, wanting to carry on their religious faith, and recognizing the importance of education for their children, the group met weekly for communal prayer and started a school. The prayer leader was Jacob Schmidt, Martin's great grandfather, known as "Der Schulmeister," who also served as the school teacher, "catechist, choirleader, organist, postmaster, and genealogist."[4]

Following the arrival of the Volga Germans in Ellis County, in 1876, Fr. Adolph Wibbert, from Salina, arrived to minister to them. However, church officials from the Kansas diocese, headquartered at Leavenworth, knew that additional priests who spoke German were needed to minister to the newly-arrived immigrants.

Providentially, several years earlier, in 1873, three German priests had arrived in Pittsburgh, Pennsylvania, from Bavaria, to set up a foundation of Capuchin Franciscan Friars. According to the website "Capuchin Friars: Province of St. Augustine," the religious order had been founded in the sixteenth century in Italy. The founders wished to emulate the life and works of St. Francis, who had lived in the twelfth and thirteenth centuries. As the Capuchin Franciscan Order flourished in succeeding centuries, its goal always was and continued to be to serve the poor and to live simply, following a life of poverty, chastity, and obedience.[5]

To address the need for German-speaking priests, the Leavenworth Diocese officials contacted the Rev. Hyacinth Epp, Order of Friars Minor Capuchin (O.F.M. Cap.), the head of the group of Capuchins in Pittsburgh. The diocesan officials implored the Reverend Hyacinth to send German-speaking priests to Kansas to take care of the spiritual needs of the newly-arrived Volga Germans. After hearing from the Leavenworth diocese, Fr. Hyacinth permitted two German-speaking priests from the Pittsburgh Province to set out for Kansas. Fr. Matthew

---

4   Blaine Burkey, ed. *"Schoolmaster" Schmidt and his "Family Album."* (Hays, KS: Thomas More Prep/Marian), 1986. 1.

5   Capuchin Friars: Province of St. Augustine, accessed June 23, 2014. http://www. capuchin.com

Hau, O.F.M, Cap., and Fr. Anastasius Mueller, O.F.M., Cap., arrived in west-central Kansas in May 1878, with a plan to serve all the small settlements in Ellis County. However, when Fr. Matthew died of cholera soon after his arrival, Fr. Joseph Calasanz Mayershofer, O.F.M., Cap. came from Pittsburgh to the Volga German settlements to take Fr. Matthew's place.[6]

With priests having arrived, and fostering their strong religious faith, the Volga German immigrants eventually built native limestone churches by hand, with the workers at times endangering their lives to build the tall spires that still grace those plains. Their faith was passed on to succeeding generations and is certainly evident in the number of individuals who dedicated their lives to religious work. As of 1986, the progeny of Jacob Schmidt ("Der Schulmeister") and his wife Anna, included "a Capuchin bishop, five Capuchin priests, a diocesan priest, a Dominican sister, two Precious Blood sisters, a St. Joseph sister, a sister of Notre Dame, and seventeen St. Agnes sisters—including a former general superior and a former general vicar."[7]

Another commonality among the Volga Germans in Ellis County was their large families, certainly helpful in the occupation of farming. For example, the marriage in 1901 of Bishop Firmin's parents, Raymond (a grandson of Jacob and Anna Schmidt) and Sophia Karlin, produced seven sons and one daughter: Jerome, Constantine, Felix, Francis, Aloysius, Joseph, Mary, and, as mentioned above, Martin (Fr. Firmin, OFM, Cap.).[8] The family of another grandchild of Jacob Schmidt, Anna Schmidt (Raymond's sister), and her husband, Frank E. Karlin, consisted of fifteen children: Laura (Sr. Mary Catherine, Congregation of the Sisters of St. Agnes—C.S.A.); Constance (Sr. Marcella, C.S.A.);

---

6   Debra Schmeidler, Myra Staab, Pam Schmidt, Dolores Schmeidler, Glenda Schuetz, ShirleySchmidt, Lawrence Schmeidler, Fr. Michael Suchnicki, Emery Schmidt, eds. *St. Catherine Church: 100 Years, 1892-1992.* (Hays, KS: Northwest Printers, 1992), 17-18.

7   Burkey, *"Schoolmaster" Schmidt and his "Family Album."* 2.

8   Debra Schmeidler, Dolores Schmeidler, Glenda Schuetz, Emory Schmidt, Christine Schmidt-Blagrave, eds. *A Genealogy Collection of Parishioners: St. Catherine Church; St. Severine Church,* (1998), Hays, Kansas, 178.

twins Isabella and Teckla; Alvin; Sylvia (Sr. Lois, C.S.A.); Germaine (Sr. Francis Ann, C.S.A.); Benno; Irvin (Fr. Paulinus, O.F.M. Cap.); Francis; Anna (Sr. Anne, C.S.A); Eugene; Wilfric; Marne; and Cletus. As is apparent, six of the fifteen children of the family entered the religious life, five as nuns and one ordained a priest.[9]

LETTER WRITER

In 1940, when Martin Schmidt left his home in Catharine, Kansas, to enter the Capuchin Franciscan Religious Order in Cumberland, Maryland, he began to write letters home regularly. Throughout his preparation for the priesthood, his ordination as a priest in 1946, and through the years as a professor at Capuchin College in Washington, D.C., he wrote letters to his family. In fact, nineteen years later, in 1959, having just been notified of his appointment as Prefect Apostolic, he wrote a letter to inform his mother and sister of the great honor that had been conferred upon him. With this appointment, he agreed to serve as the chief administrator of the Capuchin mission in the Southern Highlands of Papua New Guinea. Accordingly, Sophia, his mother, and his sister Mary, received a letter, dated April 26, 1959, an excerpt of which began as follows:

Dear Mother and Mary,

I'm writing this letter in confirmation of my telephone call of yesterday. Undoubtedly, by this time the news has been spread of my appointment, but I want to add a few details. First of all, I should like to quote the telegram that I received from the Apostolic Delegate in Sydney. It reads "I officially communicate that His Holiness Pope John XXIII has deigned to appoint you Right Reverend Firmin Schmidt Prefect Apostolic of Mendi, Papua, New Guinea. Please accept my heartfelt congratulations, and assurance of my prayers for success in your important Mission – Archbishop Carboni, Apostolic Delegate."

9   Debra Schmeidler, et.al. (1998), Hays, Kansas, 56.

Really this appointment as Prefect Apostolic confers a very high honor. But corresponding to the honor is the great responsibility. I could think of reasons why I am not deserving of this position, but now that the appointment has been made, I know that in a short time I will become completely dedicated to that work. While I'm aware of the problems and obstacles involved in this assignment, I am delighted and thrilled. I must admit it was a real shock at first; but after I recovered somewhat I gradually came to realize that this is undoubtedly one of the finest things that ever happened to me.

In short, the letter Fr. Firmin received in 1959 was the beginning of a whole new life for the theological scholar. From teaching theology to priests in formation, he began his new assignment as the head of a mission in the Southern Highlands of Papua New Guinea. He served six years as Prefect Apostolic of the Capuchin Mission in Papua New Guinea. Then, in 1965, Monsignor Firmin was ordained a bishop, the first bishop of the newly-formed Diocese of Mendi, in Papua New Guinea. Subsequently, he served as its head until he retired in 1995. After he retired, he returned to the States and lived in the Hays, Kansas, area, at St. Joseph's Friary and St. John's Rest Home. He passed away on August 4, 2005, at the age of 86.

After his appointment as Prefect Apostolic, Firmin Martin Schmidt continued to be a prolific letter writer, writing hundreds of letters to Mary from Papua and other locations. As noted above, Mary was the only daughter born into a family of seven sons. Though she had limited formal education beyond grade school, she was intelligent, with an engaging personality, and took a lively interest in the world and everything around her. She never married and chose to remain in the family home in Catharine, taking care of her mother Sophia as she aged. When Sophia died, Mary took the job as a cook at the local Catharine grade school, preparing weekday lunches for the students there. Mary had always had a strong, enduring bond with her brothers, including Monsignor Firmin. Thus, it was natural for him to continue to carry on a correspondence with her as he carried out his new assignment.

Although the letters he wrote were addressed to Mary, Monsignor Firmin knew they would be shared among his brothers, sisters-in-law, cousins, nieces, nephews, and friends. In short, besides Mary, a group of relatives and other interested individuals in the Catharine area made up his audience. Accordingly, he writes about events and activities in Papua that he thought would interest them. The letters reveal characteristics of his personality: his signature quirks, wit, and sense of humor. The letters also reveal Bishop Firmin's strong faith, habits of thought and personal traits, keen interest in events related to his family, and responses to life in Papua New Guinea and events in the world.

Often consisting of one-to-two, single-spaced, typed pages, the letters included here are filled with details of his daily life and the challenges he faces as the newly-appointed head of a Catholic mission. He describes progress being made at Mendi and at other main stations. He also tells of trips to out stations to administer the sacrament of Confirmation and visits with priests and staff. The letters reveal his total commitment and dedication to the success of the Mission. By consulting the Capuchin missionaries already in Papua, he comes to recognize and address the needs of the Mission. He makes efforts to secure sufficient staff, both religious and lay missionaries. He also expands the Mission where possible, by establishing more main stations and out stations in the Southern Highlands.

Informative and engaging, Monsignor Firmin's letters are of religious, historical, and anthropological interest. They are written in a somewhat formal tone and organized in a generally predictable pattern. The letters frequently begin with a statement of appreciation for and comments about letters from Mary and other relatives, along with mention of any events in the Catharine area. He may also include comments about the weather in New Guinea's Southern Highlands and in Western Kansas. Most often, he will describe his work agenda for the next week and beyond, including possible visits to Mission stations.

Typically, the letter continues with an account of progress made at the Capuchin Mission at Mendi, including events and activities related to the schools and the school children. Finally, he may tell an anecdote about the natives whom he encounters frequently or recount a story told to him by other Mission staff. Readers may notice that Monsignor Firmin's word use in the letters occasionally includes terms that suggest to today's readers a Western colonial attitude and condescension toward the natives. One must keep in mind that in Papua, these terms were typical of the casual speech of Australians with whom Monsignor Firmin came in contact. In the early 1960s, Westerners were much less self-conscious about using condescending or racist terms.

Editor's note:

My uncle, Monsignor Firmin wrote many letters between 1959 and 1995, not just to Mary, but to other relatives and friends, including priests and other religious. Fortunately, the letters written to Mary from 1959 to 1972 were saved, organized, and preserved by Doris Wellbrock Schmidt, my sister-in-law. My mother, Angela Beilman Schmidt, requested that she preserve them. For this book, I chose fifty-five letters, a limited selection of those written between Fall 1959, when Monsignor arrived in Papua, and Fall 1963, when he left New Guinea to attend the Second Vatican Council in Rome. The letters highlight the variety of his experiences and the notable progress made in the Capuchin Mission.

The letters included here are his own words, with only minor occasional editorial changes. Unless otherwise indicated, the letters were written from the Mother of Divine Shepherd Friary, at Mendi, Southern Highlands, Papua, New Guinea. Through publishing this selection of letters, I wish to make known to a wider audience an historic, first-person account from Monsignor Firmin Martin Schmidt, in his position as the head of a Catholic Mission in Papua New Guinea.

Fr. Firmin Schmidt (second from the right) with Sophia and Raymond Schmidt, his parents, Tommy and Phyllis, his nephew and niece, in a wheat field on the family farm (circa 1949).

Left to right: Mary, Raymond, Fr. Firmin, and Sophia Schmidt, on the day of Raymond and Sophia's 50th wedding celebration, in Catharine, Kansas, 1952

Formal Photo, taken on the occasion of Msgr. Firmin M. Schmidt's appointment as Prefect Apostolic of the Capuchin Mission at Mendi, Papua New Guinea.

Formal Photo, taken on the occasion of Msgr. Firmin M. Schmidt's appointment as Prefect Apostolic of the Capuchin Mission at Mendi, Papua New Guinea.

Back row, left to right: Aloysius, Joseph, Severin, Francis, and Felix; front row, left to right, Mary, Monsignor Firmin, his mother, Sophia, and Constantine.

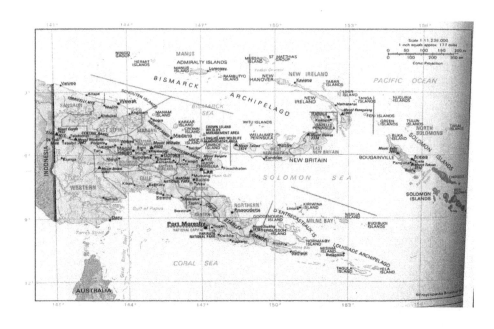

Map of Papua New Guinea, Encyclopedia Britannica, 15th ed., 2007.

LETTERS

Chapter 1

APRIL 1959–SEPTEMBER 1960
A NEW LAND, NEW PEOPLE,
AND BUILDING A MISSION

Capuchin College
4121 Harewood Rd, N.E.
Washington 17, D.C.
26 April 1959
Dear Mother and Mary,

I'm writing this letter in confirmation of my telephone call of yesterday. Undoubtedly, by this time the news has been spread of my appointment, but I want to add a few details. First of all, I should like to quote the telegram that I received from the Apostolic Delegate in Sydney. It reads: "I officially communicate that His Holiness Pope John XXIII has deigned to appoint you Right Reverend Firmin Schmidt Prefect Apostolic of Mendi, Papua, New Guinea. Please accept my heartfelt congratulations, and assurance of my prayers for success in your important Mission – Archbishop Carboni, Apostolic Delegate"

Really this appointment as Prefect Apostolic confers a very high honor. But corresponding to the honor is the great responsibility. I could think of reasons why I am not deserving of this position, but now that the appointment has been made, I know that in a short time I will become completely dedicated to that work. While I'm aware of the problems and obstacles involved in this assignment, I am delighted and thrilled. I must admit it was a real shock at first; but after I recovered somewhat, I gradually came to realize that this is undoubtedly one of the finest things that ever happened to me.

The position of a Prefect Apostolic is something like a Bishop in a diocese, except that the "Diocese" or prefecture is not very highly organized. It is the task of the Prefect Apostolic to develop and organize the church in the prefecture. The Prefect Apostolic as a matter of fact can do just about everything that a Bishop does, except confer major orders. The title is, according to the Canonists, and the telegrams I have been getting from Bishops: Right Reverend Monsignor. Also, regulations require me to change my garb to something very similar to a Bishop's. Of course I'm not going to worry about that now. Someone from Pittsburgh called me yesterday and offered to provide all the regalia for me. I'll probably get that shortly before or after I leave for my assignment. I'm sure I won't have it on my visit next week.

Capuchin College was a scene of joy Saturday morning. After I got the telegram and had notified the Provincial, I had one of the Fathers read it to all the students. They just about raised the roof with their cheers. Everyone came to extend his congratulations. The friars here seem to be as thrilled with this appointment as I am. I gave the boys the rest of the day off, and declared Monday a Mission Day and a free day.

I have no idea when I will have to leave for New Guinea. It probably will not be for a few months. Certainly, I am planning a visit to Kansas in addition to my visit next week. I hope these few words will help you to understand at least somewhat my new position.
Your devoted son, brother, Fr. Firmin

~~~

Capuchin Mission
Dec. 7, 1959
Dear Mother and Mary,

I hope all of you are coming along as well as ever. I was intending to omit this letter since I am planning to get the rest of Christmas mail out this week. I sent some Christmas cards by ordinary, surface mail at the end of October. The post office simply set that date and we presume their estimate was accurate. However, I got out only about half my mail at that time. I was in Port Moresby at the time. In spite of my plan to send Christmas letters this week I thought I might precede them with a little summary of my activities the last few days.

As I had mentioned in my last letter, I went to Tari on Thursday (Dec. 3) and stayed there until Sunday. Tari is about a half hour by plane to the west and a little north. Fr. Paul, Berard and Brother Mark are stationed there. Tari is one of the most developed main stations. From the main station at Tari there have been established at least ten outstations, taken care of mainly by Fr. Berard. My visit at Tari was rather pleasant. The people gave me as fine a reception as I received anywhere thus far. My first day at Tari I devoted to inspecting the main station. On my second day I went to an outstation about eight miles distant. I had a choice of walking, riding on a tractor, or taking a motorcycle. I chose the motorcycle. This was the first ride I had on one of these in about twenty-five years. The last time I rode one, Al and I had somewhat of a mishap. I think we got into a fresh graded road at the time. Anyway, I managed all right, and really surprised myself in view of the fact that the road wasn't very smooth in spots. I went to the outstation mainly to see the advisability of acquiring a 30-acre strip of adjoining land. We found the natives friendly all the way. At a few places we stopped and spoke with them with interpreters.

Saturday (Dec. 5) was another memorable day. In the morning the school boys had an excellent program for me. It lasted a good half hour. After the program I received a number of gifts—six home-made arrows, a home-made fancy frame with a picture of the Sacred Heart (made by one of the native teachers), a ceremonial (sing-sing) emblem, and a small cotton handbag made by the Papuan wife of one of the native teachers. I might send one or the other of these small things to you sometime in the future.

In the afternoon on Saturday I baptized three natives—Firmin Pandigo, and Joseph Ango, and John (I don't remember the last name). Firmin and Joseph are two fine young fellows about the age of sixteen. Both have completed the fourth grade and are quite intelligent. They speak English well. John is the month-old son of a native Catholic couple. The father of this child is the cook at Tari. By the way he is really an excellent cook. After the Baptism I gave a talk to the large crowd that was present. An interpreter translated it into the native language. The church was almost filled. In the evening the father (a pagan) of Joseph had a feast for the newly-baptized—including a pig-kill, etc.

On Sunday I had the main Mass at 9 o'clock. The crowd was so large we had the Mass outside. I am sure there were more than 400 in attendance. At that Mass Firmin Pandigo and Joseph Ango received their first Holy Communion. They were dressed neatly in white lap-laps and white shirts, just the same way they were dressed for their Baptism the day before. Besides these two first communicants about thirty others went to Communion. The people observed fairly good order at the Mass. The women were on one side, and the men on the other. The school boys were in the front. These led the rest of the congregation in prayers and in singing.

Their singing was surprisingly good. To keep order in the congregation, Fr. Paul appointed two ushers. These are two of the native men. They wear a special sash and carry a stick. They really keep an eye on everyone. No one dares to move. I suppose they would beat up a person if he caused any disturbance. I think they have them well trained by this time. At least there seemed to have been little or no disturbance, with the exception of the crying of a few children. Besides the men and women, boys and girls, the pigs also have a place in the congregation. Usually, the women have them on a rope. It's a bit of a distraction at first, but a person soon gets used to that. At both Tari and Kagua, the women often bring the pigs along to church. There were a couple of pigs present when I baptized the three natives at Tari on Saturday. A number of pictures were taken at the services at Tari. I hope to obtain copies of them. I meant to mention that a complete roll (50 ft.) of 8 mm. movie was taken of my visit to Kagua. I will have it developed, and if it turns out well, I hope to send it on to you eventually. That will take at least three months by the time you will receive it.

Yesterday all the missionaries came to Mendi for the retreat which started last night. It will close on Friday a.m. We hope to have a fine get-together on Friday and Saturday before they return to their respective stations.

Assuring a special remembrance in my prayers and daily Masses, I remain,
Your devoted son, brother, Msgr. Firmin

～

17 Feb. 1960
Dear Mother and Mary,

Your letter of Feb. 11 arrived this morning. That's really excellent service. Many thanks for the news. As you surmised, the fudge sent at Christmas time has still not arrived here in Mendi. There is still a chance that it may come. I'm glad you were informed about Fr. Otmar's and Brother Mark's attempt to come to Hays. I'm sure they'll get to Catherine sometime in spring. I still have not had a letter from Fr. Otmar, but he sent a cablegram telling us that the two young Fathers, Timon and Benjamin were assigned to New Guinea. Of course, we expected that. You met both of these Fathers last August when we had a banquet on the farm at Felix and Angela's. I'm writing today because I'm scheduled to leave for Tari early tomorrow morning. I'm going to have my first Confirmations there on Sunday, Feb. 21. I intend to return to Mendi again on Monday, Feb. 22. I used my pontifical equipment, mitre and all, the other day when I consecrated my chalice. I'll have some pictures taken at Tari, and eventually send them to you.

Yesterday I had another unique experience here, namely attending a huge sing-sing. I described the sing-sing I saw here at Mendi on Jan. 1 and 2. I thought that had been big. As a matter of fact, the one here at Mendi in January was only a very slight sing-sing in comparison with the one I saw yesterday. I have no idea how many thousands took part in this. According to my estimate it was at least ten times the size of the one here at Mendi.

This latest sing-sing actually lasted for a full week. Yesterday was the final day. It took place at "One" (two syllables), about five miles north of here. Fr. Gregory and I drove up in a Landrover. All along the five-mile route we saw large groups of natives heading for the sing-sing grounds. When we got within a mile of the place, we had to park the Landrover, and walk the rest of the way because the place was just swarming with natives, and we didn't want to run over any. It was with difficulty that we got through the crowd and finally arrived at the "Tambaran" House," the center of the activities. (I'll explain the tambaran later.) Even from a distance we had seen the smoke of the fires used for roasting the pigs. As we came closer, we could smell the roasted pigs. The smell wasn't very sweet. I don't know how many hundreds of pigs were slaughtered for this occasion. A conservative estimate, according to our native interpreters and guides, placed the number at least over 300. When we got to the center of the activities all the pigs were in the process of being roasted. They do this by building trenches, fill them with hot coals or ashes, put the pigs on top and between them, and seal it with leaves and all kinds of greens. The odor was not too pleasant. I don't know what was worse, the odor of the roasted pigs, or the natives smeared with grease. The trenches with the pigs extended over hundreds of yards. We were there in the vicinity from 10-11 in the morning.

I suppose they started to eat at about three in the afternoon. I know it extended way into the night. In every direction from us there were thousands of natives, dancing and singing their monotonous pieces. Their make-up consisted mainly of dark or black paint, covered with oil or grease. There were only a few with bright colors. We took a few colored pictures. I hope they turn out well. But any one picture could only have a very small fraction of the huge growd. Some of the people there, we heard, came as far as Kutubu, which is at least one week's walking distance. As we walked through the crowded area, we couldn't help but bump into some of those oil-covered natives. It took me a while to wash off the oil from one of my hands, where I had scraped against a native.

The purpose of this sing-sing was to honor and placate the Tambaran. Tambaran, in general, means a spirit, and usually of the ancestors. They have good tambarans, bad tambarans, and tambarans that are partially good and partially bad. This sing-sing was for the last, partially good and partially bad tambaran. At a certain place, in the center of the sing-sing grounds, a house for the tambaran is erected. Only a few of the men are allowed inside. It is a sort of a sacred place, especially if the tambaran is a good one. According to the natives, all evil is caused by the tambaran. When someone gets sick or dies, the natives blame the tambaran. At a sing-sing like this one at One, the idea of killing the pigs, pouring the blood over the tambaran stone, and dancing, is to placate the tambaran or get on the good side of him. Most of the natives really have very little to do with the tambaran as such. Only a few of the men, the chiefs, are concerned with the tambaran.

For this sing-sing at One, the natives for miles and miles around prepared for over three years. Over three years ago the tambaran house was built. Next, they built long houses in the vicinity, where some of the natives can sleep while preparing for and while taking part in the sing-sing. When I say long house, I mean just that. Some of the houses I'm sure are at least four hundred yards long (a quarter of a mile). These houses are not necessarily straight. They curve, and follow the contour of the lands. I guess they are about fifteen feet wide and about six or eight feet high, all constructed of native bush material. I saw at least four of these long houses on the way to One. Besides building the houses the natives must raise a sufficient number of pigs for the slaughter. Storage houses are constructed near the sing-sing area shortly before the fiesta starts. These store houses are like open booths, with roofs. They vary in length anywhere from around twenty feet to 200 feet. In those booths they store water, wood, native salt, greens and whatever may be needed for the slaughter or roasting. The slaughtering is done by the men. The women are given the entrails. How well this is observed I don't know. I saw a number of youngsters booting around a pig's inflated bladder. I don't know how they managed to get these. As a rule, I heard, the women eat the interior elements of the pigs.

When the pigs are done, they start to eat or over-eat. Our native interpreters and guide told us that the meat is never really done. Frequently it is only warmed, and they simple eat that raw, but warmed meat. Everyone helps himself. No one is excluded from eating. If we had stayed, one the natives surely would have offered us some meat. Not only do they eat the meat, but also the greens which were used to pack the pigs in the trenches. Almost everyone gets sick, I'm told, either because they eat too much, or because the food has spoiled, or because it is not sufficiently done. Eating of the pig is the final element of a native sing-sing held in honor of a tambaran. As a result of the slaughtering of all the pigs, the natives have to go without meat for several months. They just don't know how to eat meat with moderation.

From what I can gather, there is almost a constant cycle of sing-sings. They either prepare for one, or are recovering from one. Within a mile or so from our mission station here one of the native chiefs, Kavivi, has been preparing for an even greater sing-sing than the one at One. About a year and a half ago they started preparations—building long houses, raising and fattening pigs, etc. In about two years the celebration will finally take place. According to our native guides, this will be almost twice as big as the one at One. Of course, they are given to exaggeration, but it must be a real big shindig if such a long preparation is required.

While at the sing-sing at One I had my picture taken with a few of the participants. They really love to have their picture taken. Even a new bride, all greased up with oil posed with me for a picture. I hope this turns out well.

I thought you might be interested in my description of this sing-sing—which is connected with the native pagan cult.

The weather here has been wonderful the last five days. The sun has been shining beautifully every day, and we have had very little rain during this time. The evenings and mornings are like the nicest day in Kansas spring you can imagine. A few days ago, I heard of the new snowstorms that have swept across the country. Kansas was mentioned as being hit by at least one of the storms in recent weeks.

Again, thanks a lot for your letters. I hope all of you continue to come along as well as ever.

Your devoted son, brother,   Msgr. Firmin

~~~

7 April 1960

Dear Mother and Mary,

If this letter gets out of Mendi tomorrow it has a good chance of getting to Catherine by Easter. In any case, best wishes for a joyous and blessed Easter. As near to Easter as possible I will offer a Mass for all of you.

Your letter of March 30 arrived this noon. Thanks a lot. I was glad to hear that the color slides arrived in good shape at Catherine. Also, it was good to hear that the carbon copy of my letter to Mrs. Motz arrived in Kansas. If she publishes the letter, I have in mind to send other letters to her at about four months' interval on various phases of our missionary work in this area.

The big news over here is that some Sisters have finally agreed to come to our mission. They are the Franciscan Sisters from Oldenburg,

Indiana. At least four will be appointed for our mission next summer. I do not know the details of the exact date of their coming, and so on. I simply received a cablegram on April 4, stating that four of their Sisters will be appointed next summer. Of course, we need many more than four Sisters; but at least this is a beginning. We would still welcome another community besides the Franciscans, since I am quite certain that no one community could take care of all of our needs in our prefecture. As soon as possible we will begin the construction of a convent for the Sisters.

A few days before I received the cablegram about the coming of Sisters from the States, I was also assured of at least six qualified lay teachers for next year from Rabaul. This will really be a good boost for our missionary work. We should have some first-rate schools in operation within a few years.

I had a very interesting week-end April 2-4 at Erave. I went down there to give the many Catholics there the opportunity of going to the Sacraments, and also to have Mass for them on Sunday. Another reason for going was to complete the arrangements for our leases on the property down there. As I mentioned in a previous letter, Erave will become a main station as soon as we have enough missionaries to assign one or two there, and it will also be the location of our central school. My stay at Erave was very pleasant. On Saturday evening movies were shown on the lawn of the government officer's home. The projector was inside the house, but the screen was about sixty feet out. This allowed sufficient room for the natives to see the movie. There were at least two hundred natives out on the lawn. We went inside and watched from the windows after it started raining. The reactions of the natives were just as we had expected. The majority of them had never seen a movie before. They examined the back of the screen to see where those people on the screen come from, or where they disappear to. They laughed and screamed for the first hour. Even though there was a heavy downpour of rain, they stayed on to watch the movie until the end.

On Sunday afternoon I teamed up with some of the government

employees in a few games of tennis. Considering that I hadn't played since about nine years ago, I don't think I did too badly. But my muscles have certainly been sore since that Sunday afternoon. If I could find the time I would play regularly. There are a couple of tennis courts on the government property here in Mendi. I'm by no means down to my peak athletic condition, but I think I'm doing quite well in that matter. My weight last week was thirteen stone. That's the way the Australians give their weight. A stone is fourteen pounds. So that means I weigh 182. I hope to lose a few more pounds. At this high altitude, or anywhere as a matter of fact, it isn't good to carry too much weight.

Monday morning when we returned to Mendi, we had our plane loaded with fruit and vegetables. Almost everything grows well at Erave. Among the things we brought back were: watermelons, pineapples, grapefruit, mulis (something like lemons), bananas, passion fruit, and a few other things I can't recall right now. The flowers at Erave are as beautiful as I've seen anywhere. I hope within a year or so we will have a beautiful spot at Erave, as well as a productive vegetable garden and fruit grove.

We hope to observe Holy Week here as solemnly as the circumstances permit. If we had all the priests here on Holy Thursday or Easter Sunday I would pontificate, but there will be only two Fathers here on those two days. The other missionaries are coming to Mendi on Easter Monday. Most likely I will be celebrant at all the services during Holy Week, with one of the Fathers acting as Assistant Priest, and the other leading and directing the singing. The singing will have to be done by the teachers and a few of the government employees. Among other things, we will have the Easter Vigil services, with the Mass beginning at midnight. When it is midnight here (Saturday-Sunday) it is eight a.m. Saturday at Catherine. We're just sixteen hours ahead of you.

Everything is still coming along as well here as can be expected. A number of the school boys are missing at this time. The reason is that we are in the midst of the pandanas nuts season. I don't know what they taste like, but the natives are wild about them. A number of the boys got permission to go out to pick a supply of these nuts for the rest of the pupils. Some of the boys went off without permission. I heard that ten boys disappeared from the government school in the last few weeks for the same reason.

With best wishes for a joyous and blessed Easter, I remain,
Your devoted son, brother, Msgr. Firmin

～

28 April 1960
Dear Mother and Mary,

Many thanks for your letter of April 20. It arrived here yesterday noon. The huge package which you sent about January 20 arrived in perfect condition a few days ago. Everything, including the fudge, was perfectly fresh. Thanks a lot. I also appreciate receiving the three pictures—one of Mother and myself in color, one of the family and a third of the huge crowd of relatives and friends of the family taken on the day of our celebration at Hays. All the pictures turned out much better than I had expected. I was especially surprised how clear that large group picture came out. I showed these pictures, as well as some of the color slides that Al sent some time ago, to the school boys and some older people. When they saw the picture of Mother, they asked how old she was. After I told them they shook their hands in amazement. Shaking their hands is their way of expressing amazement. By the way, do you want me to send the pictures back? Please let me know in your next letter. I intend to send Al's color slides back within a week or two. All the friars saw them on their visit to Mendi after Easter. As I mentioned in the last letter, I sent the 16mm movie reel of the Confirmation at Tari to you at Catherine. Since I sent it airmail, it should have arrived by this time. Please keep it until Fr. Otmar comes for a visit in June. At that time ask him to take it along to Pittsburgh where the mission office will want to use it for propaganda purposes. Be sure to let me know when the film arrives.

This past Monday, April 25, was Anzac Day. It is the equivalent of

Memorial Day of May 30 in the U.S.A. At the celebration sponsored by the government I was invited to give the main address. Naturally I accepted the invitation. It was a fine celebration. The weather was perfect. Besides all the government personnel, there were more than a thousand, perhaps closer to two thousand, natives, including about thirty or forty native policemen, and about thirty native medical helpers of the Southern Highlands.

In the afternoon of April 25, I blessed and dedicated our new school here at Mendi. We began to use the school the next day. I am quite certain that this is the first permanent structure used as a school in the Southern Highlands. The government doesn't have anything to compare with it. We should get a high rating at the inspection by the District Education Officer. Now if we only had competent teachers. Besides having Sisters next year I'm quite certain we will have qualified native teachers in the schools of all our main stations.

I've written to you about our former cookboy, Tundu, or Shorty. He still has not been found. Our first surmise is probably correct. His "brother" (really his cousin) probably killed him so he could get his kinas. The government got nowhere so far in investigating the matter. Now that Tundu is gone, we had to get a new candidate for cookboy. The name of the new fellow is Pot. That's an appropriate name for a fellow who will work in the kitchen: Pot cleaning pans. He seems to be a willing fellow, and eager to learn. One of the first lessons we have to teach fellows like this is cleanliness. So far, he seems to be keeping himself neat and clean. Yesterday Thomas More Mia gave Pot a haircut. I guess he is serious about staying neat. Of course, their haircuts are nothing to brag about.

Tundu had been quite a popular fellow around here. When he was reported missing one of his fellow workers by the name of Manget took a knife and wacked off part of his ear as an expression of sorrow. I saw him bleeding, and asked what had happened. I was told he did this to show his sorrow for Tundu. I had heard that this is a normal way of expressing sorrow. I have seen similar expressions of sorrow or sympathy on a number of occasions for lesser things. Several weeks ago, a man brought his friend to the hospital because of fever. While the doctor was treating the fellow with the fever, the other man chopped off one of his fingers with a hatchet as an expression of sorrow. Of course, then the doctor had two patients instead of one. One of our school boys who was baptized last Christmas had one of his fingers chopped off when he was a little kid. Someone in his family had become ill. So, the Mother chopped the boy's finger off as a sign of sorrow. There are a number of women in this area with one or two fingers missing. It's hard to understand that type of mentality. Those who have been associated with our mission for some time are beginning to see the foolishness of such mutilations. The young convert with one of his fingers missing certainly knows how silly some of the traditions of his people are.

Sometime during May I am planning to visit the oil fields in the Gulf district. I am going to write to the manager of the Australian Petroleum Company in Moresby to make arrangements for my travel. Those oil fields are in my territory, but so far, we have been unable to assign one of the missionaries to that area. Since there are a good number of Catholics employed by the oil company, I thought it advisable at least to visit that area once a year. I don't think I'll be leaving for that area until about the middle of May.

I was sorry to hear that the wheat doesn't look so good. With all the moisture that you had from the snow, something should be growing this spring. I hoped it won't be just the weeds that grow this year. Here in Mendi the weather has been ideal the last week. Although this is only the end of April, the sun has already moved noticeably to the north. I think I can notice the difference from day to day.

I hope all of you are coming along as well as ever.

Your devoted son, brother, Msgr. Firmin

I hope you will have a Happy Mother's Day. I will observe that day by offering a special Mass for Mother.

[Sophia Schmidt, Monsignor Firmin's mother, died on May 4,

1960. Upon hearing of his mother's death, Monsignor Firmin wrote a letter to his family offering consolation, comfort, and appreciation for her long life. He thanked Mary and other relatives for the care they had given her in her last illness. He also wrote of the Masses that he and other Capuchins would offer for her soul. Subsequently, Monsignor's letters were addressed only to Mary.]

~~~

23 June 1960

Dear Mary,

Many thanks for your letter of June 16. It arrived this noon. Thanks also for the check for $182. I will deposit it immediately, and of course I will offer the Masses [for his mother's soul] regularly over a long period of time. I don't think you will receive the cancelled check. Here in New Guinea, as also in Australia, the banks never return a cancelled check. In any case, you know I got the money and deposited it safely in our bank here. This $182 brings the total you have sent so far to $282, including the five dollars from Mr. Weiser.

On Tuesday (June 21) we ended the worst rainy siege we have had since my coming into New Guinea. For at least three weeks we saw the sun only briefly on a couple of days. It rained heavily every afternoon and evening and through the night during all that time. The last ten days it rained also in the mornings in addition. Our yard was just one big sea of mud and water. Very few planes were able to fly in this weather. Our pilot didn't get to Madang until yesterday. This was the first time in two weeks. This rainy weather may explain why my last letters took longer than usual in getting to Catherine.

We had planned to have a big Corpus Christi celebration last Sunday. We spread the word to the surrounding area. One of the kanakas (name for bush natives) even brought in green rope for decorating the church. The green rope is something like the decoration used around home at Christmas time. We had planned to have a procession outside. Unfortunately, the weather was still bad. In spite of the bad weather we had a huge crowd, but we couldn't have the procession outside. It was the largest crowd we ever had here. The church was jammed beyond capacity. A good number of the people were outside at the entrance of the church.

This noon I received about a dozen transparent photos of the funeral [of Sophia, his mother]. They were sent by Fr. Paulinus. I don't know who took them. Will you please thank Fr. Paulinus for me just in case I won't write to him soon. The pictures are excellent. I don't know whether you saw them. A number of them were taken in the front yard at home; two or three were taken at the church, and about four at the cemetery. Everyone in the family was in at least one picture. Please let me know whether I should return these pictures.

It was good to hear that the wheat is coming along well. I hope you get good weather from now on. And above all I hope there won't be any hail. The news from the States a few days ago mentioned the forecast of rain and hail for parts of Kansas and Nebraska. I hope none materialized. Quite possibly you will be harvesting by the time you receive this letter.

Fr. Stanley is here in Mendi right now in preparation for his trip to the States. He will leave for Goroka tomorrow. By July 3 he will leave Sydney. According to his itinerary, he is to stop in Kansas around July 10. It is possible that he will pay a visit to Catherine.

I think in one of my previous letters I mentioned that our school kids here are perfectly satisfied with sweet potatoes, known locally as "kaukau," for their meals—morning, noon, and night. They will go for weeks without eating anything else but kaukau. Here at Mendi there is frequently a shortage of kaukau. Whenever we don't have enough kaukau we have to give them rice. I don't know exactly how much each kid eats every day, but my estimate is that it is about eight to ten pounds. As you can judge for yourself, that is a lot of potatoes for one person per day. As they put it themselves, "when their bellies are tight, they have enough kaukau." We usually buy the kaukau from the natives. Ordinarily we pay the same price that the government pays—¾ pence a pound. Occasionally we buy it with kina (mother-of-pearl) shells. A few days ago, a bossboy from Wa (about an hour walk from Mendi) came to our station, and asked us to come to his area to get kaukau. We told him we couldn't get it, but we would like him to bring in a supply. So, this morning at 9:30, about thirty-five or forty women came to our mission loaded down with kaukau. They brought a total of about 1600 pounds. We bought that for two kinas and a few extra pence. Kinas vary in price. These kinas were worth about five dollars each, according to the local market. You should have seen these women loaded down with the sacks of kaukau. Some of them carried not only about fifty pounds of kaukau tied to their heads, but in addition had a little baby sitting on the top of the kaukau or on top of the head. I should have taken their picture.

This morning on my way back from our school, where I had given catechetical instruction to the kids, I met a brand-new bride. In a former letter I told you that a bride over here is easily recognized by the black oil that covers her entire body, from head to toe. It's like thick crankcase oil. Her face was painted yellow and red. I told her with sign language and a few words of the native language that I know, that I wanted her to stay there while I got a camera to take her picture. I went to the house and started talking with one of the Fathers and almost forgot about the bride. In fact, I got a haircut in the meanwhile. When I finished with the haircut, I recalled that I had requested the bride to wait until I got the camera. I went up towards the school, and sure enough, she was still waiting, anxious to have her picture taken. Most natives like to be photographed. I hope this picture turns out well. It will be a beaut. While I was taking her picture, about fifty or more natives were on the side watching. I'm sure every one of them was hoping I would ask him or her to pose also.

I hope you're coming along well. I wish I could help you with the harvest, but I guess since I'm not there, I won't be missed too much. I know I could do justice to the meals if not to the work. Best regards to all. Your devoted brother, Msgr. Firmin

〜

30 June 1960

Dear Mary,

Thanks for your letter of June 22. It arrived this noon. Four hundred and seventy-two dollars is really a lot for Mass stipends. That is at least some indication of how popular Mother was. Of course, you know that in addition to the Masses that are being said for these stipends, there were many other Masses offered. I personally received a few cards, which I also acknowledged. Besides these, all the Capuchin Fathers in our Province offered at least one Mass for Mother. In every large house of our Province there was a Solemn Requiem Mass offered. This is not usually done. I think it was done at the suggestion or request of Fr. Giles. The apportioning of the stipends, I think, was good. Over a long period of time I will be able to take care of the $277, which you sent me. I think I have averaged about four or five [Masses] per week.

You spoke about having a lot of rain. For Kansas I guess six or seven inches per month is a lot. Over here we wouldn't have that little even in a dry spell. I heard on the radio this morning that at Middletown and Barikewa, where I visited the oil fields, they had 78 inches of rain during June. I think this was the highest amount for June on record. Here at Mendi it has been normal during the last ten days—rain every afternoon and evening, but beautiful sunshine in the morning. I hope by this time you are having favorable weather for the wheat.

Last Sunday, Brother Claude and I decided to take a walk to the more populated areas around Mendi. I don't know how far we walked but it took us about two and a half hours of steady walking. Even though there are no villages in the proper sense, each area has its proper name. For example, the real name for the spot where our mission is established is call Kumin. The places we passed through were Kombegibu, Longa, Tenbe, Umbimi, and I don't remember the name of the others.

We took our two workers along, Thomas More Mia and Pot. They know the surrounding area blindfolded. As soon as we got started on the trail, about fifteen or twenty native boys and girls followed us. We stopped at a few houses to greet the people, especially those known to us. The first house at which we stopped belonged to a fellow by the name of Mendiba. He is a boss boy in his area, appointed by the government. He considers himself a good friend of ours. He comes to church every Sunday even though he is a pagan. About twenty feet from his house I saw a structure, something like a small crib. On the top were hanging three skeletons, or rather three skulls. I was told that these were the skulls of friends in his line who had died years ago. I was told that formerly the natives did not bury their dead. They simply erected a crib, about four feet above the ground, and allowed the corpse to disintegrate that way. Now, I'm told, they bury their dead. What I saw at Mendiba's house could possibly be a remnant of the older custom.

The next house I stopped at was a sort of community, or town hall. It was a house about six feet high in the center, three feet on the side, about twenty-five feet long and about twelve feet wide. They were just displaying kinas (mother-of-pearl shells). This, as I mentioned before, is their money. There must have been at least thirty kinas, neatly placed on the inside along the wall and on the ground. A beautiful cushion of leaves supported each kina. It was quite dark inside, and only after I was in there a while could I see the kinas clearly. About twelve men were in a circle, saying very little. Occasionally, one would get up and examine a few of the kinas. As I found out, this was a "payback." This means simply that something was owed by one line to another. What happened is this. Years ago, in a battle between the two lines in question, one more man was killed in the one line that in the other. When the score is uneven, it has to be straightened out—hence, the payback. If the government wouldn't forbid it, the payback here would be by killing a man from the line that was one ahead. Now, since the government doesn't allow killing like this, they pay back with kinas or pigs. In a later letter I'll tell you more about paybacks. Here at this house I witnessed a real payback.

After we left this quasi-community house, we passed a big sing-sing ground which will be the site of a sing-sing in two or three years. They have been preparing for this for two years already, and it will take another two or three years before everything is ready. The most influential native, Kavivi, lives right off these grounds. It is from him that we purchased our mission land. His word seems to be law among the natives. I know he is wealthy—by New Guinea standards—because he has seven wives. As we walked along, I saw a large field of kaukau, which was being worked. At first, I spotted only two women. After looking more carefully I saw four more women digging the ground, preparing the soil for a crop. The color of their skin blends almost perfectly with the ground. I found out that this was Kavivi's ground. The six women I saw were his wives. Where the seventh was I don't know. He had just married her the day before.

A few hundred yards from the sing-sing ground we came upon four long houses. These were built in preparation for the sing-sing. They are being used as sleeping quarters and storehouses for wood, and anything that may be needed for the sing-sing. Each of these houses was about 6 feet high in the center, about three feet on the side, and about five hundred feet long. That's right: 500 feet. I took pictures of them I hope they come out well.

As we were walking along, I noticed occasionally at the side of the mountain a place for taking a drink. You can always tell whether the water is good. If a big banana tree leaf or something similar is fastened to the stream coming out of the bank or ground you can be sure it's good (the leaf forms a sort of a spout, making it easy to drink). It's strange how these natives can tell you right away whether the water is good or not. For us, the presence of the leaf, or if natives drink from a stream, we know it's good. It was beautifully clear water that came out of some of those places. The leaf forms a sort of a spout, making it easy to drink.

Next, we met a fellow by the name of Wangalu, who is also a friend of our mission. He met us outside his house with a hand full of kana-ka (wild) bananas, which he had just finished cooking. He offered us some. Brother Claude took one and so did I even though the hand in which he was holding it was filthy. The kanaka cooked banana tasted something like a cooked potato, only a little less tasty. There was nothing sweet about it. I took one bite and kept the rest of the banana in my hand until we had left Wangalu, and I secretly tossed it away. I didn't want to offend him by throwing it away in his presence.

We met a few more kanakas along the way. On this walk I saw more evidence of the carefree lives of these people. They just do what they please and when they please. They have no schedule to meet. They have no definite plans. They have no definite place to go and no definite time to return. Youngsters, from six years on, wander all over the area, not caring when or if they will get back home. None of them ever seem to get tired of walking. They can walk with the greatest of ease up the steepest hill.

By the time we got back to Mendi, only our two workers, Mia and Pot, were still with us. The rest just wandered in various directions.

Last Saturday, the girls whose picture I sent to you, came running down the road with their hands full of flowers. They told me they picked them for the church. We put them in vases and placed them on the altar. Sure enough, the next day (Sunday), they came with a few more girls with them to attend Mass. They were proud of the fact that their flowers were on the altar. I asked them to bring some more this Saturday. I'm sure they won't forget.

I had a letter from Doctor Murphy in answer to the Hays paper clipping that I sent him. He said he was surprised that he had not heard from you about Mother's death. He sends his best regards.

I hope this letter finds you and everyone else around Catherine coming along as well as ever.
Your devoted brother, Msgr. Firmin

∼∼

27 July 1960
Dear Mary,

As I'm starting this letter (7:30 pm), it's raining very hard. It has been raining since 2:00pm. It is quite possible that we are beginning another wet season. Until this afternoon the weather has been most delightful for about three weeks. In fact, every afternoon and evening was most pleasant. Almost every night after supper I was able to take a walk outside.

Yesterday was the anniversary of my investiture in Pittsburgh. The occasion brought back many happy memories. It certainly doesn't seem as if a whole year has already gone by. Here is a brief description of how I celebrated the anniversary. While I was still at breakfast (at about 7:20 am), a cargo boy from the government came to our door all out of breath. In his pidgin he told us that a fellow cargo boy from the government was dying at the hospital, and I should come quick to baptize him. Since all the other Fathers were out at their bush stations, I rushed to the hospital, and, sure enough, found the old fellow in very bad condition. He had been taking instructions at Wabag, but moved out to get a job with the government before he could be baptized. His Catholic cargo boy friends knew of his association with the Catholic Mission. So, after going through a brief instruction and preparation in pidgin, I baptized him, giving him the name Joseph. Less than twenty-four hours later he was dead. I buried him here this afternoon. Before I give you a description of the funeral, I want to give you a few more details of my first anniversary. At 9:30 I gave catechetical instructions to our school kids. Right now, I am teaching them the Mass prayers in English. In a few weeks they will be ready to pray the entire Mass. At 1:30 pm, I went to the government school to conduct catechism class there. I have about forty-five kids in that class. They respond beautiful-ly. From 2:00-4:30pm, I did a bit of manual work, but mainly directed the cargo boys how to haul and stack some lumber for our new con-vent. After supper I wrote some letters and spent the rest of the evening reading. It is really a typical day, except for the emergency Baptism.

Now for a brief description of the funeral. As far as I know, we have the only real cemetery, designated as such by the government in the Southern Highlands. This afternoon, the Catholic cargo boys from the government came down the road with a stretcher, carrying the corpse. They took the corpse directly to the cemetery, and then they came to the door and asked me to bury him, since he was a Catholic. There wasn't even a grave dug as yet. So, we gave the fellows some shovels and marked out the spot and had them dig. Before they started digging, they carried the corpse to the cargo boys' house. In the meanwhile, Brother Claude built a coffin out of plain wood. By 2:30, everything was ready for the funeral, but already it was raining very hard. We waited until 4:00pm and finally decided to go ahead with the burial in spite of the rain. Our cook boy Thomas More Mia, carried the umbrella for me as I said the prayers. By the way, I had Mia act as the sponsor at the Baptism. When we got to the grave, one of the pallbearers slipped and fell into the grave. After he finally crawled out, all muddy, they tried to put the coffin down. Unfortunately, the gravediggers cheated a bit and didn't make the hole big enough. So, one of the carpenters, Andy, finished the job while we waited. The ceremony was very simple and ordinary from there on. After it was all over, one of the deceased man's friends gave Brother Claude ten shillings (about $1.12) and said: "Tell Monsignor to say prayers to make dead man good, so he go up above." Now we have three buried in our cemetery, each with a cross to designate the spot and identify each. The other two were children. This was an old man in physical age, but a child spiritually just born by Baptism.

Last Sunday we had a pay-back sing-sing at Kombegibu. As I described in a former letter, years ago Kombegibu had a war with a neighboring tribe and killed more than they had killed of their own. The score, the native tradition, must be kept even. In former times they would simply have killed one or two of Kombegibu natives to make the score even. Now, the government insists that pay-backs may not be in human lives, but with kinas or pigs. A few weeks ago, Brother Claude and I witnessed the discussion and actual bargaining for the pay-back. This past Sunday we went to see the pay-back sing-sing. This is the ceremonious presentation of kinas in payment for the uneven score. It wasn't a large crowd. Perhaps there were about eight hundred natives in all. There were at least 300 kinas displayed beautifully on green leaves and cushions. How many were used for the pay-back I don't know, probably about thirty. The rest were for display and buying pigs for a future big sing-sing. About thirty or forty men started the war dance and sing-sing carrying axes, bows and arrows, and other weapons. We got good pictures of this. Every few minutes they stopped the dance and the chief from the one tribe would present a kina to the other tribe, and sing something as he did so. We took pictures for about two hours. Everyone wanted to pose for us. You see, we show these pictures at our mission on our slide projector, and they love to see themselves. We got a few good shots of the chief of Kombegibu, by the name of Kavivi. Next Sunday is the finale of the pay-back sing-sing. Brother Claude and I will again make an effort to see the celebration. Actually, many of the natives in that area have asked us to come to take pictures.

Please tell Al I received his letter today. I hope to write to him as soon as I can conveniently do so. This evening I am also writing to Mr. and Mrs. Melvin Walters. I am describing a New Guinea marriage, and will enclose a picture of a New Guinea bride. Please ask Ellen to show the picture. In fact, it would be desirable if she would leave the picture with you or Al. I think I have sent a number of transparent pictures to you. I would like to have them kept together. Ellen won't have any use for it after she sees it once. —I hope you had a fine trip to Colorado Springs. Best regards to all.

Your devoted brother, Msgr. Firmin

～

3 August 1960

Dear Mary,

Your letter of July 20 arrived here on August 1. I don't know where it was held up. There could be any number of places here in New Guinea where it could be delayed several days because of bad weather. Usually your letters arrive in a week or less. Wednesday is our best mail day. Today, however, nothing arrived—due to bad weather. A couple of planes did come in around noon, but they came from a different direction. –I was glad you enjoyed your trip to Colorado. Don't worry about having missed Fr. Stanley. In the first place he changed his schedule somewhat. Besides, he is not coming back to New Guinea. He has been assigned to Rochester, Pa.—after his vacation. It is possible that Frs. Timon and Benjamin stopped in Kansas on their way to New Guinea. You met them last summer when I was home. These two new missionaries and Fr. Otmar and Brother Mark left California for Sydney on August 2. After a few days in Hawaii, and probably more than a week in Sydney, they will arrive in Papua most likely after the middle of the month.

As I had planned, I attended the sing-sing at Kombegibu last Sunday. It was a cloudy morning, but by noon it began to clear up. I guess there were over three thousand people there. It was much smaller than the sing-sing I saw at Tende about five months ago. I got a number of fine pictures, including a few of the chief, Kavivi. I also had my picture taken with him. He had already removed some of his of his ornaments and make-up, but he still looked fairly good. He offered me a piece of sugar cane to shew on. Of course, I accepted it, and chewed it, just as he did. I think this was a sign of friendship. The sugar cane is very sweet, much sweeter than the cane or sorghum we used to chew on the farm. These are also much bigger—about an inch and a half in diameter, and as long as 12 or 15 feet.

The dancing at the sing-sing was as monotonous as all the rest, and so was the singing. There is really no beauty to it all. Their make-up and painting, however, is always attractive. They started early on Saturday and many of them, including our cookboy, went straight through the night. I heard them during the night and early on Sunday morning. Very few of the bush kanakas showed up for Mass at the Mission on Sunday. The sing-sing came to an abrupt end at 2:30pm with the death of the chief's father. The old boy had been dying for months. I saw him about a month ago, and wondered what kept him breathing. I went to the place of the old fellow's death. I never saw anything like that in my life. They dragged the corpse out into the yard, and then hundreds of natives crowded around, wailing and crying. The wailing was so loud, Brother Claude and I could hardly hear each other even when we spoke as loud as we could. I saw a number of men tear out their beards as an expression of sorrow. Undoubtedly, later on, some of them chopped off a finger or an ear to express sorrow over the death of Kavivi's father. The wailing and moaning kept up, without interruption, two days and two nights until the burial yesterday afternoon. We could hear it plainly at our mission. This afternoon at about 2:00 pm there was another loud wailing and crying. We still don't know what that was for. Of course, the sorrow of almost all of them is merely a show. The old boy was not a Catholic, nor did he ever show any interest in the Church. I guess he was too old to realize what this is all about. However, many of the natives in that area come regularly to Church. Incidentally, the old man's wife (who is also Kavivi's mother) is still living. She looks old, but is still very strong. She comes to the mission occasionally. She keeps a careful eye on her son who is the chief, but she doesn't accomplish much with him. Two Sundays ago, at the exchange of kinas, she objected to his giving certain ones away. He simply kicked her aside and did as he pleased.

I am enclosing a few pictures. I have quite a few more coming in the next few weeks. I think I labelled all the pictures adequately. Two are of our mission. The white zig-zag streak on the one is a defect in the film. I didn't indicate the spot of the convent, which is already under roof by this time. It is located on the other side of the church. The longhouse is a little over a mile east of our mission. I have two more pictures of the longhouses in the same area. I will send them on later. Perhaps, I will send one or the other along with my next article for the Hays Daily News. The picture of the native with the two kinas is Kavivi, the chief. He looks quite tough, and I guess he is stronger than any of the natives in his area. I'm sure, though I could beat him up without any difficulty. It is a fact that none of the natives here know how to fight except with weapons, axes, clubs, bows and arrows. And they are not very accurate with arrows. If they have nothing in their hands, they're helpless.

While I was home last August and September, I showed the document from the Pope whereby our Prefecture was established. About six weeks ago I asked a wood expert here by the name of Jock McGill to put it in a frame. He did the most beautiful job I have ever seen. He did a first-class in-lay with five different kinds of wood: black palm, white palm, Mendi hardwood, Papuan black walnut, and Bulolo pine—all from Papua or New Guinea. The black palm is from a bow and arrow used in a tribal fight near Kagua a few years ago. It is supposed to have been used in killing 12 natives. Jock spent about 400 hours in producing his work of art as my frame, but he refused to accept any pay for it. He is an expert wood-joiner. He has made and sold some famous violins. His latest big project is a carving of Boris Pasternak.

Please extend my best regards to the Karlins. I understand they're having a family reunion. I was going to write to them, but I'm a little pushed for time right now. If I find the time, I still may write. Hope everything is coming along well.

Your devoted brother, Msgr. Firmin

~~~

10 August 1960

Dear Mary,

Thanks for your letters of July 30 and August 4, respectively. The one of July 30 arrived here on Monday, August 8, and the one of August 4 arrived this noon (Aug. 10). I was happy to see the clipping of Bill Staab and his family. If I'm not mistaken, you mentioned some time ago that he was going to settle down in Arizona. I suppose by this time he should have a bit of money salted away in the bank. That, along with his pension, should keep him going. Undoubtedly, he will get into some kind of work or business.

I was happy to hear that Frs. Timon and Benjamin stopped in on their way to the coast. They had difficulty getting reservations as quickly as they had hoped in Honolulu. According to the latest letter from Fr. Otmar, they weren't expecting to get to Sydney until August 9 or 10. I'm sure they will stay at least ten days in Sydney, doing some shopping and renewing some of our contacts there. I really don't expect them to get to Mendi until about August 24. I'll be delighted to hear the recording that was made during the Fathers' visit. I'll also search their luggage for the fudge, in case they don't present it upon arrival. As you could probably tell even from the brief visit, they are very fine young priests.

I returned right before dinner today from a trip to Goroka—which is an hour by plane almost directly east of Mendi. I went there to attend the installation of their new Bishop Schilling. Apart from a bit of bad weather we hit about ten minutes from Mendi, it was a delightful trip. Goroka is undoubtedly the finest city in the highlands. It is in the Western Highlands of New Guinea. At an altitude of about 5100 feet, it has a climate almost like that of Mendi, but it is not quite as damp there. There are at least four first class general stores there. As all the stations and missions in the highlands, Goroka is located in a valley with high mountains in every direction. Bishop Schilling belongs to the S.V.D. group from Germany. His mission was cut off from Alexishafen. There has been missionary work done in that area for at least thirty years. One of his parishes, Mingende, is probably the most Catholic in New Guinea. I heard that it is not unusual to have four to five thousand communions on a Sunday. Although Bishop Schilling's Vicariate contains a number of well-developed missions, he has only fifteen priests. That's only a couple more than we have. For the installation ceremony at Goroka, there were about thirty priests present from neighboring missions. I was the only Capuchin. Besides myself, there were only two other heads of missions, Bishop Noser and Bishop Arkfeld—both Americans. Bishop Arkfeld is probably the best-known missionary Bishop in the world. He is known as the "Flying Bishop." He is one of the best pilots in New Guinea. As far as I know, he does regular pilot work just about every day of the week. Bishop Noser,

Bishop Arkfeld, and Bishop Schilling wore their regular solemn episcopal garb for the ceremony. I also wore my best outfit. By the way, the priests, as well as the people stared at me, I could tell they had never seen a Capuchin Monsignor. After the services I was called back outside for some pictures.

After everything was over, dinner and a little reception, two of the Bishops and I went to a plantation residence for the night—about six miles from Goroka. The former owner of the plantation built a very classy home there, probably the classiest in the highlands—with wall-to-wall carpeting, huge picture windows on one side, big open porch, doors of silky oak, several acres of green lawn, etc. Bishop Arkfeld bought the plantation. The house came with it. The plantation yielded fifty tons of coffee this year. He is selling the coffee right at Goroka for about fifty cents a pound. Of course, the expenses are quite high. –This morning there were at least twenty priests at the airstrip, all waiting for their flights back to their respective missions.

Everything is still coming along very well here at Mendi. One of the history-making accomplishments here is the construction of a market for the natives. In a square, a short distance from the government offices, the natives put up two long booths, each about 130 feet long. Every Saturday forenoon the natives are to bring in their produce: kaukau, potatoes, corn, etc. The idea behind this is to get the natives in the habit of raising more than they consume themselves. The first Saturday the market was open the place was completely over-run. There were a few thousand there I suppose. Because there were so many, they weren't able to sell all their goods. As a result, no one showed up the next Saturday, and only about three the following Saturday. Eventually, they will get some order into this market. We ourselves buy kaukau and vegetables directly from the natives. They bring it in to the mission. The price we pay for kaukau, potatoes, or corn is a little less than a cent a pound. Most of the time we pay in shillings or pence. We have two-shilling pieces, one shilling pieces, sixpence and threepence (Australian exchange). They always prefer to take two one-shilling pieces in preference to a two-shilling piece. The money they get from their produce is usually saved until they get enough to buy a kina, which ranges in price from one pound ($2.25) to as high as five pounds or more. Occasionally, however, they will use the money to buy various objects at the government trade store. The most popular things they buy are: belts, mirrors, lap-laps (ordinary piece of cloth they wear instead of a home-made net or leaves), and shirts or sweaters. A belt is the first thing a youngster starts to wear. He or she may go for a couple of years—to the age of four or five—without wearing anything else. The natives love the mirrors. They admire themselves in a mirror for hours at a time. When they prepare for a sing-sing, I'm sure they spend more time before a mirror than the best-dressed bride in the States. It is only gradual that the natives will learn to buy things from the store and not save everything towards a kina.

I see I'm getting close to the end of the page. By the way, be sure to send me the address of Sister Marian, C.S.A. I would also appreciate it if you would identify her for me. Hope everything is coming along well.

Your devoted brother, Msgr. Firmin

~~

17 August 1960

Dear Mary,

Your letter of August 12 arrived this noon (August 17). Thanks a lot especially for that huge check of $162.87. You can be sure I was not expecting anything like that, and I know you could very well have used that amount yourself. If the will made allowance for this, I'll keep it. Otherwise, I think you should have kept it. If I keep it, you can rest assured that I will use it well—Thanks also for the clipping of the members of the Capuchin Educational Council. I had heard that they were going to meet in Kansas this summer, but I hadn't heard the exact date, until I got your letter. I was happy to hear that some of my former fellow-lectors of Washington stopped to say hello. Fr. Norbert is really a wonderful priest. I was stationed with him about nine years. I'm sure he, as also Frs. Myles and Neal, enjoyed their visits with the Schmidts. Too bad that meeting took place in Kansas when I was no longer in the States. Remember the last time we met for such a meeting in Kansas? It was in 1952. A few days after that meeting Fr. Myles went with us to Colorado Springs. I had a letter also from Fr. Giles today. He also mentioned that he was hoping to pay a visit to Catherine. By the way, he was delighted with your letter on the occasion of his Silver Jubilee.

Fr. Otmar and his fellow-travelers still have not arrived here in Mendi. In fact, I haven't heard from any of them since they got to Sydney. Most likely they will get here in about a week from today. The Sisters who have been assigned to our mission are beginning to make arrangements for their trip. Three of them have a Bachelor of Science degree in education; the other Sister has excellent training and practical experience as a nurse. I think that's an excellent combination to answer our needs here in the Southern Highlands. The convent which is being built for the Sisters is making good progress. At the present time they are working on the ceiling, the outside being all completed. It's going to be a very fine structure—68 ft.x30 ft.

Everything is continuing to come along well here at Mendi and the other stations. The people at Kombegibu are still in mourning. Two weeks ago, I told you of the death of the father of the Chief (Kavivi). Upon his death all, or almost all, the women and girls covered their bodies completely with gray clay. Many of them also wear white beads, as you must have noticed in some of the pictures I sent home. Today about ten of the girls, ranging in age from nine to about twenty-five, stopped here at the mission. All were completely caked over with mud. Even their eyebrows, eyelashes, and eyelids are covered. Their heads, including the hair, are covered with a solid shell of this dried clay. It must feel like a helmet. I asked them how long they were going to keep covered with this mud. I got no definite answer. I suppose they have some kind of rule as to the time limit, but I haven't been able to find out. I do know that some of the women in this area have been covered with clay ever since I arrived last October. Either they are doing this to express very great sorrow, or they are doing it because of show. I suspect in many cases it's just a question of showing off. The girls who were here this afternoon seem to be embarrassed in being covered with clay. Actually, they feel so embarrassed they haven't come to church since they covered themselves with the clay a couple of weeks ago. I'm sure these youngsters would rather omit this part of their tribal custom, but no one dares to take the lead. Before they left today, they agreed to come to Mass on Sunday in spite of the clay.

I don't think I have told you much about facial make-up and hair-do among the natives. The women and girls here in our area invariably have their hair cut very short. It is rare that you see any woman or girl with hair longer than an inch. Frequently their heads are practically shaved. I think one reason they do that is for the convenience of carrying their bilum, or bag, slung over their head. The women are never without this bag. The men, in this area, as a rule have bushy hair, grown quite long. They put so much grass, flowers, twigs, etc., in their hair, it's often hard to tell what is their hair and what isn't. Their hair is so thick that they can hide almost anything in it. Frequently we watch them as one fellow will look for, and smash, the lice on another fellow's head. This is true also for the women, as far as the lice are concerned. What I have said about the women's hair being cut so short is not universally true in New Guinea. On the coast, and in other areas where the natives are more sophisticated the women and girls wear their hair long, and of course they're very bushy.

Many of the natives, both men and women, carry permanent tattoos on their bodies. Frequently, their faces have all kinds of fancy designs. I saw a number of native Sisters at Alexishaven and Yule Island who have these tattoos. I guess they are deeply impressed in the skin and cannot be outgrown. It is some process of burning. This tattooing is not as common in the Southern Highlands as it is on the coast or in the Chimbu area. One native woman, a Catholic from Chimbu, who comes to church every Sunday has a face like a checkerboard, with a mess of dark blue lines crossing each other. I guess the natives look upon these as a work of art which enhances their beauty—in their minds—or the lack of it. –It is rare that you see a woman or a man around here without bracelets, or I should say, armlets. They wear these above the elbow. These bracelets as a rule are woven out of bark from a certain type of tree. Before they put them on, they soak them. After they're on a day or two they become real tight. I don't know how they can stand them—Sometime in the future I'll tell you a little more about their other make-up, their earrings, and nose rings.

I am enclosing a picture of my house. I can't recall having sent one before this. I'm having the Miltenbergers live in there now. The two cream-colored tanks catch water from the roof. It is then pumped into the blue tank, which provides the force for running water in the house. I'm having other pictures printed. They should be here in a week or so. –Have you found yet who Sister Marian is? A few days ago, I had a nice letter from Frank Schmidt's Sister (Sr. Francis Marie). Her school kids sent some mission articles.

Again, thanks a lot for the letter and the huge check.

Your devoted brother, Msgr. Firmin

~~~

14 Sept. 1960

Dear Mary,

Since I have nothing to send along this time, I'll use an aerogram. I'm writing at this time hoping that there will be a plane out of Mendi tomorrow. The weather has been quite bad, and as a result the flying for the highlands has been limited. Evidently, we're in another rainy season. A few days ago, I'm sure, we had over two inches during a ten-hour period. I guess we've had at least a half inch of rain each day since the beginning of September.

My trip to Mt. Hagen last week was quite enjoyable. I went there for the Installation of Bishop Bernarding as the first Bishop of that area. The ceremony was held outside because of the large crowd. Conservative estimates placed the crowd of natives at five thousand. The following day (Sept. 9) the natives had a sing-sing as their expression of welcome to the new Bishop. I witnessed part of the sing-sing. As far as I could judge, the crowd was a bit larger for the sing-sing than for the Installation. Fr. Ross, the pastor of the parish at Mt. Hagen, told me there were 8,500 people in his parish. The average number of communions on an ordinary Sunday is around one thousand. They have a large population there, and as far as I know the mission is around thirty years old.

While at Mt. Hagen I met a number of friends I had known for some time in New Guinea. One of these was Dr. Ivinskis, who had been stationed at Mendi until about three months ago. He is an excellent Catholic and a very good doctor. He is also a good public relations man for the Capuchins. Everywhere he goes he sings the praises of the Capuchins.

The morning I went to Mt. Hagen (Sept. 8) there was a tribal fight down the valley here at Mendi. Natives from all over were heading down to witness the battle. The government (native) police also went down in full force. Our plane flew in the general direction of the fight, but we couldn't see anything from the air. When I returned on Friday, I found that the battle was actually stopped before it got under way.

Our two cookboys are still as interesting as ever. Today Mia bawled out Pot for not trying to learn pidgin. He just knows a few words in pidgin. Fortunately, he knows a few terms used around the kitchen. But as a rule, he'll stick to his native language. Maybe I'll be able to pick it up more quickly that way.

A few days ago, I noticed that Pot was missing around noon. I asked Mia where Pot had disappeared to. He told me Pot went down to Wa to cry. Some relative of his had died, so he thought he should go down there and express his sorrow. It is the custom here that when someone in the same line or tribe dies, the rest in the relationship come to cry. In recognition of that, a pig is killed and the meat distributed among those who come to cry. I suspect some go to cry merely to get the meat. When Pot returned that evening, I asked him whether he was finished crying. In a matter-of-fact way, he said he was finished now. Evidently, he stopped after he received his part of the pig.

Within a week I'll send my next letter to the Hays Daily News. Actually, I have the letter written. Right now, I'm waiting for a few pictures from the photo company. I had a few pictures taken reading the Hays Daily News, flanked by a few kanakas. I think it will be a fine bit of publicity. One of the pictures shows one of the natives with a Coca Cola trademark on his arm. As soon as I receive the pictures, I'll mail Mrs. Motz the letter and a few pictures. At the same time, I'll send you a carbon copy. Possibly until that time you can round up a few pictures that would be desirable to publish with the article. It deals with a brief summary of my trip to the Gulf of Papua, a description of the native concept of marriage, the bride price, the marriage ceremony, and family life. I had intended to include a description of a sing-sing, and the native pay-back philosophy, but it would have been too long. I'll include these items in a later letter.

I trust you're coming along well in your work at the school. I'll be interested in hearing how you're managing to provide the food for such a crowd of youngsters. I suppose Pamela and Marla are again staying at Catherine, while they're going to school. Will you please tell Ellen I appreciated receiving her letter and the clipping of the wedding from the paper. According to the description, the wedding must have been very beautiful.

Has Joe ever closed the deal at Mankato? I was very much interested in how that was going to turn out. I hope it paid off financially for all the trouble it caused.

One of the Fathers will be heading for the bush country tomorrow for almost a three-week stretch, so I had better bring this letter to a close, and spend a bit of time discussing his work. Best regards to everyone. Hope everything is coming along well at Catherine and at the school.

Your devoted brother, Msgr. Firmin

September 15, 1960

Dear Mrs. Motz:

Just a year ago I spent a four-week vacation in Ellis County in preparation for my missionary assignment in New Guinea. At that time, I met hundreds of friends who showed a genuine interest in this remote part of the globe. Some were interested in New Guinea from an ethnological point of view, others from the cultural angle, and still others from the missionary prospects. Now that I have lived a full year as a missionary among the natives of the Southern Highlands of Papua, some of my experiences may offer the raw material for deductions on the various levels of interest. However, I must caution against generalizing. What is true of one section is not necessarily true of another section of New Guinea.

Even though New Guinea is not big in comparison with the United States, it is a country of great variety. The many languages are a good illustration of what I mean. A linguistic expert told me last week that there are at least 521 basically different languages in New Guinea. Imagine what complications there would be in the United States if there were a special language for each state. And then imagine how these complications would be multiplied if there were a special language for each county. As Americans we would say that would create an impossible situation. But really such an "impossible" situation exists in New Guinea. The language difference is just one phase of the variety in New Guinea.

Before I describe some of the practices and customs of the natives whom I have contacted in the Southern Highlands of Papua, I want to tell you of my expedition to the Gulf of Papua and the interior along the coast. As Prefect Apostolic of Mendi, I have ecclesiastical jurisdiction over all of the Southern Highlands and also over the Gulf district between Bell Point and the mouth of the Purari River, roughly about nine thousand square miles in addition to the 10,000 square miles of the Southern Highlands. Since the Gulf territory is my responsibility for missionary work, I decided to make an exploratory trip and assess its mission prospects.

It was through the courtesy of the Australasian Petroleum Company (APC) that I could make the trip. The Petroleum Company has been searching for oil in that area for over ten years—without success. When I requested to visit that district, the APC was just in the process of clearing an area at a place called Iehi for sinking another well.

The APC provided all the transportation, including a Catalina seaplane, a Beaver seaplane, a barge, a canoe, and a Sikorski helicopter. The canoe ride of thirty-eight miles up the Kikori River was the most interesting and most advantageous for inspecting the place for possible mission work. The canoe which I boarded at the mouth of the Kikori River was at least forty feet long and not more than three feet wide. It was carved by the natives out of one huge piece of timber. A forty-horsepower outboard motor propelled the canoe. The APC gave me two native boys as companions for the trip. One of the lads steered the canoe, and the other placed himself in the prow of the canoe to keep an alert eye on logs or other dangerous objects coming down the river. Seated in an easy chair in the center of the canoe, I found the trip most comfortable, even though the sun was at its hottest in that tropical area. With the powerful motor, we travelled close to thirteen miles per hour against a very swift current. Because of the many whirlpools, the river is rather treacherous. It averages about two hundred yards in width, and occasionally widens to three hundred yards during the first thirty-eight miles from its mouth. The channel is deep enough to allow large oceanliners to go as far as Middletown, the APC depot, twelve miles from the mouth of the Kikori.

On both sides of the river, there was a solid mass of luxuriant growth amidst tropical trees. Occasionally I could observe a stream coming from the dark jungle and emptying into the Kikori. Evidently, it is these streams that create some of the whirlpools in the river. I was told that there were many crocodiles and dangerous snakes in and near the river. I saw none.

Over that thirty-eight-mile stretch up the river I saw only three small villages. The largest didn't have more than ten native houses. All these houses were built on poles about twelve feet off the ground. I could think of three reasons for this: first, because of the extreme heat; secondly, because of the danger of a flooding river; and thirdly, as a protection against unfriendly reptiles.

My three-day stay along the Kikori River and my trip with the helicopter to the interior, and the inspection tour with a Beaver seaplane over the delta area confirmed the fact that there are very few natives living in the Gulf section. It is almost impossible for people to live there in large numbers, because of the food problem. Almost no ground can be found for cultivation. Sago, a bit of seafood, and a few coconuts near the coast would be the only means of subsistence.

The weather is considerably different from that of the Southern Highlands. Being at sea level and only a few degrees from the equator, it becomes uncomfortably hot. The heavy rains don't help much either. At Kikori, it rains 200 inches per year; at Middletown (12 miles from the mouth of the Kikori), it rains 250 inches per year; at Barikewa (38 miles up the river), it rains at least 350 inches per year. This past June alone, they had seventy-eight inches of rain at Barikewa. There were two heavy downpours while I was there. I never saw so much water come down in such a short time.

While the trip to the Gulf and the stay on the Kikori River were most interesting, I was happy to return to my headquarters in the Southern Highlands. Although the population in the gulf district is sparse, within a few years we hope to operate at least a few mission stations there. We already have a lease of several acres at Vaimuru, which seems to show signs of becoming a shipping center eventually, and possibly the gateway to the Southern Highlands.

Getting back to our mission area of the Southern Highlands of Papua, I should like to present some of my observations and experiences that may be of interest to you and to the subscribers of the Hays Daily News. Actually, every day among these pagan, primitive, illiterate, and backward natives offers the opportunity for new and unexpected adventure. However, at this time I shall confine my observations to the native outlook on marriage and family life.

Marriage among the natives in the Southern Highlands is primarily an aspect of tribal economy. Obviously, human nature is the same in New Guinea as in other parts of the world, and therefore there is a mutual attraction between a boy and a girl. However, from all indications, love is not a prerequisite for marriage. Neither does personal beauty or charm play a vital role in the selection of a bride. The prime consideration appears to be the "bride price," and the working ability of the prospective bride. The "bride price" is the amount of money, or its equivalent, a man must pay to the father of his prospective bride. Unless the payment is made, there is no marriage. This is one reason why baby girls are so popular with native parents. Each girl represents an increase in wealth, in the form of the bride price, when she reaches the age of marriage.

Frequently, marriages are arranged without the knowledge of the bride, or at least without her approval. It is mainly a business transaction between the father of the bride and the husband. The man who wants to get married approaches the father and asks how much he wants for his daughter. If the prospective husband can pay the price, arrangement is immediately made for the marriage. As a rule, the girls will comply with their father's wish. However, occasionally, the girl may object. This happened near our mission a few months ago. A young man by the name of Tundu wanted to marry Masomi, the daughter of Tomis. Tomis and Tundu agreed on the price. On the designated day Tundu brought his payment. Tomis was delighted, until he learned that Masomi had disappeared. Nowhere could she be located. To escape the marriage, she simply hid in bush territory for several months. Tundu, unhappily, didn't get his bride. Tomis, the father of Masomi, was most unhappy over the loss of the kinas, axes, and the rest of the bride price. He threatened to kill Masomi as soon as he found her. It has happened in some cases that a girl committed suicide to avoid a particular marriage arranged by a father or an uncle. In this case, Masomi returned after a few months, when she had heard that her father had calmed down. Now Tomis is anxiously waiting for another eligible man to ask for his daughter, and so collect the bride price.

The aftermath of this attempted marriage was that Tundu calmly gathered up his possessions, went a mile or so down the valley and negotiated for another bride, the very next day. Unfortunately, the father of this second "possible bride" demanded too high a price. Since Tundu didn't have the number of kinas, axes, and pigs the father requested, he gave up for that week, hoping to find a "bargain bride" sometime later.

The price for a bride fluctuates from place to place, depending on the "supply and demand" and the wealth of the prospective husband. The basic economic rule of "supply and demand" concerning brides applies here. A typical price for a bride in the Mendi Valley right now would be fifteen kinas, three pigs, an axe, and a handful of salt. (A kina is a mother-of-pearl shell that can be bought in this area for the equivalent of about $3-$6.) This may not seem terribly expensive by American standards, but it is extremely high for most natives in this section. Mendeba, a neighbor of our mission, began transactions for a bride two years ago. At that time, he was able to make a down payment large enough to take the bride, but he didn't have enough to make complete payments. Now he is working for the government to earn the required number of kinas. However, according to my calculation, he won't reach the required sum for another ten or fifteen years. Some less fortunate men never earn enough to make even the initial payment. These remain unmarried. In some sections of New Guinea, the bride price has become so high that the government had to step in and place a ceiling. In one district, I know the government set the equivalent of $125 as the maximum. The coastal natives assure us that in some of the more advanced areas, a bride price of the equivalent of $600 is not unusual.

Since the "bride price" is part of the native economy, the government is reluctant to outlaw it completely. In fact, even converts to the Faith cannot ignore the "bride price." It is simply part of the native way of life. Perhaps it could be classified a dowry in reverse. Because of the attractiveness of the "bride price," you can imagine the opposition there will be on the part of the parents, if a young convert finds herself attracted to the religious life. Problems have arisen in this matter in more advanced districts.

Concomitant with the bride price, another factor that enters into choosing a bride is the girl's ability and willingness to take care of the gardens and pigs. Here in the Southern Highlands, it is the woman who is the "bread-winner" in the family. She must take care of the gardens, raise kaukau (sweet potatoes), look after the pigs, and in general provide the food for the family. The men and boys roam about as they please, hunt, and congregate in groups to exchange stories. The government has tried to impress on the natives that men must work also. For this purpose, the government has provided jobs, and even forced men to repair roads and improve airstrips. But this policy on the part of the government has had no effect on the native custom of having the women provide the food for the family. A man looking for a wife will therefore be interested in a girl who has been well trained by her mother in the taking care of gardens and pigs.

Polygamy is permissible by the native code of morality. Frequently, a man's wealth can be gauged by the number of wives he has. If he could afford a bride price for more than one girl, he is fairly well-to-do by native standards. A plurality of wives is also a sign that a man has a number of gardens to be tended. Kavivi, one of the most powerful chiefs and one of the wealthiest in the Mendi Valley, has eight wives. According to reports, he intends to get four more. It seems his eight wives are not adequate to take care of his extensive gardens. So, you can see that even such a primitive area as the Southern Highlands, there is an unfair distribution of wealth.

The marriage ceremony among the natives is a very casual matter. I observed one of them recently. Here is how it happened. On the designated day, the prospective husband, Wangalu, and the father of the prospective bride met in a native house, which is the equivalent of a community room. The bride price was already agreed upon a few days previous. On this, the wedding day, Wangalu, the hopeful groom, brought the pay. Wangalu lined up the kinas on the ground along the wall inside the house. For each kina he had an ornate cushion of banana tree leaves and bark of the finest trees in the area. (They treat kinas as an American would handle a precious jewel.) At the far end of the room he had a steel axe (bought from the government). At the entrance to the house he had two pigs tied to a peg. As I entered the room, I could hardly see anyone. There are no windows in the native houses, and the door is usually too small to admit much light. After my eyes became somewhat accustomed to the dark, I could see the price for the bride lined up against the wall. On the one end of the room was the father of the bride and the bride. About a dozen friends or relatives were scattered about in the room. Hardly a word was spoken. The fact that the girl was present, and her "bridal dress" was a sign that she was willing to become a bride. The man who was buying the bride sat closest to the kinas, noticeably proud of his wealth. For at least two hours they sat with hardly a word spoken. The father of the bride and the prospective husband were smoking a pipe during all this time, obviously giving the impression of deep concentration and reflection. Every ten or fifteen minutes the father examined one or the other of the kinas. Almost as often, the anxious groom arose to dust off, or polish, one of the kinas. Finally, the bargain was completed. The father accepted the price, and thereupon "gave away" the bride.

It is almost impossible to describe the bride for this occasion. She was covered completely from head to toe with black oil, derived from the sap of some kind of tree near Lake Kutubu—several days' walk from Mendi. She actually looked like someone who had been completely dipped in black crankcase oil. Even her skimpy and abbreviated grass skirt was soaked in that oil. Her face was the only part of her body not soaked in that oil. Instead, it was painted a bright red. While she was not exactly a blushing bride, her face certainly was a striking red.

What the significance of the oil covering is for a bride, I haven't been able to find out. However, I was told that after the payment and acceptance of the price, the bride and groom separate and don't see each other again, or at least they do not live as husband and wife until the oil has worn off. There seems to be no definite time for this. I have seen some brides wearing this oil-covering for at least a month. Only after this "bridal dress" has disappeared, or worn off, will the married couple live as husband and wife.

While the natives of the Southern Highlands have some concept of the family as a unit and of family life as a basic training for life, in practice the family is a loosely-knit portion of this primitive society. For one thing, the native husband and wife of the Southern Highlands do not live in the same house. In fact, there is no home life among these natives here as it is known in America. To be sure, the husband and wife see each other frequently—in the garden, near each other's houses, in the bush, and in other less conspicuous areas. According to the testimony of the natives, the men rarely go to the house of the women, and women never enter the house of the men. The husband lives in the house of his father, or brothers, or relatives, or if at all possible, he will have his own house. The wife lives in the house of her mother, or sisters or female relatives. When children are born, they will live with the mother. When the male children reach the age of about five or six, they move in with the father or uncles. The female children remain with their mothers, or aunts.

There is no such a thing among these natives as a family dinner, or a family get-together, or a family outing. The father and the boys receive their daily kaukau from the wife or mother. They eat when they feel like it. As soon as the girls are old enough to work, they will help their mothers in the garden and help themselves whenever they want kaukau. Their time for eating likewise is not guided by any kind of schedule. They simply eat when they become hungry. Frequently, men and women as well as boys and girls can be seen nibbling on kaukau or sugar cane as they walk about, and that is almost any time of the day.

The loosely-knit family life is not universally true, for other parts of New Guinea. In the more advanced districts, where the natives have been in touch with civilization and Christianity for a longer period of time, family life is beginning to follow the pattern of the Western World. It will take many years before this will become the common practice here.

There is surely a mutual parental-filial love among these natives, but at times it is not easy to discern. For example, several months ago a lad of fourteen or fifteen returned to Mendi after a year's absence in a coastal school. Upon arrival there was no embracing, no kissing, not even a handshake between the son and his parents. We know, as a matter of fact, that this particular lad has a genuine love for both his father and mother, but it evidently was not manifested even after a year's separation.

Obedience to parents is likewise a vague concept among these primitive natives. According to the testimony of a number of the natives in this area, when a boy is big enough to roam about—presumably about the age of six or seven, he will go and come as he pleases, regardless of his father's objections. The little girls seem to be trained at least a little more carefully by their mothers, but their idea of obedience would also differ considerably from the Christian and American concept. It is not rare that youngsters, instead of returning to their own house at night, will stay with their friends.

The natives in general are very good to the children. It seems that children are welcomed and treated well everywhere. About five months ago four of our school boys—between the ages of 7 and 12—ran away from school and without any provisions took off for Ialibu, a good two days' walk. They didn't go hungry. The natives, even though total strangers, offered them food along the way. Such walkabouts by native children without provisions are rather common.

From this summary description of the natives' view of marriage and family life, you can see what problems confront the missionaries in their attempt to inculcate a Christian way of life. Since the family is the basic unit of society, and since the sacredness of the home is inevitably a part of the sacredness of marriage, in order to raise the tone of this primitive society, we must impress on the natives the basic lessons of the natural law about marriage and family life while we introduce them to the Christian way of life. The natives must learn that marriage is a sacred mutual contract between one man and one woman, and not a one-sided economic transaction; that marriage is monogamous by God's own decree written in the law of nature, and not by economic necessity or expediency; that the marriage state is a personal vocation involving social responsibilities and not a convenient, selfish arrangement.

Changing the native way of thinking and their way of life in these matters is a slow process. While limited progress is observable among the adults with whom our Capuchin missionaries have maintained contact for five years, hope for the future rests mainly with the youngsters of school age. These, we hope, will absorb the Christian way of life while they are being given a basic grade school education.

I hope these few reflections on the native marriage customs and family life will be of interest. In a future letter, I hope to describe other aspects of native life. Until I came to New Guinea, the "primitive culture" meant for me an era of history that was receding farther and farther into the past. New Guinea, strangely enough, brought "Ancient History" back to life again for me. By a jet plane I came from the twentieth century culture to 5,000 B.C. culture, within a matter of hours. I hope my brief description will have some of the living reality that I am observing every day.

Yours sincerely,

    Rt. Rev. Firmin M. Schmidt, O.F.M.Cap.

    Prefect Apostolic of Mendi

<center>~~~</center>

Chapter 2

OCTOBER 1960–SEPTEMBER 1961
SISTERS ARRIVE,
GIRLS COME TO SCHOOL,
TRIPS TO OUTSTATIONS

12 October 1960

Dear Mary,

Many thanks for your letter of October 1, and the letter and birthday card of October 4. The first arrived on Tuesday October 11, and the birthday card and letter arrived here today—well timed. Many thanks also for the five dollars. I hope to use it well. I was happy to hear that my letter to the Hays Daily had a favorable reaction. I had a letter from Mrs. Motz today. She was well pleased and is looking forward to my next letter. She also sent another check for $25. In her letter she expressed her appreciation for the letter she received from you. She didn't call you before publishing the letter, she said, because she wanted it to be a surprise. I intend to write to her in a day or two. I wonder if you could send me a couple of copies of the letter, as published in the News. You need not send the entire paper, and you can send the copies by ordinary mail, since I'm in no hurry to receive them. I'm sure Mrs. Motz will give you extra copies if you tell her they are for me. She offered to send some copies in her letter.

I am writing this letter from our cargo shed where we will be living until the Sisters' Convent is completed. I spent most of today, my birthday, moving out here. Actually, this isn't bad at all. We have a nice wooden floor, and an aluminum roof, of course no ceiling. It is raining right now, and the noise on the metal roof is a bit disturbing, but I'm sure we'll get used to it. The Sisters are expected here on Friday October 14. One of these days I'll take a picture of this new temporary home of ours. Speaking of the Sisters, we got two of the bush girls to clean up, and gave them some dresses, and have them ready to work for the Sisters when they get here. Both have been to our school. One of them is Masomi. That's the girl I referred to in my letter. That's the girl who was to marry Tundu, by her Father's arrangement. She simply ran off, as I mentioned in the letter. She is a very bright girl, speaks English fairly well, and is very enthusiastic about meeting the Sisters.

I am enclosing a few pictures taken last week on my visit to Tari. I have them well marked to tell you what they're all about. The one at the outside altar where I distribute Communion seems to give you the impression that I am almost bald. As far as I am aware, I have as much hair now as I had last year. However, I'm getting a good percentage of gray hair. The pictures taken inside were taken with a polaroid camera. The picture is automatically printed in a few seconds. Too bad the outside picture at the altar doesn't show the big crowd of kanakas. I bet there were easily six hundred people for the Mass. I read the gospel in pidgin and gave a short talk in pidgin during the Mass, for the benefit of the natives employed by the government. After the Mass, I preached to the people in English while one of the native teachers translated the sermon into Huli, the native language.

My trip to Tari was most pleasant. The friars stationed there are

Fathers Paul, Berard, and Timon, and Brother Mark. I taught the three Fathers for four years in Washington, and Brother Mark was stationed in Washington for about five years while I was there. Among the highlights of my visit at Tari was a visit to the initiation area of the local tribe. I won't describe the entire procedure of the initiation, since it would take me several pages. Briefly, it amounts to this. The initiation to the secrets of the tribe is open only to the boys, and that only to some of the boys. The initiation takes three days. One phase of the initiation is an instruction on the obligations in life. Practically, these obligations are close to the ten Commandments. The initiation ceremonies take place during the night, ending usually at dawn on each of the three days. I arrived at Tari the night before the last phase of the initiation. Brother Mark and about five of his cargo boys were planning to attend. They asked me to go along. I accepted the invitation. At about one o'clock in the morning we set out for the initiation grounds, a half-hour walk. About two hundred yards of the walk went through a bad swamp. I sank in up to my knees. The cargo boys, noticing that I wasn't used to this type of walking, wanted to carry me. I insisted I could walk as well as they.

When we finally arrived at the initiation "hall," we found they had held it early this night, probably because of the threatening rain. However, I saw the house or hall in which the final ceremonies take place. It is a narrow house, about ten feet wide, three feet high on one end, and about twenty feet on the other, all built out of branches of trees and bush. Both sides of the house, which was about sixty feet long was lined solidly with the old timers of the tribe. Down the center was a ditch about a foot deep. The ditch was almost a solid fire. The last part of the initiation I was told, saw the young lads running along the ditch, through the fire, in the meanwhile being beaten with whips by the men lining the two sides. This is supposed to be proof of their manhood. I went into the house, and almost suffocated because of the smoke. I don't know how they can stand it. Since everything was completed, we decided to return to the mission. On our way back we were caught in a heavy rain. Too bad we miscalculated the time. I would have appreciated to have seen the last part of the ceremonies.

As I may have mentioned before, we have a quasi-central school at Tari. The best boys from our other stations were sent there for special schooling. I was amazed how well they're doing. They speak fairly good English, and in general, seem to be well trained. Their manners are as good as any kids I've known in the States. As I arrived at the mission, the school kids were lined up at the entrance of the house, and sang two numbers for me. One of the pieces was sung in two voices. I must say it was well done, certainly as good or better than kids of comparable grades in the States. The morning I left they (the whole school) sang again for me. One of the numbers I recall was "My Bonnie lies over the ocean." I gave them a free day. They were delighted. All of them accompanied me to the plane. They were still waving after we had taken off. –The first time I had Mass in Church I was surprised to hear all the kids answer the prayers in Latin. All of them know the Gloria by heart, as well as all the prayers said by the altar boy. That's not bad, when you realize that none of the kids are beyond the third grade.

I see I am getting close to the end of the page. I had better not start another, since it's getting close to nine o'clock. Our pilot didn't come back today because of the bad weather. So, I don't know whether this letter gets out tomorrow or not. I guess by this time you have found the irregularity of the mail delivery from here.

I hope you will continue to get along well at the school. Best regards to all – Felix and Angela, Al and Nora, and the rest. I hope the report of Tommy's condition is going to be favorable.

Your devoted brother, Msgr. Firmin

~~~

19 October 1960
Dear Mary,

The biggest news over here this week is the arrival of the four Sisters of St. Francis and Louis Ciancio, the first lay missionary from America.

The Sisters arrived as scheduled on Friday morning, October 14, at 11:05 am. It was a beautifully bright morning and the Sisters were given a royal reception. They are the first Sisters to have set foot in the Southern Highlands. Ever since their arrival they have been objects of curiosity. I think some of the natives are still not sure whether they're real. All the school boys were lined up along the road at the mission for welcoming the Sisters. They all had been prepared for the coming of the Sisters by washing well, and wearing a clean lap-lap. As the Sisters stepped out of the Jeeps, the school kids sang out: "Welcome, Sisters, to Mendi." Besides the school kids, a number of bush girls and women were on hand to welcome the Sisters. Ever since their arrival the bush girls in this vicinity have been hanging around the mission. One of the first things they asked was when they could come to the Sisters' school.

The Sisters seem to be a very fine group. You probably saw their pictures and the article about them in Capuchin Challenge. The article refers to them as "frail." They are anything but frail. They're all fairly young. Even the superior can't be much over thirty. They were very favorably impressed with the reception given them and with the mission in general. They are full of enthusiasm, and they are well qualified, and have a wholesome attitude towards the natives. They should prove a tremendous boost for our mission. They can't wait to get started. I think we'll have them start teaching next Monday. I have no idea how many of the bush girls will show up. I have a hunch that in a few months we'll have as many as we can handle. I suppose one of the first things the Sisters will do is put at least a few stitches of clothes on these bush girls.

The Sisters are delighted with the two girls, Masomi and Tio, whom we gave them as house girls. When the Sisters arrived, they were waiting at the door of their house, dressed in beautiful dresses. Both girls have been helping them in the kitchen, cleaning house, keeping the fire going, and so on. The girls on their part seem to be enjoying their working with the Sisters. Neither of them is Catholic, but Masomi knows quite a bit about the Catholic religion. I think one of the Sisters will be giving instructions to these two girls, Tuviam (mother of Mary Philomena), and a few of the other women around the place. The mother of the Chief (Kavivi) made a special trip to the mission to meet the Sisters. She has been back a couple of times since then. She is very friendly. I think we should be able to get a lot of natives to come to the mission through her influence. She must be at least sixty years of age. I have a picture of her somewhere. One of these days I'll send it to you.

Our two cookboys, Pot and Thomas More Mia, are still working for us, even though they're not cooking. They carry the food from the Sisters' house to the cargo shed where we are living now. The Sisters with the help of Masomi and Tio are doing the cooking for all of us until the convent is completed. Thomas More Mia baked twice already since the Sisters arrived. He did a beautiful job both times. He loves to show how important he is. I guess the Sisters had high praise for him. In any case, they're happy to have someone like Thomas More Mia do the baking.

A few weeks ago, I mentioned that Pot was in the process of getting married. This past Sunday I asked him about his bride. He said he got rid of her. What happened is this. She tried to get Pot, but Pot wouldn't pay the required kinas to her father. This is a clear sign that he didn't intend to marry her. When I asked him where the girl was, his answer in his best pidgin was "Mi rouse meri finis." This means: I sent her away for good.

Pot knows very little about our religion, even though he comes to Church every Sunday. He is still filled with the superstition of his own people. Last Sunday he told us that his sister's baby was sick. So, he said, he had to go to build a tambaran. This is a sort of a shrine to the evil spirit. Whenever something goes wrong, natives say it's due to tambaran. So, to placate the evil spirit, and get on the good side of him, they build a crude little hut to tambaran. And that's what Pot did last Sunday. Something like this is quite common among these natives. Many, including Pot, I'm sure have only a vague idea of tambaran and the evil spirit. It is a slow process to rid the natives of their strange notions in this regard. Of course, those who are baptized have been well enough instructed that they don't participate in the respect shown to tambaran.

A few days ago, as I was sitting at my desk, a young school lad knocked at the door. I answered the door to see who it was, and was surprised to find this young lad with a gash in his head, and blood coming down all over his face. The boy had fallen and hit his head with the full force on a huge nail. I took him to the hospital. The medical assistant fixed him up. The young lad didn't cry a bit. In fact, he didn't even wince when the medical boy put iodine on the gash, and put a few stitches in to sew it up. After he was finished, I asked whether it hurt. His simple answer a no. Those kids are really tough. I guess they have to be to survive. When a boy has an accident of this nature, even though it wasn't his fault, he always feels a bit guilty. When he came to the door, he gave me the impression he was afraid I was going to scold him. These kids are certainly interesting.

I received Al's letter today together with a new tape recording. Please tell him thanks. I'll answer him at my first opportunity. Right now, I don't know when I will be able to play the recording back. The machine is in Tari at the present time. Please also tell Nora thanks for the birthday greetings and the letter. I am a bit back in my correspondence. I guess I'll catch up by Christmas.

Your devoted brother, Msgr. Firmin

P.S. Were you able to make out my recording from over here?

~~~

26 October 1960

Dear Mary,

Many thanks for your letter of Oct. 15. It arrived here on Friday, October 21. I appreciate also the clipping from the paper about the Capuchin Fathers donating a complete set of books of St. Lawrence of Brindisi to the Catholic University of America. They evidently had quite a big celebration. Fr. Giles wrote and told me there were well over 350 Capuchins on hand to take part in the celebration. I understand the big Shrine at C.U. was filled to capacity for the Mass, which was part of the celebration. I had received a special invitation, and was asked by the committee on arrangements to attend. Of course, I wouldn't think of going that distance just to attend the celebration. Besides the great distance involved, it would require me to be absent too long from the mission at this time. As you might realize, with the opening of a new main station, the establishing of the Sisters in our mission, and the planning and building of a new central school in our mission, with all these things to tend to, I wouldn't feel free to be absent for any length of time now.

I was happy to hear that our recording turned out all right. Before I sent the tape to the States, I played it back to the boys. They thought it was terrific. They have asked me a few times since then to make another recording.

The Sisters seem to be coming along very well. They started teaching this past Monday, October 24. They were eager to get started, even though they were a bit worried about the reaction of the kids. But after one day of class they felt wonderful about the school. Besides the forty-eight kids we had in school, spread over three classes here in Mendi, fifteen girls showed up the first day of class. The second day there were twenty. However, a problem arose on the second day. Four of the girls came to the Sisters late in the afternoon, parked themselves at the entrance to the Sisters' house, and refused to go home. They told the Sisters that their fathers and brothers threatened to kill them because of their coming to school. Hence, they were afraid to go home. The Sisters didn't know what to do. So they sent word that they wanted to see me. I went over and talked to the girls for a while, but didn't seem to be making much progress. One girl said that her father had an axe ready to chop her up as soon as he saw her. I finally told them that if their fathers or brothers harmed them in any way, or if they opposed their coming to school, they would have to deal with me or the law. I assured them I would check on them in the morning. Evidently, this made an impression on them, and at about 5:30 pm, they headed slowly in the general direction of their homes. They had told me some of the other girls had already escaped and had hidden in the bush. This morning, to my surprise all the girls showed up for class, and, in addition, five more school girls came along. I haven't asked any of them about their fathers or brothers, and therefore I don't know whether my threat had anything to do with their coming back to school.

Since we do not as yet have a dormitory for girls, we can only accept local girls for class. If we would have a girls' dormitory, I'm sure we could have a few hundred girls in school without any difficulty. Some girls actually came in from Ekari, about a four-hour walk from here. We told them we had no place for them to stay. In spite of the fact that we told them we had no place for them right now, and that they should return home, they remained in this area for a few days. We haven't the least idea where they stayed at night.

Getting back to the men's reaction to the girls' attending school, we weren't too surprised over their opposition. In this area, as in most of the Southern Highlands, the girls are looked upon as very little more than beasts of burden. It is their task to cultivate the gardens and raise the pigs. Hence, when the men didn't see the girls working in the gardens, they became a little disturbed. Perhaps, they're also worried that the girls will learn too much in school, and then look down upon their bush life, and look for husbands among the more educated or sophisticated. As far as the girls are concerned, I was a bit surprised that they were afraid of their fathers. Usually, they ignore their parents and are not worried over their reaction at their age. When their parents become a bit too upset, they simply take off for the bush and hide for a while. I really think the girls will continue to come to school since the three daughters of Kavivi, the Chief, are attending school. Of course, it could be that he doesn't know about it. Eventually when we will have a dormitory for the girls, we hope to get Kavivi's mother to look after them.

She's really a very fine woman. Since Kavivi is about forty years old, I guess she must be around sixty. She is strong and healthy, and much older than most people get around here. She is very friendly toward the mission and as a rule she attends Mass on Sundays. I think I may have mentioned that I took a picture of her and Kavivi at a sing-sing some time ago. She was thrilled when I showed them to her, and she wouldn't leave the mission until I finally gave her the pictures. I also had to give a couple of pictures of Kavivi.

The Sisters are doing a wonderful job in general. As far as I can tell, they are really in love with their work even though they have just gotten started. A couple of them are good musicians. One is an expert at playing an accordian. Fortunately, we have an accordian here. She has put it to good use. Until we get an organ, I think she will play the accordian in church for High Masses and other services requiring singing. She hasn't played the accordian in church as yet, but I gave her permission to play. –I took a few pictures of the Sisters with their pupils. Eventually, I hope I'll be able to send you some of them. To make room for the increased enrollment, Brother Claude and his helpers are building another school. When this second school is completed, we will be able to take care of about 120 pupils right here in Mendi.

We're coming along quite well living in the cargo shed. Since we have a roof of aluminum and no ceiling in the shed, it's quite noisy during a heavy rain. Last week one day, we had a hailstorm. It made such a noise it was impossible to carry on a conversation. Otherwise, it isn't too bad.

I hope all is coming along well at Catherine. Hello to Felix and Angela, Al and Nora and the rest.
Your devoted brother, Msgr. Firmin

〜

3 November 1960
Dear Mary,
Your letter of October 22 arrived here on the 29th. Thanks a lot also for the clippings of the Hays Daily you had enclosed. In your letter you mentioned that you intended to send copies of my latest letter in the

Hays Daily to Dr. Murphy and the Papanos. I would appreciate it very much if you would do that. Please let me know whether you are able to send those copies to them. Both, I'm sure, would appreciate receiving them. Thanks also for the information about the St. Joe Alumni Day this year. I had not had anything about it this year. Possibly I'll receive a newsletter from the Association in a day or so. It was good to hear that Severin was being recognized in the Silver Jubilee celebration. I wrote to Severin last Sunday (Oct. 30). Most likely, he didn't get my letter until after the Alumni Day.

If this letter gets to you later in the week than usual, it's because I was gone all week. I just returned this noon from Ialibu where I went this past Monday for a brief visit. Frs. David and Gary are stationed at Ialibu. Fr. David is the one who came with me to New Guinea last year. Fr. Henry also belongs there, but he hasn't come back as yet from his vacation. He is returning by way of Europe, India, and Hong Kong. I had letters from him all along the way. He is in Sydney right now where he will be archpriest at a First Solemn Mass on November 13. Perhaps you heard before that Fr. Henry was pastor of a parish in Sydney from about 1948 until 1955. So, he should have many friends.

My visit to Ialibu was very pleasant. I hit excellent weather, even though the night before I arrived there the thermometer dropped to 45 degrees. While I was there Fr. Gary left on an expedition to the Wiru Plateau. This area was just opened for missionary work. As far as I know, Fr. Gary is the first white missionary to go into that area. However, he barely had set out on his trip, when a group of Protestants, Lutherans, and East-West Bible group followed. A day later he sent word back telling us that the Protestants are causing him a lot of opposition. Of course, that's our usual story over here. The Protestant missionaries are fanatics. However, I have no doubt that Fr. Gary will make the best impression on these people. The expedition was all on foot. I think Fr. Gary was accompanied by about fifteen cargo boys and a few native catechists. He will be in the Wiru area for at least two weeks. During that time, he intends to start about ten stations.

I found the natives at Ialibu as friendly as ever. They are undoubtedly the most friendly people I have met in New Guinea. Large crowds met me again at the plane, and larger crowds came to the mission to greet me and to shake hands. On November 1, I had Mass at 6:00 pm. The Church was almost completely filled with bush people. They were told that I would have the Mass, but when they saw me as I entered the sanctuary for Mass, they all in unison called out something in their native language, which is an expression of delight or admiration. Remember, this took place in church. After the Mass, even though it was already getting dark, they waited in church until I finished my Thanksgiving. Then they accompanied me outside. I spoke with some of them through an interpreter. Within a few years, we should have a large, active congregation there.

Here in Mendi everything is coming along quite well. The Sisters are doing a bang-up job in every way. At the last count, there were around forty new pupils here since the Sisters started teaching. Almost all of these are girls. The men still object to the older girls' coming to school, but they continue to come. It will take us a while to break their attitude. The Sisters seem to be making good progress, in teaching the older girls sewing. The younger girls are being introduced to regular classroom work. The chief, Kavivi, has approved of his three girls coming to school, and has expressed that he is glad the Sisters are teaching. This should help us to break down the attitude of the rest of the bush kanakas.

One little girl by the name of Porkiami has been floating around our mission for several years. Her father has been working for us about five years. Porkiami must be closer to six years than to five, even though she looks as small as a three-year-old. Occasionally, the friars have given her a dress. Every time that happened, she didn't take her dress off until it fell off or rotted off. When the Sisters came, Porkiami ran around the place without wearing anything. And of course, she was completely covered with dirt. Last Saturday the Sisters were doing some washing when they spotted Porkiami. They called her over and threw her into a tub of soap water and gave her a good scrubbing. Porkiami enjoyed this very much—to the Sisters' surprise. After she was clean, and dried off, the Sisters gave her a cloth to wrap around herself. Porkiami took the cloth and simply wore it over her head. Sunday, the Sisters finally found a dress for her. Porkiami was delighted. She's been hanging around the Sisters ever since. Porkiami was following them, and she remained in front of the church until the Sisters came back out—an hour later. Porkiami is the sister to Masomi, who is the house girl for the Sisters. One of these days I hope to get a picture of Porkiami. If I do, I'll send you a copy.

In a former letter I mentioned that one of the Sisters plays the accordian. Last Sunday, the feast of Christ the King, she finally played the accordian in church. It sounded very good, almost like a small organ. While she played the accordian, the kids sang a few hymns. They did a very good job. In the afternoon we had Benediction. Again, the Sister played the accordian, and the kids sang the "O Salutaris." They didn't do too well on the "Tantum Ergo." In a few weeks, I'm sure they will have the kids well trained to sing in church. I have hopes that they will be able to sing the High Mass for Christmas.

I hope everything is still coming along well around Catherine. Please extend my best regards to all in the family, and to Uncle Jake's and Aunt Anna's.

Your devoted brother, Msgr. Firmin

~~~

30 November 1960

Dear Mary,

Your letter of November 19 arrived here in record time—November 24. Thanks a lot also for the clippings from the Register about the President-Elect Kennedy and the article about the American heiress, Mrs. Dills, becoming a nun here in Wewak, New Guinea. I was surprised to hear that my surface Christmas mail has already reached its destination. That surface mail between here and the U.S. is really unpredictable. We followed the advice of the postal department in sending off Christmas mail. I have a number that I will send airmail. I guess I sent over a hundred by ordinary mail sometime in October. –It was good to hear that the news of the arrival of the Sisters of St. Francis was being spread. I hope it will put a little push into the Sisters of St. Agnes. We definitely are expecting them to come to our Mission at least within a few years. In our optimism concerning more Sisters, we started building a convent at Tari, and will start one at Ialibu shortly. We are planning to take the Sisters to our other stations for a few days' visit. They are slated to go to Tari this Saturday.

The school kids continue to come to school in large numbers. According to Sister Noreen, the Superior, at least sixty new kids have reported for school in recent weeks. Of course, they don't all come every day, but still the attendance is good. Yesterday, I visited the sewing class. At the present time, Sister Noreen conducts that class either in the living room or out in the yard. When they have class in the living room, they don't bother with chairs. They sit right down on the floor, just as they do outside. It seems that this is the most comfortable position for the natives anyway. They love to use the needle, and, according to the Sister, some of them are doing quite well. Their project right now is making blouses for themselves. The Sister cut out the cloth from a plain pattern, and the girls sew it all by hand. The idea is not merely to teach them to sew it all by hand, but also to make something they can wear. Actually, they will have to learn how to wash and keep clean before they will be told to wear clothes. Some of the girls in the sewing class come from Kavivi, the Chief's, line, and therefore they are still in mourning over the death of Kavivi's father. At least five months have passed since he died, but the girls and women of that line still walk around with the clay smeared all over their bodies. The Sisters have tried to make them wash. Some have washed, but a few days later they come back with a new coat of "mud-pack." It is simply a native custom or tradition that cannot easily be eliminated. –Incidentally, I don't remember whether I told you that the name of Kavivi's father was

Jacob. It is difficult to figure out how such a name got into an area like the Southern Highlands. –Getting back to the sewing class, I took a few pictures of them yesterday. There are usually about eighteen in the class. A few were missing when I took the picture.

I think you realize that the native bush people have no concept of time. They have no idea of an hour or minutes. If you ask them how long it takes to walk from Mendi to Komia or some other area, they have no idea what to answer. If it takes a short time, they tell you it takes "liklik" time. If it takes long, they speak of a "big fellow walk-walk." About the only thing they know as far as time is concerned is sunrise time and sunset. Because of this difficulty, you can imagine the trouble the bush kids have in trying to come to school at a certain time in the morning. School starts at 8:30, but the kids have no idea when it is 8:30. Consequently, they come to the Mission as soon as the sun shines in the morning. In case it is cloudy, it's hard to say when they will show up. Some of the kids have been here as early as 7:00 am, and they have come as late as eleven or twelve. Our church bell rings at 6:25 and 7:10 every morning, but many of the kids are too far away to hear the bell. Among the bush kanakas, time really means nothing. They are never in a hurry to go anywhere, nor are they in a hurry to leave. I have seen some of these natives sit along the mission road or in our yard for three or four hours at a time—just talking or doing nothing at all. In fact, when they come to talk or to discuss something, they would be disappointed if you simply gave them only a few minutes. Some "important" discussions of theirs go on for days. And during that time, they repeat the same thing again and again. The American close-time schedule would drive these people mad.

Both our cook boys are still on the verge of getting married. Thomas Mia has already paid for his "bride," but since he is a Catholic, he will have to get married in the Church. It's hard to tell their ages, but I don't think Mia is more than nineteen. –Pot is in a dilemma. He got rid of the girl who was lined up for him some time ago. Now a new one, or her father, is after him. Due to some preliminary agreement, Pot made a down payment for the bride with a pig and two kinas. In the meanwhile, Pot decided he didn't want her. As far as I could find out, the girl's father and friends have already eaten the pig. This makes it very difficult for Pot to call off the deal, since part of the payment (the pig) can no longer be reclaimed. In spite of this, Pot finally decided not to take the girl. The girl, on the other hand, has threatened to jump into the river and commit suicide if Pot won't take her. To prove that she is serious, she has already prepared a garden of kaukau for Pot. This has upset Pot. He walks around quite sad these days. Every now and then he comes to discuss troubles. Yesterday he said equivalently that this trouble has made him think too much, and when he thinks too much, his belly hurts. As he put it, in his inimitable Pidgin, "Belly belong mi, him all buggered up. Mi tinktink too much." I guess it is nothing else than a sign of nerves. And this is amazing. I didn't think any native could suffer in this way. I guess that's also a sign of brains. Today, Pot came up with what he thinks is the solution. He will go and hide in the bush for a month or two. During that time, he says, this girl will leave and find another man. Then he can return to the Mission, a free man. He really loves the Mission and doesn't want anything to come between him and the Mission.

I am enclosing a few pictures of the Sisters. I have a few better ones, which I may send sometime later. I think I have labeled each adequately. All the pictures I am sending were taken right here on the Mission. Other pictures were at the airstrip.

I hope you, and all those around Catherine are coming along as well as ever. Hello to all in the family.

Your devoted brother, Msgr. Firmin

〜

29 December 1960

Dear Mary,

This letter will get out of Mendi at least a day later than usual. I usually write to you on Wednesdays, but this week I didn't get around to it until today. I've received a good number of Christmas cards and letters, but I'm sure many others have not been delivered as yet. It isn't that the weather was bad. Actually, it has been unusually good for flying. However, here in New Guinea, the people, Australians and others, believe in celebrating. I know a number of pilots who took off from Friday before Christmas until the following Wednesday. This is Thursday, Dec. 29, and we haven't had a mail delivery since last Friday, Dec. 23. That really is nothing unusual. I hope to acknowledge some of the cards I received as soon as I can. In the meanwhile, I would appreciate it if you would tell Al and Nora, Felix and Angela, Uncle Jake and Aunt Clara that I am grateful for their cards and letters. Also, if you see Joe or Hubertine, please tell them thanks for their card and letter.

As we had anticipated, Christmas was a most beautiful celebration. I can recall very few of the past that I enjoyed more. The weather was delightful. We had a rain on Christmas Eve, but it cleared up at least three hours before Midnight Mass. On Saturday, December 24, at 10:30 in the morning, nineteen boys were baptized in our church here at Mendi. While Fr. Otmar administered the Sacrament, I explained the ceremonies to the people. One of the boys, Bede, who was baptized last year, translated my explanation into the Mendi language for the benefit of the large crowd of natives who were present. All nineteen were dressed completely in white, shirt and pants. The sponsors were native boys who had been baptized a year ago. These were dressed in white shirts and grey pants. It was really a beautiful occasion, from every point of view. The nineteen boys range in age from about eight to seventeen. By the way, little Andiu, of whom I wrote recently, was also baptized. He was as happy as any native boy I have ever seen. He took the name of David. I had a picture taken with him and another small lad, which I hope to send to you if it turns out well. Among the names taken by the newly baptized are: Firmin (Waliba), Raymond (Walu), Martin (Wabunk), Otmar (Osup), Simon (Otu), Edward (Piwi), John (Nono), Stanley, Senan, Kevin, Charles, Clement, Carl, George,

Claude. We had a lot of pictures taken of the group. I hope mine with Raymond, Firmin, Martin, and David turn out all right.

All of the newly-baptized received their First Holy Communion at the Midnight Mass. The midnight Mass itself was very beautiful. At about 11:30pm, all the school kids, about eighty, came to the Church in procession, while the older boys in the church sang, "O Dear Little Children." In the procession were also the newly baptized, all in white. The girls were dressed in red blouses—which they made themselves under the direction of the Sisters. The other lads all wore dark red lap-laps. At the crib, which was beautifully decorated, I gave a talk to the youngsters after I had blessed the Christmas tree and the crib. This was followed by the singing of Christmas carols by the children. Accompanied on an accordian and directed by Sister Noreen, they did a beautiful job of the traditional carols.

The Midnight Mass was a High Mass, at which the boys sang again and very well. At the Mass, I had a Christmas and First Communion sermon for the youngsters. It was as impressive a first Communion celebration as I can remember. Besides the newly-baptized, there were at least fifty natives who went to Communion at the Midnight Mass. After my midnight Mass, I offered my other two Masses immediately. After my thanksgiving following the third Mass, all of us had a fine lunch of ham sandwiches, coffee, and cookies at the Sisters' house. It was close to 3am by the time we finished. That was about 11:00 am, Dec. 24, Catherine time. –Fr. Otmar had the nine o'clock Mass in the morning, and again the church was jammed with natives. The youngsters again sang their Christmas carols. –The rest of Christmas Day was rather quiet, except for a brief visit by the District Commissioner, and the Doctor. The District Commissioner is not a Catholic, but he has the highest regard for our mission. The doctor is a good Catholic. In the evening at 6:00 pm, we had a big Christmas dinner, prepared by the Sisters, one of whom is an excellent cook. Looking back now, I must say it was as fine a Christmas as I have had. The Sisters, as far as I could judge, really enjoyed Christmas also.

The day after Christmas we had games for the school kids—races of all kinds, tug-o-war, dart throwing, rope jumping, etc. We tried to have each youngster win at least something. It may interest you to know that a certain Firmin Waliba was by far the fastest boy in the foot races. He runs like a gazelle. Besides being a good athlete, he is a very fine lad. He has the heartiest laugh I have heard among the natives. (While Firmin Waliba is very fast, I think I could outrun him, now that I am regaining my athletic form.) According to the scale I stepped on at Erave about two weeks ago, I weighed 176. I hope I will be able to stay that low. I don't think I have ever felt any better. I haven't had a cold of any kind for over a year. I had a slight cold shortly after my arrival in October 1959. I haven't had a touch of anything since that time.

After the games on Monday, Dec. 26, we told the school kids they should go home for a few days. We told them to be back by Friday. In spite of our urging, a number of them preferred to stay at the Mission. Others who went home, returned on Wednesday or today. Only a few of them were not back by this evening, Thursday, Dec. 29.

There is a big sing-sing scheduled here in Mendi for Monday, January 2. For at least a week, we have been hearing the beating of drums and singing, in preparation for the occasion. Usually the drumming and the singing goes way into the night. I'll try to have the Sisters go to the sing-sing grounds so they can be seen by the natives. I'm sure they'll command a lot of interest.

I had intended to write to Fr. Raphael for Christmas, but simply didn't get around to it. Perhaps I will be able to write to him sometime in January.

Best regards to all and best wishes for the New Year.
Your devoted brother, Msgr. Firmin

~~~

11 January 1961
Dear Mary,

I have been answering letters for a couple of days, and still haven't caught up. I had hoped to be able to write to all that require an answer, but I may be forced to postpone a few. Just in case I won't be able to write to Regina and Charles Polifka, will you please tell them thanks for the photo they sent of Judy and Leroy's wedding. –The mail service has continued to be quite bad since Christmas. It all gets to its destination eventually, but very slowly. I guess the airlines are a bit overworked this way. The weather has been unusually good for flying during the last week.

Although officially according to government schedule, this is summer vacation from school, the Sisters started class again this past Monday. In the short time the Sisters have been teaching there has been an increase of at least 65 pupils. During this week and next week, I'm sure there will be a further increase of at least twenty or twenty-five. –Last week I mentioned one of the bigger girls by the name of Lumi, who was to be married to some fellow according to the arrangements of her father. Since the father was unsuccessful in getting Lumi to accept the fellow, he is now trying to marry off Lumi's younger sister, who is about fifteen years old. The old boy must really want the bride price badly. The younger girl refused to cooperate too. She also is coming to school here. Yesterday as the younger girl was coming down the road to school, she noticed her father coming towards her—about four hundred feet away. She screamed and immediately headed for the bush with her father after her. He couldn't catch up with her. An hour later she was back in school as if nothing had happened.

The case of Pot and his possible marriage seems to be solved temporarily. Pot went to Kagua about a month before Christmas to get away from the possible bride. Before he departed, he told the girl who wanted to marry him, that he wasn't coming back. She thereupon returned to the bush, sad over her loss. However, a couple of days after Christmas, Pot returned to Mendi. A few days ago, I asked what happened to the girl. He said she has given up, but in her sorrow, she chopped off one of her fingers. From a few reports, I heard she also stole a pig that belonged to Pot. At least, he was going to report his pig as missing to the government officer, and he was quite certain that this girl took it.

Our other cook boy, Thomas More Mia, finally got married last Sunday, January 8. His bride's name is Bolu. Negotiations for this marriage started way back at the end of October. The bride price was paid sometime in November. About three weeks before Christmas, Fr. Otmar had a final discussion concerning the bride price with the parents of both, and interested relatives. The agreement was to everyone's satisfaction. I don't remember the complete price. As far as I recall, Thomas paid about seven kinas, a big pig, about . . . $13 and a couple of axes. Bolu is a real bush girl. She left the bush only a couple of months ago. The Sisters have been trying to teach her a few things, but she has a long way to go. The Sisters say she has picked up something. – As I may have mentioned before, it is very important that the complete bride price be paid before the marriage takes place. Before the complete price is paid, either party can back out.

The marriage ceremony was rather casual in comparison with other marriages I have seen in the States. Since Thomas is a Catholic, the marriage had to take place before a priest. The ceremony was held in church at 4 pm last Sunday. Two Catholic boys were the witnesses (best man and bridesmaid). We teased one of the fellows about being the bride's maid. –Somewhere a dress was found to fit the bride. She is a rather hefty girl. Unfortunately, no one showed her how to wear the dress. She had it on backwards. She didn't seem a bit nervous about the ceremony. In fact, she didn't seem to be concerned about anything. She was sitting in her usual way on the ground in front of the church chatting with a few of her bush friends. Thomas wore a pair of trade shorts and a fancy blue shirt. Of course, both were barefooted. Bolu had been coming to church for several months now, but she usually parked herself on the floor—a good distance from the altar. She seemed a bit shy when Fr. Otmar told the bride and groom to come forward. She seemed a bit embarrassed when she was told to hold hands with Thomas, as part of the ceremony. She giggled when she was asked whether she would take Thomas as her husband. Everything was done in the local language, the only one she understands. When everything was over, the bride immediately left the Church, while the groom stayed inside a while to say a few prayers. When I came out of the church a few minutes later, the bride was already heading down the road with a few of her bush friends. We called her back for a few pictures. I hope to remember to send you some. We kidded Sister Noreen about playing the accordian for the ceremony. She almost believed that we wanted her to play "Here comes the bride." To make everything complete, we typed out a formal invitation to the wedding for the Sisters. At the bottom of the invitation we put: Reception at Bolu's bush house at 8:30 pm -R.S.V.P. –This, by the way, was the first marriage of locals. I mean where both were from the immediate vicinity. There have been many marriages of locals with outsiders.

This coming Sunday I will have Confirmations at Ialibu. On the 22nd of January I will administer Confirmation at Mendi, and on the 25th at Tari. For the next few weeks, I will be roving about somewhat. I also intend to pay a short visit to Kagua, and possibly to Erave. If my next letter gets to you a few days later than usual, you know the reason why.

I am enclosing a few photos. I think I marked them adequately on the back. I may have a few more to send along the next time. You can see that both Raymond and Firmin are fine looking lads. Raymond is always full of mischief. He is a very delightful character. I thought I had a photo made of myself with Martin, but I can't find any among the prints. Martin is one of the brightest boys we have in school. He is a bit older than the rest of the fellows. He seems one of the most promising native boys we have in school right now. Too bad he is so old.

I hope everything is coming along well at Catherine. Hello to all.

Your devoted brother, Msgr. Firmin

15 February 1961

Dear Mary,

Your letter of February 4 arrived in Mendi on the 11th, but I didn't get it until my return from Erave on Tuesday Feb. 14. Many thanks. I was surprised to hear that you have not had much snow this winter. The radio reports left me under the impression that the Midwest and West as well as the East had been hit by a number of heavy snow storms. Perhaps by this time you have gotten some. If you would receive as much snow as we receive rain, you would be snowed under for a couple of months a least. This is only the 15th of February and already we have received seven inches of rain since the first of the month. –I was sorry to hear that your sciatica kicked up again. I hope it isn't serious. Maybe you need a warm climate like New Guinea. –The news of Roseann's Colleen was wonderful. This noon I received her very fine letter and five dollars. I certainly will write to Colleen either today or tomorrow. I have a hunch that the Sisters in school urge the children to contribute to the Holy Childhood Association, which is really meant to help all the missions. In any case, I was happy to receive the gift from Colleen.

I mentioned that I returned from Erave on Tuesday, February 14. I went there on Saturday (Feb. 11) morning to see how things are going there at our latest main station. We started it as a permanent station towards the end of October. It is dedicated to Our Lady of the Angels. Besides having a large lease of land (311 acres) for coffee plantation, vegetable gardens, fruit trees, and farming, we started our central school there. This year we have sixty-two boys there –thirty-four in Grade 3 and twenty-eight in Grade 4. About forty-five of these boys have already been received into the Church. We have two native teachers there from Rabaul. Each has had ten years of education. They seem to be well qualified. In addition to the two native teachers, a lay missionary by the name of Lou Ciancio is the infirmarian, director of activities, and instructor of music. Fr. Gregory Smith is in charge of the station. Almost the entire 300-plus acres are covered with trees and bush. Right now, there are clearings of about fifteen to twenty acres for the missionaries' house, the school and church, the dormitories and gardens. It is slow work getting a place like that ready for use. For a number of weeks, Fr. Gregory had over fifty cargo boys engaged to cut down the trees, clear the ground, and construct the buildings. There is a wooden structure house there for the missionaries. The carpentry work on it is rather rough. It will be fine when it is finished. The climate at Erave is quite a bit warmer than here in Mendi. In fact, it gets rather hot during the day. At night a person can be comfortable using one or two blankets. The rainfall there per year is about 140 inches. That's even more than we get here.

My stay at Erave was rather enjoyable. The boys at the school are full of life. They all seem to miss their home areas, Mendi, Tari, etc., but they still seem to enjoy life. We had organized games for them on Sunday morning. In the evening the teachers organized a singfest. They really had a lot of volume. I'm sure they could be heard over the greater part of the Erave Valley as they sang such numbers as "Darling Clementine, "Glory, Glory Hallelujah," "I've Been Workin' on the Railroad," and a few with the native touch. These kids are great for writing letters. I'm sure at least three-fourths of them gave me letters to their friends. They're proud of the fact that they can express themselves in English. Of course, the English of some isn't the best. A few of them, however, are very good.

Our enrollment in the school here at Mendi is continuing to grow. Sister told me they had over a hundred kids in school, not counting the bigger girls who are in the sewing class. Within a few months, we may construct a dormitory for the girls, who would like to come to our school from the outstations. This will mean another increase in enrollments. In addition to teaching the kids at our station, Fr. Otmar and two of the Sisters go to the Government school twice each week to teach catechism.

We're still living in the cargo shed. However, last week Wednesday we finally got the flooring in for the convent. If all goes well, we should have everything ready for the Sisters to move in the convent by Easter time. There is a lot of painting to be done, and a number of time-consuming jobs. Anyway, it's good to know that the end of our cargo shed living is in sight.

On a number of occasions, I mentioned about young girls being forced by a father or brother to marry simply because of the bride price. There was an interesting case of that recently about a mile from here. As is frequently the case, the girl was not consulted about a proposed marriage. When the arrangements were all completed, the girl objected. When everything else failed, she jumped into the Mendi River, attempting to commit suicide. It just happened that a native policeman, a Sergeant, was passing nearby. He immediately dove in and rescued the girl. I haven't heard the results of that as yet. Most likely, she'll be tied up temporarily, until she agrees to accept the husband selected by her father.

Among the school boys here at Mendi, there is a fellow called Wengenem. Yesterday his mother came to the Mission, for the first time as far as we know. The first person she met was Sister Claver. Through an interpreter they started to speak with each other. No sooner did Sister Claver tell her that she was teaching Wengenem in class than the mother of Wengenem threw her arms around Sister Claver and embraced her as an expression of joy and appreciation. As Sister Claver expressed it, "She slobbered all over me. I felt like I needed a real good washing after that." But she enjoyed this expression for the work done here at the Mission. If you could see how crusty and dirty and greasy these natives are who come from the bush, I think you could understand why Sister Claver felt she needed a complete scrubbing after this native's demonstration of affection. In any case, I believe this is a sign of how much others also appreciate the work done by the Sisters here. I hope everything is coming along well at Catherine.

Your devoted brother, Msgr. Firmin

22 February 1961

Dear Mary,

Thanks a lot for your letter of February 11. It reached me at Ialibu on the 18th. I had gone to Ialibu on the 17th for a visit to the bush. I'll tell you about that later. I was glad to hear that you liked the Confirmation pictures. Some of the ones taken here have not been developed as yet. Eventually, I'm sure, I'll get more to you. –Thanks for the clipping of the Ohio family that is coming to New Guinea. They're slated for Mt. Hagen, a neighboring Vicariate. Mt. Hagen is a little less than twenty-five minutes by plane form Mendi.

Speaking of lay missionaries, I'm beginning to get quite a few applications. It is quite possible that I will get a lay missionary as a pilot. I have a very good prospect from Australia. The contract of our present pilot will expire in July. Besides this new prospective pilot, I have also a possible manager for our farm and coffee plantation at Erave, as well as a couple of teachers lined up. In addition to these, two new Capuchin Missionaries have been assigned to our Mission a week or two ago, Fr. Samuel Driscoll, and Brother Alfred. They will get here by the end of April. Fr. Roy Schuster is slated to get here in August sometime. So you can see, we are beginning to expand a bit. We could use at least eight more priests right now. Everywhere I go the natives have asked me to give them a priest to take care of their people.

I had a most interesting week-end –Feb. 17-20. On my Confirmation visit to Ialibu around January 15, a delegation of about fifteen people from a place called Orei asked to have a priest permanently assigned to their area. After talking for a while, I finally agreed to visit their station to see how sincere the natives were in this request. I set the date for Sunday Feb.19. That is why I went to Ialibu last week. On Saturday morning, Fr. Gary and I set out for Orei. It is eighteen miles from Ialibu. Fortunately, a fairly decent road permitted us to go by motorcycle almost all the way. I guess I had to walk only a little more than a mile. Everywhere along the way the natives came out to the road to say hello and to shake hands. Fr. Gary is really popular among those people. We arrived at Orei not quite two hours after we left Ialibu. What a welcome we received. I bet there were at least 150 people right at the mission station to meet us. After we got clear of the crowd, we had a cup of coffee and a light lunch.

In the early afternoon we visited the village near the Mission. This, by the way, is the first village I saw in our Mission. There are no villages in or near other stations. The natives were all delighted to see us. I went in, or rather crawled into, one of the houses. It took me a while to see anything inside because of the fact that there are no windows, and the door is only about thirty inches by twenty inches. After my eyes were adjusted, I could see the stalls for the pigs, as well as the "beds" for people. All these of course in the same house. The rest of the houses were the same. One of the bigger houses I visited was occupied by about twenty-five men – all seated along the inside wall, with a fire in the center. We found out they were cooking something special for themselves. As a rule, the women cook the kaukau and other ordinary food. But occasionally the men find something special. This the women don't even get to see. They told us they had caught some fish in the nearby stream. I later saw the traps with which they catch the fish. They're cleverly constructed. As far as I could tell, the fish they were speaking of were eels. They roasted them wrapped in leaves. I'm sure they ate them with great relish, since this is a rare treat for them.

I mentioned the river nearby. Two big waterfalls, each at least 100 feet high, empty into the river. They are very picturesque and the rumblings of both can be heard at the mission house.

Later in the afternoon I met all the catechumens at Orei. Fr. Gary has an active catechumenate there. About thirty belong to it. They range in ages between sixteen and thirty, divided almost equally between boys and girls. A catechist is assigned to this group to teach them their religion. For over a year, they have been having catechism class five days each week, not counting Sundays. Some of them have been coming to this class for four years. Not only do they learn their catechism this way, but also prayers and songs. I took their catechism and asked them a few questions in Pidgin. No sooner had I asked the question than the whole crowd answered in unison. I discovered that they know the entire catechism by heart, and they understand the explanations, as was clear from Fr. Gary's quizzing. This is remarkable when you realize that the majority of them can't read. They just learn by repetition. After we were finished with the catechism lesson, we prayed the rosary in Pidgin. A hymn to the Blessed Mother brought the session to a close. This, by the way, is the daily procedure. At least twelve and possibly twenty, of these catechumens will be baptized at Easter time.

On Sunday morning I had the main Mass. There were well over 400 people in attendance. The mass was out in the open. Fr. Gary took some pictures of the crowd. I hope to get them eventually. There were about twenty Catholics present. They all went to Communion. After Mass I distributed the blessed ashes to the Catholics and to the Catechumens. After my sermon, which was put into Pidgin and into Umbongi (the local language), Fr. Gary had a Baptism of a child of one of the Catholic couples there. He baptized her Catherine. We told the parents that the name of my hometown was Catherine. They got a big kick out of that.

The people did not leave after Mass. They remained until about six p.m. Throughout the afternoon I met and talked with the natives, through an interpreter. I bet I shook hands with almost all of the 400 that were present. It was a great day for them. The majority had themselves either painted up or greased up. This they do only on special occasions. Incidentally, my hands were coated with several layers of grease by the time I was finished meeting the natives. Many an old man or woman pushed his way through the crowd just to get a "look at the bishop," as they put it, and to shake his hand. They were so pleased with my visit, that they spontaneously took up a collection and got £1.19.3 (about $4.40), which is a lot of money for those people. They gave me this, they said, to "pay for my legs." This is simply the way they put it in their language. Before they departed from the Mission on Sunday evening, another official delegation came to ask for a priest "to sit down all the time" at Orei. They assure me they would give us all the land we need to put up a big church and a new school. Naturally, I couldn't make any definite commitment. Fr. Gary is taking care of about sixteen outstations right now. But it was certainly good to see such natives as these, and their interest in the Church. It should become a flourishing Catholic Community in another ten years or so. When Fr. Gary doesn't get to Orei on Sundays, which is not too rare, a good number of the natives walk to Ialibu for Mass, a distance of eighteen miles.

On Monday morning at about nine we headed back for Ialibu. In spite of the heavy rain during the night and the consequent slippery roads, we covered those eighteen miles back in less than an hour and a half. A couple of hours later our pilot came by to bring me back to Mendi. I arrived in Mendi in a heavy rain. It has been raining for almost two days now. Yesterday the rain was so heavy that the airstrip had to be closed to all aircraft. As far as I can recall, this hasn't happened for at least six months. It is only the 22nd of February, and already we have had ten inches of rain this month.

I don't know whether you will hear from me next week or not. I'm scheduled to go to Goroka on Feb. 27 for the Bishops' Meeting. I don't know how long it will last. All the Bishops of Papua and New Guinea will be present, including those of Rabaul, the Solomons, Bougainville, and New Ireland. The Apostolic Delegate will also be present. I invited him to come with me to Mendi. I don't know whether his schedule will allow it. I hope you're all coming along as well as ever. Hello to all in the family.

Your devoted brother, Msgr. Firmin

~~

12 March 1961

Dear Mary,

Your letter of March 4 arrived yesterday (March 11). Thanks a lot also for the clipping of the Cadet basketball team you enclosed. They really must have a powerful basketball team. Speaking of the Cadets, I received a letter about a month ago from the editor of their school paper, requesting that I write a column for their paper. Unfortunately, the boy, Bergagnoli, sent the letter by ordinary surface mail. It was mailed on November 17 and took almost three months to get here. I haven't answered as yet, presuming they're not in a hurry. I have had a number of letters from other schools with similar requests. Naturally, I'll always answer requests like that, if I can. —Was sorry to hear of the death of Kate Staab and Regina Schmidt.

According to our plans, the Apostolic Delegate, Archbishop Maximillian de Furstenberg, arrived here in Mendi on Tuesday morning, March 7th, at about ten o'clock. He was given a formal welcome. The District Commissioner had a formal Guard of Honor at the airstrip, composed of about twenty native policemen. This is an honor extended only to the heads of governments, or official representatives of those governments. As the ecclesiastical superior of the Mission, I gave the first official welcome, and then I presented the Delegate to the government officials. For this, as well as for the Reception in the afternoon, I was dressed in my white suit. After the formal welcome, we took the Delegate and his secretary, Msgr. Rottuno, to our Mission station — about a mile from the upper end of the airstrip. The school children — about 140 — lined both sides of the road in front of our house. We had given them bright, blue and green lap-laps for the occasion. As the Delegate stepped out of the car, the entire crowd of kids sang out at the top of their voices: "Welcome to Mendi, Your Excellency." The Sisters had practiced with them the previous day. It certainly pleased the Delegate to hear these words of welcome from the children, a number of them out of the bush for only a few weeks.

After a brief visit in the house, I took the delegate to visit our schools. Instead of a formal program by the kids, I decided to have the Delegate visit the classrooms, and see for himself how the Sisters actually conduct class. I'm sure it was greatly appreciated, and I know also it was the first time that he saw how classes are conducted for these natives, from those who don't know a word of English to those who can read, in the first and second grade. We started at the top class (grade 2) and went down to the lowest –prep (equivalent to kindergarten). The first group was given a lesson in oral English, and then Sister had them read. The first grade did the same. The smaller youngsters were given a lesson in arithmetic, abc's. All of them closed their respective demonstrations with a song.

—After it was all over with, one boy in grade 2, by the name of Lui, started to cry. The reason, as Sister found out, was that she did not call on him to read. So, with Sister's permission, he came to the house afterwards, and asked to give the Delegate a demonstration of his reading ability. He came with two readers, one for himself and one for the Delegate to follow. Then he sat down on the floor in front of the Delegate and read. Everyone got a big kick out of that. When Lui was finished, he closed his book, and with a smile from ear to ear left, satisfied now that he had shown the Delegate how smart he was.

The Delegate's stay was very pleasant. As I mentioned, in the afternoon, the District Commissioner had a formal Reception at his home. Almost all non-native residents of Mendi were present. The Reception lasted from 4 – 5:30. Unfortunately, the convent isn't quite ready for occupancy, so we had to make suitable accommodations in our cargo shed. We spent a full day cleaning it up. I even rolled out a carpet for the room in which the delegate stayed. This is the carpet the natives gave me when I arrived in 1959. The Delegate didn't seem to mind these conditions. Actually, I had warned him of our living in the cargo shed, when I sent him the invitation. He seemed to feel at ease, and I was really glad he could get at least a slight taste of mission inconveniences. –When we were at the Reception in the afternoon, the Sisters really set a beautiful table for our dinner, which we had at 7 p.m. The Sisters also prepared a very delicious meal. I don't think the Delegate will hit anything better anywhere along the line in New Guinea.

The Delegate and Secretary were very favorably impressed with what they saw in our mission. Among other things they were surprised how well the school children prayed along at Mass. As I told you before, they say the Mass prayers at every Mass they attend. They were also surprised to see how well our buildings are constructed – the friary, convent, schools, and also our cargo shed. The church, they observed, was very devotional. I think the Delegate carried many happy memories with him after a one-day visit in our Mission. Because of his brief stay, we could not take him to our other stations, —Tari, Ialibu, Kagua, and Erave.

It will take another two weeks or so before the Sisters can move into the convent. At first, lack of materials held up the work. Now, lack of workers is holding up progress. Two of Brother Claude's most reliable and skilled native carpenters beat up a few fellows at the government station. All of them were thrown into calaboose for three months for riotous behavior.

Remember, some time ago I told you about one of the older schoolgirls by the name of Lumi, who refused to accept the husband selected by her father. That same girl, Lumi, is now working for the Sisters. She is working with Masomi, another girl who refused to take the husband selected by her father. I mentioned Masomi in one of the articles I wrote for the Hays Daily News. Tio, who had been working with Masomi, prefers to spend her time in school. The time out of school she spends with her sister, Tuviam, the mother of Mary Philomena. Lumi is one of the best and most promising girls around here. She is an excellent worker. She is only 4'8" tall, but is built like a tank. She is delighted to be working for and with the Sisters. I'm sure her father will have great difficulty in trying to marry her off to someone. Incidentally, we call Lumi, Aunt Jemima. I think the name fits her perfectly.

In your second last letter, you mentioned that you were able to have scheduled High Masses respectively for Mother's and Dad's anniversaries. I was glad to hear that. I think you recall that you sent me $282 in Mass stipends for Mother towards the end of May or June. By this time, I have said exactly eighty-eight of those Masses. By May 4th

I will have said at least 120. At that rate it will take me at least another year and a half to finish the $282. I could offer them more quickly, but I like to spread them out a bit. Of course, I have said a few others, in addition to the ones for the stipends. I hope everything is coming along well around Catherine. Hello to everyone in the family.

Your devoted brother, Msgr. Firmin

~~~

17 April 1961

Dear Friends of the Hays Daily News,

Since my last letter to the Hays Daily News, six months ago, there have been a number of favorable developments in the Capuchin Mission of Papua, New Guinea. First of all, we have had an increase of Capuchin Missionaries, assigned by the Province of St. Augustine, with headquarters in Pittsburgh, Pennsylvania, the same Province that is staffing St. Joseph College at Hays, St. Francis Seminary at Victoria, and caring for the parishes of Ellis County. Secondly, a group of four Franciscan Sisters from Oldenburg, Indiana have come to this Mission to help in leading these pagan natives to Christianity. Thirdly, lay missionaries have begun to arrive from America to work in our Mission.

FRANCISCAN SISTERS

The presence of the Sisters in the Mission will be a big help not only in raising the standard of education in our schools, but also, and especially, in correcting the natives' pagan attitude toward girls and women. According to the primitive native mentality, women and girls have practically no rights. It is their unenviable lot to work the gardens, raise the pigs, and in general be a slave to the man. Even in entering marriage, the girl as a rule has no choice. She must submit to the choice made by her father or brothers, or uncles. This usually amounts to nothing more than living with the man who offers the best kinas or pigs as payment of the bride price.

It is quite obvious that there can be no genuine progress in our efforts to Christianize these people unless we are able to have them recognize woman's God-given rights and personal dignity. With the help of the Sisters, we have hopes of achieving our aim. In the six months that the Sisters have been in charge of our school at Mendi, a noticeable change has already taken place. The girls have been coming to school in large numbers in spite of the opposition from the native men in this area. And once the girls have gotten to know the Sisters, and have come to a few classes, they can be kept away from school only with difficulty. A number of the men have tried to keep their daughters at home to work the gardens and take care of the pigs. Almost without exception they have failed. One native father tried with physical force to keep his two daughters from coming to school. Through some trickery the girls escaped, and hid in the bush for a few days. After the storm blew over, they returned to school, and have been attending ever since.

A number of the native men are beginning to respect the work that is being done by the Sisters. Two of the most powerful chiefs in the Mendi Valley have publicly expressed their approval of the work of the Sisters, and are sending their daughters to school. At the Christmas sing-sing in Mendi, which was attended by about 7,000 natives, the Sisters proved to be the center of attraction. Through interpreters they spoke with many fathers and mothers, and as a rule found them most willing to send their youngsters, girls as well as boys, to school.

The problem of raising the status of girls and women in this pagan land is by no means solved. However, the work of the Sisters in this Mission is probably one of the most effective means of attaining our goal. Within the next five months, the Franciscan Sisters of Oldenburg will assign two more Sisters to this Mission, bringing the total to six. These six will staff two main stations. However, many more Sisters will be needed. It is hoped that at least one more Community of Sisters will come to our assistance in this urgent work within the next year.

LAY MISSIONARIES

Another significant development in our Mission is the arrival of the first lay missionary from America, with the hope of getting a number of others. A lay missionary is a man or woman who freely offers his services to help achieve the aims of the Mission. The work done by lay missionaries is of a wide variety. Thus, in our Mission we can utilize the help of qualified teachers, carpenters, nurses, mechanics, electricians, and even skilled farmers. Since there is usually a shortage of missionary priests and brothers, lay missionaries are frequently indispensable in carrying out our work with any efficiency. Any lay missionary from America who is accepted in our Mission agrees to render his services for at least five years. In exchange he receives no monetary remuneration, except his keep and a reasonable amount of spending money. Since the first lay missionary from America arrived in October 1960, three more volunteers have been found acceptable. It is hoped that a good corps of lay missionaries will be built up to insure the steady progress of this Mission.

NATIVE SUPERSTITIONS

Even though there has been an increase of Missionaries, priests and brothers, and even though Religious Sisters and lay missionaries have begun their important tasks in the Southern Highlands of Papua, progress is necessarily slow. In Christianizing as well as in civilizing a people, it is not merely a question of giving instructions. Knowledge is indispensable but by itself not adequate. There must be constant training. These natives are products of their environment, which for generations has been saturated with pagan practices. Their lives are immersed in superstitious practices. By way of example, if a child gets sick, there is no prayer offered to God. Instead, Tambaran (the evil spirit) is immediately called upon. Frequently, a pig is killed to placate the evil spirit, or Tambaran. When a man accidentally burns his foot as he rolls into a fire in his sleep, Tambaran must have been angry, and needs to be appeased. When someone dies, the blame is again shifted to Tambaran. And so this particular superstition pervades their entire life. An instruction about God and His attributes certainly can be grasped by a native mind, but his knowledge will not immediately and easily blot out all superstitious practices. From experience we know that only gradually will the superstitions be replaced by a Christian life.

PAPUAN JUSTICE

There are many pagan barriers that must be broken before Christianity can enter the hearts of these natives. One of the biggest barriers is the pagan concept of justice as opposed to Christian charity. Christianity has been rightly labeled as the Law of Charity. When we speak of charity in relation to Christianity, we have especially supernatural love in mind. However, it also embraces any manifestation of charity. Hospitals, orphanages, homes for the aged, all kinds of charitable institutions, and personal acts of charity are the signposts of Christian culture. If this is true, then these pagan Papuans are a long way from Christianity.

Among the pagan natives of the Southern Highlands of Papua there is no such a thing as a gift. There is only exchange of one thing for another. As a result, the expression "thank you" is practically meaningless. It is still doubtful whether the word "thanks" is part of the native vocabulary. One of the Missionaries who has been working on the Mendi language recently discovered a word which broadly means "well done." Even if this is comparable to "thanks," it certainly does not have the same connotations that we usually attach to it.

Since the native mentality measures the value of everything by its power of exchange, real gifts are almost valueless as far as they are concerned. If nothing is demanded in return for a gift, they conclude, it must have no value. Discovering this fact has been a surprise for many a new missionary in New Guinea. While the natives' sense of values may be twisted, they do expect that everything that is given to them must be "backed" or repaid in some way. In fact, they think a man is a bit whacky who gives something away free. But this does not mean that they are not good at bargaining. Among themselves they talk for days over a simple deal. With mission and government personnel, they resort to every trick they know of to make a good trade. For example, when they bring potatoes, tomatoes, corn, or other produce for sale, they are very careful to put the best on top of the bag, and the smaller ones and rotten ones at the bottom. At Mendi most of the buying of produce has been done with kinas (mother of pearl shells). The bigger the kina, the greater the value it has. No matter how big a kina the purchaser for the Mission presents, it is always a bit too small for the natives. After a few weeks of trading, the missionary will get on to the tricks of the native traders. While a native likes to "haggle and bargain," as a rule he has very little respect for a missionary who gives in too easily to his demands. They seem to admire a "strong" man who sticks to his price.

STEALING, BIGGEST CRIME

In keeping with the native mentality that nothing is ever given away gratis, they have a very strict code of justice. Stealing seems to be the greatest offense according to the primitive native code of laws. If anyone is found guilty of stealing, the punishment inflicted by a native court usually far outweighs the offense. For example, one of the native lads who is working for the Mission told me the other day that a few years ago a man who was found guilty of stealing a pig, had his hand chopped off as a punishment. In other cases, we have heard that men have been put to death for stealing a pig. The government is gradually taking care of handling all offenses in its own court. It is well known that the government is much more lenient in inflicting punishment than native courts. Consequently, whenever a native is accused of any crime, especially stealing, he immediately runs to the government officer. At the government court, he will get a fair trial; his punishment will be reasonable; and besides, the native court would not dare to reconsider the government's decision — at least not openly.

VALUE OF SYMPATHY

Since according to the native mentality absolutely nothing is given away free, even sorrow and sympathy must be paid for. When a man accidentally cuts his hand as he trims a piece of wood, and receives an expression of sympathy from another, it is understood that he must repay the sympathizer by giving him his knife. A few months ago, one of our new missionaries hit his thumb while driving a nail into a board. A native on the scene immediately expressed his sorrow over the misfortune, and thereupon claimed that the hammer now belonged to him as a payment for his expression of "sorrow." To be sure, we do not go along with this native idea of "justice." We are in fact trying to impress on their minds constantly that charity is a more perfect virtue than the justice of which they speak.

On the occasion of a death of a native, it is the accepted practice that relatives, friends, and anyone in the same line or tribe express sympathy by crying. It seems the more important the man who dies, the louder the crying. At the end of the "wake" and funeral, there is a huge pig-kill for the mourners. Although I have not heard the significance of this, I suspect that the pig feast is in payment for the sympathy. It isn't difficult to imagine that many a "sympathizer" is already thinking of a feast when he goes to the funeral. At least he knows his sympathy will not be offered for nothing.

VALUE OF PROPERTY

The natives in the Southern Highlands of Papua have no deeds to property, no titles to prove ownership, nor any written record of possession or rent. However, every acre of land, every tree and bush, everything of any value belongs to someone. There are no visible boundary lines between neighbors, but each knows where his property ends and where his neighbor's begins, and everyone must respect that invisible line. The same is true in the case of trees. Here at the Mission we are compelled to buy trees for constructing buildings, for firewood, and for other purposes. We have found that, even in a small area of a few acres, there may be as many as ten to twenty owners of the trees, and the owners of the trees are not necessarily the same as the owners of the ground on which they grow. On a spot about fifteen minutes from the station at Mendi, Brother Claude (our general carpenter) tried to buy five trees to cut into stumps for one of our permanent buildings. To his surprise, he had to deal with five different men.

When we buy firewood from the natives, they bring it to the station over a period of a week or two. It seems they keep track of every little sliver. As soon as one small piece has disappeared, they immediately come and demand payment. This is another example of the fact that they know every little item that belongs to them, and they won't give anything away without pay.

WAR AND PAPUAN JUSTICE

Not only do the individual natives insist on "justice" and pay for every object, but also tribes observe this in relation to each other. A good example of this is the pay-back that usually follows a native war or tribal fight. Whenever more men are killed on one side than on the other, the score must be evened by counter-killings. If you listen to the natives relate their past history, it seems the score in the matter of deaths is never really evened. Since the government took control of the territory, killing by way of retaliation has been almost completely eliminated. However, a good number of tribal wars of years ago — before the government came — have created an imbalance that is still outstanding. Since the government has condemned retaliation murders, and since the tribal law demands a pay-back, a compromise had to be reached. The government allows the pay-back, but it must now be made with kinas, pigs, or tomahawks.

A few months ago, I had occasion to witness such a pay-back. Years ago, there was a war between Kombegibu and Wa. A few more men of Wa were killed than of Kombegibu. So, the tribe at Kombegibu had to even matters by giving them kinas and pigs, and tomahawks. It was a solemn ceremony, involving singing and dancing, and also killing of pigs for a feast. I got the impression that the chief of Wa was a bit embarrassed about accepting these objects as a pay-back. Undoubtedly, he and his tribe would have preferred to kill a few of the men of Kombegibu.

I witnessed not only the actual pay-back but also the preliminary negotiations. The preliminary negotiations amounted to a discussion on terms — how many kina shells would be required, how many pigs, etc. The discussion lasted for weeks. I saw only a couple of days of this. The government, through its own show of power, has been able to talk the natives out of pay-back by taking human lives, but it has not as yet succeeded in making the natives forget the pay-backs altogether. In the mind of the native of the Southern Highlands no power on earth can allow the non-payment of a debt, no matter how it is caused.

Occasionally, we hear of tribal paybacks which escape the notice of government officials. Such a case happened a couple of months ago at a place which is only a half-hour walk from one of our outstations. The government found out about the revenge killing and immediately brought about 200 men from that particular tribe into calaboose, where they will be subject to a few months labor on the roads. While only one or a few of them committed the murder, it will be a lesson to the entire tribe that they can't take the law into their own hands in a pay-back.

PAPUAN GIFTS

Even in the more advanced areas of Papua and New Guinea the idea of pay-back is not completely forgotten. Toward the eastern border of our Mission quite a few natives who had been driven out of Papua and into New Guinea proper years ago in a tribal war, are now returning to their ancestral homes. On the New Guinea side, these natives had been in touch with the government and the Mission for a number of years. The leader of a part of a returning tribe came to one of our Missionaries, Fr. Gary, and asked him to come and take care of his people, to offer Mass for them, baptize their children, take care of the sick, and teach all of them about Christ. As a sign of his sincerity, he gave Fr. Gary a donation of over three pounds Australian (about $8). Fr. Gary hadn't run into anything like that among the natives before this. A month later, the same native leader returned and gave Fr. Gary another pound ($2.25). Lest there be any misunderstanding in the future, Fr. Gary said, "I will give you a nice kina, in exchange for your money. "Oh no," replied the native, "I don't want anything for the money. This is a gift." Fr. Gary thought to himself, "Here is finally a native who has learned the Christian virtue of charity." But his optimism took a quick plunge, when the native added: "I am giving you this for nothing." We can be sure that this native remembered every penny he gave to Fr. Gary, and no one will be surprised when some day he will come and demand all of it back — for nothing.

Our Missionaries are trying to instill a spirit of charity among all who come to our Mission. It is a slow process. However, occasionally one can see signs of progress. Shortly after my arrival in the Mission in October 1959, I visited all of our main stations. At each I received genuine gifts from some of our local natives. At one place I received a mat woven from native cane; at another place, a native bow and arrows, along with a ceremonial armband; at another I was given a beautiful hand-carved frame for a picture, and a native-woven handbag. None of them asked for anything in return. None expected anything except my delight in accepting the gift, at least as far as I could tell.

It is a slow process to teach these natives that there is something better than their concept of strict, selfish, and distorted justice. It will take years, and perhaps generations, to indoctrinate the adults. Our highest hope is with the children in school. Once they spontaneously say "thank you" for something that is given to them or done for them, we know they have taken a big step away from the traditional tribal and pagan justice. A person who is grateful for charity is not far removed from acts of charity himself.

The barrier of "pagan justice versus charity" is only one of the many that must be broken among these pagans in Papua before we can hope to have a Christian atmosphere in the Southern Highlands. With the help of God's grace, and the patient efforts of the Missionaries, along with the unfailing assistance of our friends back home, we hope we will gradually lead these Papuans out of the dark night of paganism into the broad daylight of Christianity.

Yours Sincerely,

Rt. Rev. Firmin M. Schmidt, O.F.M.Cap.

Perfect Apostolic of Mendi

~~~

In 1959, Msgr. Firmin's official arrival at the Capuchin Mission at Mendi, with the group of Capuchin Fathers with whom he will serve and Bishop Adolph Noser, SVD, of the Madang Diocese.

Monsignor Firmin with school boys at Kagua, November 1959

Confirmation, at Tari, Msgr. Firmin, standing, (center left). On the left, individuals to be confirmed dressed in white. On the right, women sitting, with woven bags (bilums), some holding sweet potatoes (kau-kau) and others holding wood, which the women carry on their backs, February 1960.

At a sing-sing, Msgr. Firmin, center front, flanked by Thomas More Mia and Tundu, 1960.

Msgr. Firmin with a native woman covered with gray (dried) mud, a sign of mourning. About thirty pounds of beads are hanging around her neck and shoulders, 1960.

Sisters of St. Francis arriving at the Mendi Mission. Left to right: Sisters Noreen, Annata, Martine, and Claver (partially visible). School boys standing in front of them, October 1960.

Msgr. Firmin greeting a native woman with her child on the way to Orei. She also carries a bilum on her back, February 1961.

Msgr. Firmin offering Mass in the Bush, in the Mendi area, 1962.

*A woman carrying a bag of sweet potatoes (kau-kau), weighing about
fifty pounds. At times, women might arrive at the Mendi Mission
from twelve or thirteen miles away, while carrying such a load.
Frequently, women would carry a baby on top of the kau-kau or on
the neck of the mother, (see photo, preceding page), July 1962.*

Natives ready for a sing-sing.

A sing-sing near Mendi, September 1962.

Preparing for a sing-sing at Mendi, 1963.

Placing the pig to be cooked on hot coals, for the meal at a sing-sing, at Mendi, 1963.

Msgr. Firmin and Fr. Paul with Church Committee Members at Tari, 1963

15 June, 1961

Dear Mary,

Thanks for your letter of June 3. It arrived here on the 10th. I was also happy to receive the clippings from the paper concerning the graduation at St. Joe's and the ham [radio] station here in Mendi. The news about our ham station came from my letter to Mrs. Motz. I wrote to her after I saw my last article in the Hays Daily News. That particular article by the way was sent to the Mother General of the Franciscan Sisters. The folks of one of their nuns from WaKeeney sent it, I think. The Mother General was most pleased. She wrote to one of the Sisters here and said it was the first good view she has received of our mission. —The same day I received your letter I also received one from Pia. Please express my thanks to her for the letter and for the stipends. I hope to write to her within a week.

Concerning the ham station here, Fr. Benjamin hasn't been broadcasting very much in recent weeks. For one thing he is waiting for his antenna. Then also he has been away at his bush station a good bit. After spending a few days here last week, he went out again to the bush, this time to Pinj, which is two valleys to the west.

Our boarding school for girls was finally started two days ago. The dormitory is not bad at all. It is an aluminum building about seventy feet by twelve feet. This includes a "kitchen," a place for cooking their meals. The twenty-nine beds fold up into the wall during the day time. The beds actually are nothing but wooden platforms about 5 1/2 ft. by 2 ft. with hinges on one end and wooden legs on the other. During the day the dormitory is an open room which can be used for classes, if necessary. The floor has a mat woven out of pit-pit, or some kind of cane. Of course, there are no mattresses, or anything equivalent for the beds. The natives prefer a hard bed. Nor do they use a pillow. In their own huts they don't even have blankets. Here we supply some blankets. Even though there are only twenty-nine beds, I'm sure there will be at least twice as many girls in the dormitory eventually. Some of the little girls who stay here are only about six or seven years old. They're all delighted with the convenience of staying at the Mission. Within a week we'll have the place filled to capacity, and then some, when we start enrolling a few of the girls from the outstations.

—An older woman from Wa, a short distance from here, is staying with the girls as their "hausfrau," and watchdog. She has been friendly to the mission but she is a real bush woman. The first night as the girls started to say their night prayers in common, they discovered that this woman didn't know how to pray. So the girls immediately got busy and started to teach her. They began by teaching her to make the sign of the Cross. I'm sure in a short time she'll know all the prayers. This particular woman has a daughter, about eight or nine years old, who goes to school here. We had thought at first of getting the mother of the chief, Kavivi, but finally decided that this younger woman would be better. Kavivi's mother must be well over sixty years old, but she is still strong and healthy. She works in the garden from morning until night, and is still able to carry a big bag of potatoes on her back. When I say she works in the garden, I mean she really works. She can't be bothered using a hoe. She gets right down on the ground, and digs with a simple digging stick. It is possible that she will also begin to stay here with the girls after a while. The old lady is certainly most pleasant. And everyone has the greatest respect for her. No matter where she sees me, she always waves at me. Frequently she goes out of her way to shake hands with me.

The Sisters are happy with their beginning of the boarding school. This will allow them to supervise and instruct more of the girls. While the prejudice in educating the girls will not be broken very soon in this area, at least now there will be hope of getting some converts among the girls and the women. Once we get a few there won't be much of a problem in getting more later on. —As you might expect, the Sisters are teaching the girls a few games. Last night a couple of the Sisters were playing a kind of cat and mouse game with the girls, out in the yard. We have a fairly bright light in the yard which remains lighted until the electricity is turned off.

I told you some time ago about the Sisters' two cook girls, Masomi and Lumi. In spite of the fact that Lumi was so thrilled with her work, the poor girl is out now. Here is what happened. A native policeman in Nipa, three valleys from Mendi, sent a note to Lumi, proposing marriage. Lumi, evidently thinking that this would be a good partner, accepted the proposal and left the Sisters without notice. After two weeks, Lumi returned, but without a husband. What happened I don't know. According to rumors, the possible husband has been transferred to a farther outpost and thus Lumi's trip was useless. Anyway, Lumi came back, hoping to return to work for the Sisters. Of course, under these circumstances the Sisters couldn't accept her, and she rather expected this, I guess. I bawled her out for running off the way she did. She probably feels bad about everything, but she still comes around to the Mission. I think she has been coming to school. You can't blame Lumi too much in trying to get married to a policeman. A policeman has a fairly good income by native standards. At least he gets enough to support a family. This would definitely have taken her out of the bush. It was only about four or five months ago that Lumi's father wanted to force her to get married to a backward bushman. I guess she still fears that she may be compelled to return to the bush. Lumi's sister, Tepo, is one of the girls staying at the Mission now. She is a very bright girl. Her English is probably as good as any of the school kids here.

According to my plans I will go to Erave on Saturday, June 17th, for a visit. I haven't been there for several months. If you remember, that is the place where we have our central school. The new lay missionary, Bill McQuillan, is also there now, along with Lou Ciancio, a lay missionary from Pittsburgh, and Fr. Gregory. Mr. McQuillan seems to be a competent man. In a very short time that he was here at Mendi I could easily see that he is not only a farmer, but knows how to help himself. He seems to be an excellent handyman, and a willing worker. He has been around a good bit, serving in the near East as a member of the Australian Army. — I said I was planning to go to Erave on Saturday. That is, if the weather is suitable. It has been raining almost all week.

Today there was no plane in the vicinity of Mendi or Erave. Some people from Mendi went to Erave for last weekend. They still haven't been able to get back, and this is Thursday evening.

Hope everything is coming along well at Catherine. Hello to all. Your devoted brother, Msgr. Firmin

~~~

25 September 1961

Dear Friends of the Hays Daily News,

While the rest of the world is being gripped by the political tensions of international politics, the natives of Papua and New Guinea remain as unconcerned and as uninterested as a carefree child. Except for the more advanced natives in coastal areas, and school children in the upper grades or in intermediate schools, the average native of New Guinea hasn't even heard of Khrushchev, much less of the rockets which he threatens to hurl at humanity. Neither radio nor newspaper can convey an international message in the language of the illiterate native. In a real sense, the natives of Papua and New Guinea live in a world of their own.

What is true in the political world is also true in the economic, social, medical and religious world. These natives are living in a world apart. It is the aim of the missionary endeavor to break down the barrier that isolates the natives, and introduce them to the spiritual riches of the world of Christianity, to which they have as much a right as any other people.

This is work that cannot be completed in one year or even in one generation. Steeped in superstitious beliefs and practices, and surrounded by a pagan atmosphere, the natives are suspicious of anything that goes against their traditions. While some progress is being made with the older people, our hope for the future rests mainly with the young. It is not rare that the adult natives themselves will tell a missionary: "What you say sounds good, but I am too old to understand. Tell it to the younger people." The real meaning behind such a statement probably implies that the Christian message is completely at variance with their pagan notions.

While the primary work of the missionary is aimed at the spiritual welfare of the natives, he cannot remain unaware of the physical conditions and physical welfare of the natives. As a matter of fact, the spiritual ministrations are frequently conditioned by the natives' physical wellbeing. However, the physical health, and the native view of health are themselves obstacles to contend with. Their health, probably as much as any phase of their being or life, is steeped in superstition and erroneous views.

HEALTH CONDITIONS

In previous letters to The Hays Daily News I described the economic and social status of the natives. Now I should like to give you a view of the health conditions of the people in this area. As a prefatory remark, I should like to mention that the government has been aware of the health problems, and had undertaken extensive projects to control diseases and to raise the standards of health. Conscientious doctors, nurses, and medical aides in every district of Papua and New Guinea are rendering a most remarkable service to the natives. However, just as in all other phases of work in New Guinea, it will take a generation or two to attain a reasonable goal of health control.

In a scientific report on the medical status of the natives of New Guinea, the Director of Health in 1954 stated that the average life expectancy of an adult native is estimated at 32 years. This estimate was based on studies conducted in three separate Districts. To be sure, that figure would be slightly higher now, since more hospitals and doctors are being added to the Territory every year. However, the natives' life expectancy is quite below that of people in other parts of the world. Infancy death rate is also unusually high.

LACK OF SANITATION

Undoubtedly, there are multiple causes for the short life expectancy and the high rate of infant deaths. High among the contributing causes must be placed the lack of sanitation and cleanliness. The ordinary native who lives in the bush probably goes for years without taking a bath or washing in any way at all. If we can judge by appearance, then it would seem most likely that the bush natives never wash intentionally. One of the Missionaries mentioned recently that in his opinion the only time water touches the bushman's skin is when he is caught in the rain without his "leaf-raincoat."

The bush house of the natives is built on the bare ground. His "bed" is the ground itself, or in some cases, chewed up sugar cane. The open fire in his house without a chimney smokes up not only the house but also the people who live in it. Ordinarily, the pigs stay in the same house that the natives use for sleeping, even though sometimes the pigs may be in a separate compartment. There is no ventilation. The only opening is a door about two feet square, and even this is closed up at night or when it turns cold. This explains why the natives usually smell like smoke or ashes.

CLAY AND OIL COVERING

Besides acquiring their "coats" of dirt and smoke, many of the natives cover themselves intentionally with clay or oil for certain big occasions. For example, when someone dies, all the women in that line or tribe must cover themselves with clay as a sign of mourning. As the clay wears off, they must renew it. This is kept up for months. I know, as matter of fact, that some women have retained their "clay covering" for more than a year. This clay is also spread over the hair and face, including the eyelids. It must be quite uncomfortable, especially when the clay dries.

There are various occasions that seem to call for a cover of oil or grease. The most common occasions seem to be a sing-sing or a marriage. For a marriage, the bride is covered completely with oil (a black substance, appearing like tar, coming from the sap of a tree near Lake Kutubu). A few weeks ago, a new bride, dripping wet with oil, came to our Mission. She had been almost completely blinded by the oil that had gotten into her eyes. The Sisters recognized her as one of the first girls that used to come to the Mission for instructions. After the Sisters had cleaned out the bride's eyes, she continued on her way, insisting that she retain the oil over the rest of her body, until it wears off naturally.

Just as these bush natives have no idea of personal cleanliness, so likewise they have no concern for the food they eat. Their kau-kau or sweet potatoes are usually roasted in hot ashes. While they ordinarily shake off the ashes before eating the kau-kau, they aren't worried too much if some of the ashes or dirt is eaten also.

In addition to the lack of cleanliness, another contributing cause to their health problems is their inadequate diet. They live practically on kau-kau, or, sweet potatoes. They know nothing of a balanced diet. They do get occasional sugar from cane, and also a bit of greens, but other foods, like meat or milk, are not part of their daily fare. They get pork at pig-kills, but these are not frequent enough to be considered part of their regular diet.

AGE OF NATIVES

We usually divide man's age into three periods: childhood, youth, and adulthood. These three periods are surely observable in these natives also. However, the respective periods do not seem to be in the same proportion as they are in the United States or in other countries with comparable standards. In the Southern Highlands of Papua, there seems to be a long period of childhood, a very brief period of youth, and a relatively longer period of adulthood. As a result, it is very difficult for us to estimate their ages. The Missionaries who have been here for five years or more have noticed that up to the age of sixteen or eighteen, children seem small and immature. But once they get to be about twenty, they age very quickly. Actually, we can only guess their ages, since they themselves have no idea whether they were born ten years ago, or twenty, or thirty. However, we can notice that once they mature, they soon seem quite old. It seems reasonable to assume that their inadequate diet is at least a contributing factor in this. We have actually seen that the children who have boarded at our Missions, who had food regularly, and occasionally a bit of variety, have become stronger and healthier and bigger in just a few years.

DISEASES AMONG NATIVES

Periodically, the government sends out patrols to different areas to introduce the natives to law and order. On these patrols while the government officers take the census, the medical men make a physical checkup. Invariably they find a large percentage of the natives with scabies, yaws [a chronic infection that affects mainly the skin, bone and cartilage], and other diseases resulting from lack of cleanliness. Steps are taken to treat the more advanced cases, but the natives are generally reluctant to cooperate.

For some reason or other, the natives from the bush are afraid to go to the hospital. There is a hospital at Mendi and also one at Tari, with a qualified doctor in each place. Other places in the Southern Highlands have first-aid stations or medical posts, with doctor boys or medical assistants always on duty. Medical service for the natives is completely gratis, even if it involves transportation. The reluctance of the natives to go to the hospital probably can be traced to the fact that someone in their tribe had gone to the hospital and died there. From this, they conclude it must be a bad place. They don't even seem to advert to the fact that many more natives die in the bush. Nor do they take into account the fact that many of those who come to the hospital waited until it was too late to benefit from medical care.

As far as I know, there have been no statistics published as to the most frequent causes of premature death among the natives of the Southern Highlands. According to the local Doctor, malaria, tuberculosis, pneumonia, and gastroenteritis would be high on the list of the causes of death. Naturally, most of the cases could be saved if the victims would come to the hospital immediately, or if they would stay, once they got there. Many of them run away after having received only partial treatment. Besides the sicknesses just mentioned, there are cases of cancer and leprosy. In recent years there has been an increase of such sicknesses, and mumps, chicken pox, and measles. It is almost impossible to enforce a quarantine when a contagious disease strikes. Consequently, a contagious disease quickly makes its rounds. Because of their improper diet, and low resistance, most of the natives are quickly run down when they fall victim to what we might consider an easily curable disease.

NATIVES CURES

As might be expected, the natives have their own ideas about sicknesses, and how to cure them. A common "cure" for a headache is to wrap a vine around the head as tight as they can stand it. Their cure for a stomach pain is the same. Whether they are serious about their "remedy" for these ailments is hard to say. Quite possibly the pain or pressure caused by the tight band around the head or stomach is so great that they are distracted from the actual headache or stomachache.

When the natives cut themselves, they stop the bleeding with a bit of mud, and then they put leaves on the sore spot, and wrap it with a vine or crude string. Undoubtedly, infections do set in, but it is surprising how well they manage with such crude and unsanitary bandages. Several months ago, Porkiami, a little girl about six or seven years old, cut the tip of her finger. She immediately pushed the finger into the mud and kept it there for a while. After a few minutes, the bleeding stopped, and she simply went her way as if nothing had happened. Of course, there was no thought of washing it off.

NATIVE POISON

When the bush natives come across a serious illness, or one that comes on very quickly, they at once conclude it is poison. A person who is "poisoned" must be given "medicine," which is secretly concocted by some of the leaders in the tribe. Whether there really is such a medicine, I have not been able to ascertain. It seems to be a secret even as to who is able to make such a medicine. But, in any case, the ordinary native is convinced that he must take the medicinal potion to get rid of the poison.

In many cases of serious illness, the natives build a house or "shrine" to Tambaran ("evil spirit"). If the poison was caused by the anger of the evil spirit, then it is hoped that the Tambaran will now be appeased and thus remove the poison. So great seems to be their confidence in Tambaran that even when the doctor in the hospital pulls someone through a serious illness, they give credit, not to the doctor, but to Tambaran.

As far as the "poison" is concerned, the natives seem to be convinced of its reality. Just as they have "certain individuals" who know the secret formula for the medicine, so also, they have individuals who know how to make poison. The threat of poison is one of the chief causes of fear among the natives. Even young children are told stories of poison.

At all out main stations we have schools which comprise children from different tribes. While these tribes are no longer carrying on open war against each other, they continually suspect each other of possible poisoning. Occasionally, the fear of poison from the children of another tribe becomes so great that they run away from school and return to their own tribe in the bush.

DEATH OF A SCHOOL BOY

At the beginning of July, a school boy by the name of Namba died unexpectedly here in Mendi. Immediately, the fear of poison struck the school children. As a result, dozens of them returned to their homes. One little boy, the brightest one in school, was actually so overcome by fear that he became genuinely sick. The next day he ran away from school. After a month, he came back, but in a few days, he disappeared again because of the fear of poison. We are hoping this boy as well as some of the others will eventually return to school.

After Namba died, his father came to take his body to his home village for burial. We had hoped to have the doctor at the hospital perform an autopsy. However, the father objected and insisted that the body be buried at once. In such cases, because of the natives' deep-seated superstitions, the government does not force the issue. — A few days later word filtered in from the bush that the natives had performed their own autopsy on the dead body, and found their suspicion confirmed, namely that Namba was poisoned. Naturally, this report caused a few more schoolboys to leave.

CURE OF A SICK BOY

An incident that happened about a month after the death of Namba may be instrumental in getting some of those schoolboys back, and in dispelling the fear of poison in general. This incident concerns another schoolboy by the name of Osup. This lad began to shown signs similar to the ones observed in Namba before his death. We wanted the boy to go to the doctor for a check-up. He was willing to go, but unfortunately his parents found out about it, and immediately forced the boy to leave school and return to his home in the bush. With the cooperation of the government officers, the parents were threatened with the calaboose, if they did not allow the boy to be taken to the doctor. As soon as they saw the native policemen coming towards their area, they knew they had to cooperate. Osup was taken to the hospital. In a short time, it was found he had one of the worst type of worms, which was sapping his very life. The worm was readily expelled, and immediately Osup picked up. He is here in school now and is making wonderful progress in every way. Whether his parents are convinced that it was the doctor who healed him, I don't know. It is possible that they saw their solution here also in Tambaran. In the meanwhile, the news of Osup's remarkable recovery is being spread throughout the valley.

In the case of almost every sudden or unexpected death, the natives perform their own autopsy, even though their knowledge of anatomy and medicine is extremely primitive. According to reports, the native "experts" in autopsy not only can discover that the victim was poisoned, but also they can tell where the poison came from and who was responsible. From the stories that circulate, it seems clear that such conclusions are nothing else than pre-conceived notions, arising from ill-feeling towards someone. In former times, death as a pay-back would have been in order. Now, because of the government supervision and control, such a type of pay-back is beginning to disappear.

TRAINING THE YOUNG

From this brief summary of the health conditions in the Southern Highlands, and the natives' view of health, it is clear that a big task lies ahead of us. Since it is difficult, and in some cases impossible, to change the views and way of life of the older people, our efforts in these matters are directed mainly towards the young. When the children present themselves for school, the first requirement is that they wash themselves completely. Those who are found to have scabies are immediately given medication. Every morning all the school children have to bathe or wash themselves in one of the streams near the Mission. At the assembly signal before the start of school each morning, there is an inspection. Anyone who has not washed himself well, is sent to the stream for a re-wash before he is admitted to the school. After a while, they seem to like the idea of washing regularly.

To facilitate and encourage their washing regularly, we give them soap. At first some of the bush kids got the idea that the soap by itself did the cleaning without use of water. They soon learned how the soap is used most effectively. However, we have noticed that frequently after they have finished their washing and have dried, they rub soap all over their body. It is quite possible that this is a means of applying a layer or covering, as a bit of protection against the cold morning breezes of the Southern Highlands. Even with the temperature in the low fifties or forties, these native kids are faithful in taking their morning bath in the cold mountain streams.

FIRST-AID STATIONS

Another important phase in training the native youngsters in hygiene and in becoming accustomed to proper medical care is in the form of first-aid stations, conducted in connection with our schools. At Mendi, where there are over 150 children in school, such a first-aid station is not only an effective way of teaching the young Papuans, but it is also a necessity. Cuts, bruises, fevers (from various causes), boils, indigestion, etc., turn up constantly. Every day, the Sisters apply disinfectant to bruises, wrap bandages, give out pills, and in general train the youngsters to take care of their health. The children appreciate more and more, as time goes on, the first-aid treatment by the Sisters. After a few months, they are readily disposed to visit the doctor, if the Sister deems it advisable.

The children's attitude toward the first-aid center at the Mission is beginning to take hold also on some adults. Many of the natives, especially women, in this area who refuse to go to the hospital do not hesitate to come to the Sisters for treatment. Some of them will even agree to go to the hospital if the Sister goes along or at least sends a note to the Doctor.

An interesting incident, along this line, happened several months ago. Kavivi, one of the most powerful chiefs in the Mendi Valley, seriously gashed his arm while working on the other side of the government station. He covered the gash in the usual native fashion and tied it with a vine and then headed for our Mission for treatment, even though he had to pass the government hospital on his way. When he arrived at the Mission, Sister Noreen, seeing that several stitches were required to close up the wound, told Kavivi to go to the hospital. Only after she wrote a note to the doctor did Kavivi agree to go. Brother Claude took Kavivi to the hospital, and there he proudly presented the note, as if to say: "Sister thinks it's all right for you to fix my arm." When the doctor was finished, he told Kavivi he would have to come back the next day again. Kavivi objected, insisting that he cannot come because he had to see Sister. The following morning, as expected, Kavivi came to the Mission. Sister gave him the note to the doctor, and thereupon he agreed to go to the hospital. This, and other similar incidents, are signs that we are convincing the natives of the importance of proper medical care.

Some of the natives undoubtedly come to the first-aid station mainly to get a bandage, which in their mind is really a decoration. However, they are beginning to recognize and appreciate the real purpose of disinfectants and bandages. On the busiest days, the Sisters have had as many as a hundred calls for first-aid treatment. However, usually the number does not exceed twenty-five per day.

MEDICINES AND BANDAGES

The first-aid station at the Mission is run in close cooperation with the government doctor and the government hospital. Incidentally, the Doctor at Mendi for the last eighteen months was Dr. Vincent Zigas, world-famous authority on the laughing sickness. Obtaining sufficient supply of medicine and bandages is always a problem. About six months ago, we received a shipment from the Catholic Medical Mission Board, which has been organized specifically to supply Mission needs. However, most of the medical supplies, including bandages, salves, disinfectants, anti-malaria pills, etc., have come through the Capuchin Mission Office, 220-37th Street, Pittsburgh, Pa. Doctors and institutions that have a surplus of supplies, or samples that are useful in New Guinea, have sent their supplies to the Mission Office, where the materials are properly packaged and sent on to our Mission. When the supplies arrive here, with the help of the local doctor, we classify the medicines. Those to be prescribed only by a qualified doctor, are put under his care, which, however, are available for our people at any time. Other medicines are kept at the first-aid center for use when needed. Bandages, adhesive tape, salves, iodine, and mercurochrome are always needed.

From my account of the medical status in the Southern Highlands of Papua, you can see what I mean when I speak of the natives as living in a world of their own. The medical barrier is only one of many obstacles that keep these natives separated from the rest of the world. Through circumstances of history and environment, the development of the people of Papua has been retarded in general. Basically, the natives here are the same as people everywhere. Given the opportunity, they will show they are not an inferior race.

The missionary work of the Capuchin Fathers and Brothers of the Province of St. Augustine, and of the Franciscan Sisters of Oldenburg, Indiana, as well as the help of the lay missionaries of our Mission is aimed at removing the most important barrier that is keeping the natives in a world of their own. I refer to the spiritual barrier. Once we remove this obstacle, the treasures of the spiritual inheritance of Christianity will be at their disposal. And this treasure cannot be gauged by the standards of this world.

I hope my letters to The Hays Daily News not only give you a view of some of the facets of primitive, pagan life, but also that they cause you to be grateful for the many blessings to which you have fallen heir simply by being born and by living in a country that is rich in material and spiritual blessings. The work of the Missionaries is inspired by the conviction that God's blessings can be best appreciated by sharing them with others.

Yours sincerely,

Rt. Rev. Firmin M. Schmidt, O.F.M. Cap.
Prefect Apostolic of Mendi

~~~

Chapter 3

———∞∞———

OCTOBER 1961-SEPT 1962
MORE BUILDING, TRAVELS TO
BUSH STATIONS, CONTACTING
MORE NATIVE GROUPS

[**OCTOBER 16-23, 1961,** Monsignor Firmin is in the coastal city of Port Moresby to attend the Papua New Guinea Mission-Government Conference. While there, he meets the Superior General of the Franciscan Sisters, Sr. Cephas, and the other nuns with her, at the airport and helps them with immigration formalities of their entry into New Guinea. After the conference, he shops for items needed by the Mission, and, finally, he meets Frs. Paul and Roy, who are coming back to the Mission after visiting the U.S.]

2 November 1961

Dear Mary,

Your letter of Oct. 14th was waiting for me in Mendi when I arrived here on Thursday the 26th. Your letter of the 21st arrived the next day. Thanks a lot. I was happy to hear that you, Fr. Paulinus and others appreciated receiving the letter from the schoolboy, Bede Dus.

— Will you please tell Angela that I received the clipping from the Hays Daily News. I hope to acknowledge it directly, in a few days after I get a bit more work cleared up here. I think Mrs. Motz did an excellent job in setting up the article. The photos also were quite good. I think the article should be well accepted by most of the readers of the paper. I still intend to write a few articles for Catholic papers, but have not as yet decided when I'm going to begin.

As I had expected, I returned to Mendi on Thursday October 26th. This was the fastest trip ever from Port Moresby. I came on a Piaggio (twin motor plane) directly from Moresby to Mendi. The flight came along the Southern Coast of Papua until we hit a place called Baimuru. From there we came straight into Mendi. It was the quickest and most pleasant flight I have had into the Southern Highlands. This plane, by the way, is scheduled to make that run once every week. However, frequently the heavy rains and bad weather cause the flight to be cancelled or diverted somewhere else.

—Frs. Paul and Roy were glad to reach their destination. Four days after landing here in Mendi, Fr. Paul was on his way to Tari. I'm sure the natives there gave him a warm welcome. Fr. Roy stayed at Mendi at least for the present. This morning he went with Fr. Benjamin on a trip to the bush. They will be gone for a couple of weeks.

Last Sunday, the Feast of Christ the King, was a big day here at Mendi. The first native local girl was baptized, namely Masami. She took the name of Mary Ann Teresa. We call her simply Mary Ann. The Sisters had her all dressed up in white. A number of pictures were taken. If they turn out well, I hope to send you some. During the High Mass that followed she received her First Holy Communion. Her sponsor in baptism was Mary Elizabeth Rame, a lay missionary who arrived here about two months ago. Now that the first local girl has been baptized, I'm sure others will follow soon. After the Mass, there was another Baptism —the son of Thomas More Mia and Bolu. Remember, these two are the ones whose wedding I described last January. Bolu is not a Catholic as yet, but she has attended instructions. The little boy was clean and dressed up very neatly by the Sisters.

The Mother General of the Franciscan Sisters, Mother Cephas, and her Counselor, Sr. Hortense, seem to be favorably impressed with the work that is being done here in the Mission. This past Tuesday I took them to Erave to visit our central school for boys. The lads really put on a good show. They even had a program, which included military marches, singing, playing musical instruments and a one-act play. Remember these lads are only third and fourth graders, and only a couple of steps away from savagery. They did a marvelous job in their singing. Three of the boys did very well in singing solos. After a two-and-a-half-hour visit, a tractor with a trailer came to the Mission to bring the Sisters back to the airstrip. (There are no cars or jeeps at Erave.) As the Sisters left the Mission, the boys did an excellent job in singing "Now is the hour to say good-bye." The Sisters are hoping that eventually the girls of our Mission will show progress comparable to that of the boys. —From Erave we went to Kagua. The Sisters stayed there for a day while I returned to Mendi. The following day they were taken to Ialibu, where they also spent a day. I feel certain that after visiting all our stations, the Mother General and the counselors will try to send us even more Sisters than are presently in their plans.

On Monday November 6th, I will accompany the Sisters to their new station at Tari. Three Sisters have been assigned there —the two new ones and Sister Annata. The latter is sorry to leave Mendi. She is an unusually fine Sister and is especially successful in taking care of the younger school kids. I'm going along to Tari mainly to bless the new chapel and convent there, and to see that everything is properly arranged. The Mother General will stay at Tari for about a week. I intend to return to Mendi after a couple of days.

Two days ago, a representative from the Educational Department from Australia stopped at our Mission to inspect our school. He had nothing but the highest praise for the work the Sisters are doing here in the school. It is his opinion that these school children will surely pass most of the coastal kids after a few years, mainly because of the excellent foundation they are getting from the Sisters. He was particularly impressed with what is being done for the girls here at Mendi. He said he hadn't seen anything to compare with this anywhere in the highlands. The Sisters were delighted with this reaction.

The Mother General and Sister Hortense returned from Ialibu at about 1 p.m. today. They had quite an experience. Fr. Henry took them out to see a bit of the outstations. On their way back (about twenty miles from the main station) the Jeep on which they were riding got stuck. They had to get out to allow the natives to pull out the Jeep. In the meanwhile, it started to rain heavily. I think they were completely soaked. Presuming they will not catch a cold, I was happy to hear that they got caught in the rain. It gives them a taste of what the Sisters run into quite frequently here.

Please tell Al and Nora thanks for their letters which I received last week and this week respectively. I hope to write to them shortly. I'm continuing to appreciate the Register. It has been arriving the Saturday before the day of publication. That is unusually good service.

I hope everything is coming along well around Catherine. Hello to all.

Your devoted brother, Msgr. Firmin

~~~

28 December 1961

Dear Mary,

Our Christmas has come and gone, and I must say we had a beautiful celebration this year. Even the weather was ideal. We didn't have any rain on the 23rd and 24th, and the greater part of Christmas Day itself. Only at 9:30pm on Christmas day did it start to sprinkle. But since then we had over four inches.

According to our plans we had Baptisms here on Saturday December 23. Fourteen were Baptized, including another girl by the name of Tio. Her Christian name is Clare Ann. The following are the names of the boys: Mark Wengenen, Stephen Yump, Benjamin Kumbesal, Matthew Erave, Damien Tumay, Christopher Konovili, Gregory Luka, Brian Alowak, Anthony Pisi, Alfred Ponege, Michael Olea, Paul Lui, and Gabriel Apo. As in the past, all of the newly-baptized were dressed in white. While Fr. Otmar went through the ceremonies of Baptism, I explained everything to the large crowd of natives who had come for the occasion. For the benefit of those who didn't understand English, Francis Kili (our most advanced school boy) translated the explanation into the native language. All the newly-baptized received their First Holy Communion on Sunday December 24, at the nine o'clock Mass. With the nice sunny weather everything turned out beautifully. When we get the pictures back, I hope to send you some, at least one of Clare Ann. By the way, Clare Ann Tio is the sister of Andrew's wife, Tuviam.

Our Christmas celebration started at 11:30 with the procession by the school children. In that procession the best boy in the baby class carried the image of the Holy Infant on a cushion, as the older school children sang, "O Dear Little Children." The boy presented the infant to me. I placed it in the crib, and then blessed the crib and led the prayers and consecration at the crib. This was followed by the singing of Christmas carols. The children did very well. The church was completely jammed; even the aisles were filled. The kids overflowed into the sanctuary, just leaving enough room for the servers at the altar. I don't think anyone counted the number who received Communion, but there must have been at least ninety—almost all natives. So, you see, the congregation at Mendi, and at all the stations, is growing.

After the Midnight Mass, I had my other two Masses right away. A number of people stayed for them. After my third Mass we all went to the Sisters' convent for a lunch. It reminded me of old times at Catherine. It was after three by the time I got to bed. – The following morning, we had a scheduled Mass at 9 o'clock. The children sang Christmas carols at that Mass. I asked Mary Elizabeth Rame (lay missionary) to record the carols. She managed to record three on one side of the tape. A technical difficulty with the machine prevented her from recording the rest. The recording isn't bad. The first two numbers were recorded in the back of the church, and the third in the front. For the last recording the microphone must have been a bit too close to one of the lads who frequently sang off key. You can tell he has a good voice, but invariably he got off key. Between the first and second carol, there is a bit of Pidgin gospel recorded. The priest reading it is Fr. Senan. I hope the speed can be adjusted to your machines in the States. The singing is recorded on fast speed, listed as 33/4. The speaking is recorded on slow time, listed as 17/8. I hope to send the tape to Al in a few days.

As I mentioned on the tape, I'm going to be traveling a bit during January and February. I intend to visit all the main stations and a few of the outstations. At four of the main stations and one of the outstations, I will administer the sacrament of Confirmation. We don't have real large classes to be confirmed at any of the stations, but in a few years, we should have big crowds every year.

I had Christmas cards or letters from all in the family and close relatives. I hope to acknowledge most of them within a week or two. I will have to get that done before I start making the rounds of the Mission next week. In a few letters I learned how weak Aunt Anna has been getting. According to one, she won't have more than a few weeks to live. I did write to her about three or four weeks ago.

Tomorrow is sing-sing time here in the Mendi Valley. The natives have been practicing all week. Besides the practicing, they have begun to paint themselves and decorate themselves. If the rains continue as they have the last few days, there won't be much of a sing-sing, in spite of the preparation. Yesterday afternoon and evening we had well over two inches of rain. This afternoon, it started to rain at about 1:30. It has been raining off and on for about three hours now. Our cook boys Pot and Mendeba, have been dressed in bush clothes for two days now.

While we have been having such nice weather prior to Christmas and on Christmas Day itself, we heard of the bad storms all over the U.S. Kansas was mentioned as one of the storm spots. While the weather has been almost ideal here in the Southern Highlands, our pilot told us there was a good bit of snow on Mount Wilhelm, about 45 minutes by plane from here. That mountain is around 16,000 feet high. It is possible that there was also some snow on Mount Giluwe, which is only about fifteen miles from here.

The day after Christmas we had games for the school kids, with the aim of having all of them win some prizes. I'm sure all of them (about 95) won at least something. Right after the games we told everyone to go home for a few weeks. In spite of our insistence that they see their people, at least thirty-five or forty stayed back. A number of those who went home on Tuesday, came back today already. They really are attached to the Mission. Of course, all the Catholic boys will come back on Saturday.

I got some transparent photos back a few days ago. I hope to send one or two of them along with this letter. I'll mark them adequately.

Our mail service this Christmas was terrible. I don't know the explanation for that, since the weather was very good. We had only one delivery of mail the week before Christmas. Most of my mail came yesterday and today. And that was the case with most of the friars.

I forgot to mention that on Christmas Day we had a delicious turkey dinner at the Sisters' Convent. One of the Sisters, Sr. Claver, is a first-class cook. It was most enjoyable. —Speaking of turkeys, we have a number of them at three of our stations. At Kagua we have 18. One of the stations sent us one for Christmas. When the natives here saw it, they almost became wild over it. A number of them wanted to purchase it. I'm sure we could have gotten several tons of potatoes for it. The natives wanted the turkey mainly for the feathers. —The end of the page tells me it's time to stop. Hello to all.

Your devoted brother, Msgr. Firmin

18 January 1962

Dear Mary,

Your letter of January 6 was waiting for me at Mendi when I returned from Ialibu on the 15th. I guess it arrived the previous Saturday. The mail service here in recent weeks has not improved at all. There seem to be enough planes in, but there must be some conflict in schedule.

—I was surprised to hear of the death of Dorothy's sister, Angela. You mentioned that Fr. George was there for the funeral. I bet Fr. Athanasius didn't make it. I doubt whether he will ever come back to Kansas. He doesn't like to travel. He hardly ever moves around even locally from the friary at Annapolis. During the ten or eleven years he has been at Annapolis, I bet he hasn't been off the property more than six times. Of course, now his health doesn't seem to be very good any more. —Thanks for the account of Aunt Anna's death and funeral. I was surprised that all the nuns were able to make it in such a short notice. Too bad the weather was so unfavorable that the Bishop was unable to attend.

As I had planned, I spent the last week-end in Ialibu. Except for the heavy rains, it was a very delightful week-end. I'm sure one night it rained well over three inches. In the last eight days they had something like seventeen inches of rain at Ialibu. The first afternoon I was there Fr. Samuel took me out in a Land/Rover to one of his stations. We got stuck twice, in spite of the chains we had on the car, and in spite of the fact that the Land/Rover is four-wheel drive. Fortunately, we had a crowd of boys along to pull us out.

I had the Confirmations on Sunday after the 9:30 Mass, as scheduled. The church was jammed to capacity. I'm sure there were at least 500 people inside. A number of the boys chose the name of Firmin for Confirmation. The previous week when they had the reception of converts at Ialibu, one of the boys was baptized Firmin. I think his native (pagan) name was Pamba. There is a Firmin now at each of our main stations. Remember, last year in February I made a trip to an outstation by the name of Orei. That is eighteen miles out of Ialibu. When the natives of Orei heard I was coming to Ialibu, a big delegation walked in those eighteen miles. A few of them asked to be confirmed at Ialibu. I told them I would visit Orei again after Easter, and have Confirmations there. They seemed delighted.

This is still vacation time here in Papua. In spite of the shortage of kau-kau, and in spite of our having told all the school kids to go home for a few weeks, there are still over forty of them hanging around. About twenty of them are boys who are preparing for Confirmation this Sunday. These lads are having religion class twice a day. They seem to be quite enthusiastic about receiving Confirmation.

Over half the kids who are here and some of our workers have been sick for almost a week. Most of them have fevers, ranging from 100-104 degrees. The cause of the fever has not as yet been determined by the Doctor. It seems that some are victims of malaria, and others simply have the flu or a virus of an undetermined nature. There were a couple of cases of pneumonia.

[In a later letter, Monsignor Firmin states that, after investigation and research, the doctor identified the sickness as ornithosis, commonly known as "Parrot's Disease." While any bird can carry the germ for it, a cassowary had attacked a school girl, and she came down with a fever. This started the spread of the infection. Medicine was prescribed and soon the illness was under control.]

Today, our second laywoman missionary arrived in Mendi. Her name is Clair Toohey. She is about twenty-one years old, but looks older than Mary Elizabeth Rame, who is over thirty. The two are scheduled to take care of the school at Ialibu. However, they will have to stay here in Mendi for a couple of weeks—until their house is completed at Ialibu.

The opening of the school year may be delayed in a number of our stations due to food (kau-kau) shortage. This shortage of food around Christmas time is an annual occurrence. For some reason or other, the natives, not only in Mendi, but also in Ialibu and Kagua, don't work for a few months around Christmas time. As a result, nine or ten months later, there is a shortage of food. (It takes about nine or ten months for kau-kau to mature in Mendi and Ialibu.) I don't think they will ever learn to space their crops right. As a result, they endure what they call "the big hunger" from the end of October to January. We are hoping that the kau-kau will begin to come in soon.

You probably heard of the eclipse of the sun that will take place on February 5. I don't know whether it will be in the States. According to reports, it will be best in New Guinea—if it isn't cloudy. Some crackpot missionaries, like the Jehovah Witnesses and some Lutherans are using this eclipse to scare the natives, and consequently forced them to join their religion. The government became aware of this and has stepped in to warn the heretics concerned.

We got a bit of a shock a few days ago on the world news. I refer to the sinking of an Indonesian ship by the Dutch off the coast of Dutch New Guinea. For many years already Indonesia has been looking for an opportunity to invade and take over West, or Dutch, New Guinea. About six weeks ago, the President of Indonesia threatened to invade West New Guinea if Holland didn't hand over that part of the island peacefully. As a matter of fact, Indonesia has no right at all to West New Guinea. We are hoping the UN will step in and settle the dispute by taking over that part of the island just as they have taken over the territory of New Guinea (bordering Papua). If Indonesia should invade, and take over West New Guinea, it would be only a matter time until they would start to move east—to our part of the island. I personally think this won't happen, since Australia cannot afford to have an unfriendly nation administering New Guinea. The news this evening seemed to indicate that the UN will start to take action soon.

A few days ago, I had a letter from Tommy. I can see he doesn't like the service too well, but he is trying to make the most of it. I intend to write to him in a few days. I am enclosing a transparency of a group that was baptized in Mendi on December 23. Mary Ann Masami, the sponsor for Clare Ann Tio is also in the picture. Mary Ann is in a blue dress, and Clare Ann in the white dress. The camera should have been a little closer for the picture.

Hello to everyone around home. I hope everything is coming along well.

Your devoted brother, Msgr. Firmin

~~~

6 February 1962

Dear Mary,

As you well know by this time, I didn't get a letter off to you last week. There simply wasn't any opportunity, since I spent almost all of last week out in the bush—from 15 to 28 miles out of Tari. I returned to Mendi yesterday morning after the total eclipse of the sun. The eclipse, total at Tari and at Mendi, was one of the most beautiful spectacles in the sky I have ever seen. I remember back in the early thirties we had an eclipse, but as far as I can recall, it was only partial. This one yesterday was one hundred percent. It actually became dark, and about five stars, or planets, were plainly visible just as at night. The eclipse started at 7:40 in the morning. It was total for about three minutes beginning at 8:45. The natives were scared to death. They expected either the end of the world, or else some unusual catastrophe. At Tari, where I was for the eclipse, the natives started coming to church before six in the morning. The Masses at 6:30 and 7:00 were jammed. After the Mass many stayed on in the church. Others, probably a few hundred more, crowded into the school rooms and covered their heads with rags so they couldn't see anything. We tried to explain to them that it was just a temporary black-out of the sun, but they couldn't be made to understand. We had a number of smoked pieces of glass, and with some difficulty, finally convinced a few of the natives to look.

They were amazed. —All over New Guinea the natives were worried and scared for weeks in advance. At one place, according to the radio, a group of natives got together and purchased seven 50-gallon drums of kerosene—hoping this would be enough fuel for the "long night" they were expecting. At a number of places, they stored up several weeks' supply of food for the dark night. On my trip through the bush last week, at every stop, we were asked about the big thing that was going to take place. No amount of explanation seemed to satisfy them. They just have no idea of what the sun is, or the sky, for that matter.

Our pilot, Ken J. Olma, had to come to Tari on Sunday. We waited to fly until the major part of the eclipse was finished. All planes were forbidden to fly between 8:15 and 9:15am. Fortunately, we had a clear sky—something most unusual for the morning in Tari. I took a few pictures, but I doubt whether it was light enough to come out well. It was about as dark as a bright moonlight night. The next total eclipse, according to the radio report, will take place in the year 2000. I suppose that is in reference to this part of the world.

Before I tell you of my Tari-Koroba expedition, I want to thank you for your two letters, one of Jan. 20 and the other of the 27th. Both were here at Mendi when I returned yesterday morning from Tari. Thanks a lot. I was happy to hear that Fr. Gary was able to stop by at Catherine. You have seen most of our New Guinea missionaries, and I think you can readily understand that we have excellent Fathers and Brothers over here. Fr. Gary is one of the finest. All of us enjoy his sense of humor. His competence and zeal as a missionary are tops.

You certainly are having a lot of cold weather this year. I wish you could have some of our delightful climate (apart from the superabundance of rain). Incidentally, we had thirteen inches of rain during the month of January.

Now to tell you of my trip to Tari and the outstations. As planned, I arrived in Tari on the morning of Jan. 26. Two days later, Sunday, I had Confirmations. I think there were about sixteen or seventeen in the group. I hope to remember to enclose a photo taken with a polaroid camera. The people at Tari are really coming to church in large numbers. I am sure there were well over six hundred people present for my Mass, which I had out in the open. In this crowd there were only about fifty Catholics. Almost all the rest are taking instructions. About 150 of them have been coming to instructions—three times a week (over an hour each time) for three full years. Many of them should be ready for Baptism. These people come to Mass not only on Sundays, but also on weekdays. On a few of the weekdays when I had Mass in church, there were well over three hundred present—at the 6:30 Mass. It seems, when the bell rings, the people come to Church.

The greater part of the week I spent with Fr. Berard out in the bush—roughing it a bit, sleeping in a sleeping bag, etc. Actually, it was a most pleasant experience. On Wednesday morning, we started out on our trip with a tractor and trailer. I rode on the trailer. Not being equipped with springs, the trailer was rather rough. It was a two-wheel tractor trailer. The tractor was a Massey-Ferguson.

The first stop was at a place or station called Iobidia. I merely visited the school there and talked with the teacher. The kids put on a brief program, as they did at all the stations. For a small group, the kids at Iobidia really could sing loud. Two of the lads are called the Katzenjammer kids by Fr. Berard. They look almost identical. Their voices are the oddest falsetto I have ever heard. They give you the impression of being ventriloquists. All of the kids know their catechism entirely by heart. Memorizing seems to be easy for these natives since they have nothing else in their heads anyhow.

Our visit at Iobidia was very brief. Our destination for that day was really Pureni—about sixteen miles or more from Tari. The last half hour of the trip we got caught in a downpour of rain. I was soaking wet by the time we got to Pureni. I soon dried off at the open fireplace in the house. Although Pureni is a relatively new station, not quite a year old, there were many natives to welcome us. Later in the afternoon I am sure there were well over 300 natives at the station for instruction in the Catechism. As also at the other stations, I was expected to speak to the natives—naturally, through an interpreter. After my talk, the first thing the natives always asked me was when I was going to send a priest to their station to stay with them all the time. Because of our shortage of missionaries, one priest usually has to look after ten to twenty stations. This allows him only a few days at each station per month. My answer to their question was usually that we are hoping to have Father stop in more frequently as soon as we got more priests. This usually satisfied them.

The living conditions in the bush—at the places I visited—are not too bad. At each place there is a simple bush house. In one corner of each house there is an open fireplace, where we could keep warm and do the cooking. Since there is no chimney, you can imagine that we got a good bit of smoke in the house. The meals, as prepared by our native cook boy, were not bad. The second day out, he even baked a few small loaves of bread on the camp stove. It was quite good.

In the evening at Pureni, as also at the other stations after we had finished supper, the boss boy—native chief—and a few of the more prominent men in the area came inside our house to talk about the Mission, future plans, etc. We sat around the fire for several hours just talking. These natives have no concept of time and they love to talk. When it got to be about ten, we told them it was time to retire. I guess they wondered why we were in a hurry since we had talked only a few hours.

On Thursday morning at about 9:30 we set out for the next station which is called Hedamari. This was about eight miles from Pureni. Again, we were given a royal welcome. Fr. Berard had told all the boss boys and chiefs beforehand that I was coming. At Hedamari, everything was practically the same as at Pureni. I enjoyed the utter disrespect for time these natives showed. At about 4:00 in the afternoon, the catechist walked around the boundaries of our Mission and blew a horn, made out of bamboo. It sounded like a foghorn. I was told this was a signal for gathering for the Catechism instructions. After a half hour, I asked the catechist where the catechumens were. He answered, they were coming since they all had heard his call. I waited and waited, but only a few had showed up by 5:00, an hour later. Finally, at six they were all present, and the instructions were immediately under way. I went to the hall and was surprised to find at least three hundred men and women present for the instructions. Again, I was amazed at their answering. At every question the whole crowd of 300 shouted their answer. These also know the entire catechism by heart, in their native tongue. I recognized their spontaneous enumerating of the names of the twelve Apostles.

On Friday, we passed on to Koroba, stopping for an hour at a new place called Tindidugl. The boss boy or chief of Hedamari went along with us. This is a real honor for them, and gives them prestige—to be allowed to ride in the Mission trailer. He sat proudly next to me as we headed out of the Hedamari area. He probably felt as important as the President of the U.S.

At Tindidugl there were at least 450 natives to welcome us. This is a young station, entirely built by the natives. They had asked our Fathers to start a Mission among them. Immediately they started to build a church. When the Church was finished, they came to Fr. Berard and said: "Now we have a church; you must come and teach us about your religion." That whole area should eventually become completely Catholic. The crowd was so big that I had to speak to them from the back of the trailer. Their reaction to my talk was edifying, considering that they are all bush people. As we were ready to move on, the boss boy of that area also rode along. Now I was flanked by a chief on the left and right. I guess they felt as if they were a formal escort through their region.

At Koroba—at least twenty-eight miles from Tari—we again received a most cordial welcome. There are about forty Catholics, government employees, in that area. Of course, all of them are natives. Every hundred feet or so, we had to stop to allow the Catholics to shake hands with me and to kiss my ring. A few who had missed me on the way, came to the Mission within a half hour to greet me.

The stay at Koroba was very pleasant, and the Catholics as well as the 400-plus pagans were most eager to do anything to make my stay pleasant. On both evenings of my stay, about a dozen of the Catholic men came to our house to talk about the work of the Mission. The Catholics in the area, with the help of the pagans, built a new church entirely on their own, without asking for any remuneration. The purpose of my going to Koroba was to have Confirmations. I confirmed seventeen on Sunday, Feb. 4. This was the first time I had Confirmations at an outstation. I'll be getting more and more from now on.

You would be amazed at the generosity of these natives at Koroba. At the collection that was taken up on Sunday at the Mass, we got over 7 Australian pounds sterling. This is equivalent to about $16. A number of Catholics also came to the Mission to give me gifts. One Catholic woman gave me onions and various types of vegetables. Another gave me a chicken. The chicken I took along to Tari. I suppose they will butcher it. —When it was time to leave, all the Catholics again came to shake hands with me and kiss my ring. Some who had missed me at the Mission stopped me on the way out. Whenever a native Catholic from the Highlands meets a Priest or Brother, his greeting is always: "God bless you." It reminds me somewhat of the traditional German greeting among the Catholics.

There were many interesting incidents which I could enumerate, but it would make this letter a bit long. However, I might mention a few. In church, the boss boys, or chiefs, still think they're in charge of matters. Occasionally, when some of the natives step out of line, the chief bawls them out, and not rarely also uses physical force. Sometimes the chief makes more noise than the original disturbance he set out to correct. —The Chief from Hedamari stayed in Koroba until we left on Sunday. Again, he sat with me on the trailer. As we came into his area, he shouted to all the natives that were standing along the road. I found out later he told all of them they were to come for Catechism instructions that evening. Actually, it is through such boss boys that we get such large crowds to come to our Mission. I guess they are afraid not to conform to the chief's way of thinking. As a result, whenever we can, we deal with the chiefs to get into a place. They are usually proud to assert their authority in favor of the Mission.

The Tari area and the Koroba area are linked by what is known as the Tagari Bridge. This is a bridge designed and constructed for the government by Fr. Berard, who is a graduate from Carnegie Tech with a degree in engineering. The span of that bridge at the Tagari River is about 100 feet. It's really a beaut of a bridge. I took a couple of pictures of it. The government feels deeply indebted to our Mission for this work. Fr. Berard has designed two more bridges for the government in the last year. Neither has been constructed as yet. One is between Mendi and Ialibu, and the other is in the Pureni area.

I was just interrupted for a few hours by the arrival of Fr. Gary and Brother Claude. They came together. Brother Claude spent several weeks in Sydney to do some shopping for us. Both look very good. Evidently the vacation of six months did them a lot of good. Both told me of their pleasant visit in Kansas. However, Brother Claude said he almost froze to death. I think he said it was 14 below zero. They'll have a lot to talk about this evening and tomorrow. Of course, Brother Claude stays here in Mendi. Father will go to Ialibu on Thursday.

I hope this letter finds all of you coming along as well as ever. Hello to everyone around home.

Your devoted brother, Msgr. Firmin

～～

27 March 1962

Dear Mary,

Since I have a little time this evening, I had better get a letter off to you, even though it is a day early. This is the second day in a row that the weather has been ideal. Just when I thought we were heading for forty straight days of rain, the weather changed. It is certainly good to see the ground dry out a bit. I hope we'll have a few days more of this type of weather. After thirty-four days of rain, a change like this is really appreciated. Many thanks for your letter of March 17. It arrived yesterday noon. Since you didn't mention anything further about Felix and Johnette, I presume both are coming along well.

We have a new "postmaster" here in Mendi, and he still doesn't know what his job is. We don't really have a regular postmaster. The government simply appoints one of the patrol officers to handle matters there for a while. Just as they are about to learn how to run things, their term expires, and a new fellow is appointed. The present fellow is about the most incompetent we have had.

This past Sunday night at about 11:00 pm we had a rather strong earthquake here. We must have had about ten since I arrived in New Guinea in 1959. This last one was probably the strongest, but there was no damage done. It is really a strange sensation. The house simply rocks back and forth. The pictures, crucifixes, and other objects on the wall are slapped about. It lasted over a minute and a half this time. The center of the disturbance seemed to have been at Lae—about an hour and forty minutes to the east of Mendi by plane—right on the coast. I don't know what the natives do during an earthquake. As all things of that nature, it is most likely blamed on Tambaran (evil spirit).

Two of the Fathers, Frs. Senan and Benjamin, who are looking after the bush stations out of Mendi—one to the north, the other to the South—started to walk to Ialibu this past Sunday. They were hoping to make it by Monday afternoon around three o'clock. I estimate Ialibu approximately 35 miles from Mendi. Half of that distance is over very rough terrain. Two deep gorges are in that area. They took the walk to see how our outposts from Mendi link up with those of Ialibu. They will walk back again by about Thursday. As far as I know, this is the first time that any of our Missionaries attempted to walk from Mendi to Ialibu.

Every Friday we have organized games for our school kids. The ordinary time is in the afternoon. However, since it usually rains in the afternoon, we switched the games to the morning. Last week, I decided to give the bigger boys a few lessons in softball. I still found I know a bit about the game, but after an hour or so, I began to realize that I can't take it as I used to. I was stiff all over. It took me a few days to get the kinks out. If I feel like it, I might try again this week. The kids do quite well, especially in view of the fact that they hadn't even seen a softball game until last year. Almost all of them have a tendency to use their feet more than their hands in stopping balls.

I don't know whether I mentioned it to you before, but we are building an extension to the friary here. We had room for seven friars. The reason we are adding more space is that we are hoping to get a few young Fathers assigned right after they have completed their fourth year of theology in Washington. According to the new regulations that came out from Rome a few years ago, the young Fathers who have completed the fourth year of theology, must devote another year of practical indoctrination in their work. We are hoping to have that year of indoctrination for our young Missionaries right here in the Mission. If that will happen, then I will again do a bit of teaching. Actually, Rome has already approved of our conducting such a school for our young Fathers here in Mendi. By the end of the Provincial Chapter— sometime during July—we'll know whether the school will function here next year. It certainly will be a big boost for the Mission, if we get it going.

The addition—to make room for four or five men—is coming along very well. Brother Claude started on the project as soon as he got back from his leave. Brother Alfred is also here to help along. After the addition to the friary is completed, we are hoping to get started on another, this time a permanent-type church. The present one is not in very good shape any more. We had a new covering of kunai (grass) put on the roof, but it still leaks badly. I only hope it will last until we can get a new church ready. Besides being in bad condition, the old church is much too small. This past Sunday, we had so many people here that there were at least fifty or sixty who couldn't get inside. And the inside of the church was jammed right up to the altar. It was difficult for the people to get to the front at Communion time. Because of the difficulty of getting decent wood in this area, the bulk of the structure will probably be of aluminum. While it most likely won't be much to look at from the outside, we do intend to make a nice sanctuary.

I suppose you're still coming along well with the cafeteria work in school. No doubt, by this time, you have things down pretty well to a system.

If you think of it, you might send me Tommy's new address. I think he would appreciate an occasional letter. Hope all is coming along well around home. Hello to all. Please tell Uncle Jake's I'll write sometime soon—before Easter, I hope. I appreciated very much the letter from Aunt Clara.

Your devoted brother, Msgr. Firmin

~~~

17 April 1962

Dear Mary,

Many thanks for the Easter card and letter of April 7. It arrived yesterday noon. Thanks also for the gift that was enclosed. I hope to offer Masses for your intentions in appreciation. You surely don't seem to have much of an Easter vacation. I'm a bit surprised that school extends to Thursday noon of Holy Week, and especially that it starts again on Monday after Easter. Traditionally, the Monday after Easter has always been considered a holiday, as far as I can recall.

By contrast, they're really having a long series of holidays here around Easter time. The holidays were announced just recently in the official government publication, and they are a string of six full days, beginning Good Friday. These six days are official. As in the past, they will probably take one or two more which are not official. The fact that they have so much time off at Easter is by no means a sign that they want to participate in Holy Week and Easter services in Church. Even Catholics (of Australia) working for the government are negligent in these. For them it happens to be a big series of holidays—of leisure. They already have drawn up a program of activities that take in just about all six of the days. Part of their program includes tennis tournaments, ping-pong matches, cricket, dances, balls, movies, etc. It usually takes a good number of them a few days to recover.

On April 25, as part of the Easter Holidays this year, we will observe Anzac Day. I told you of that last year, or the year before. It is something like our Memorial Day. This year, as in the past, I have again been asked to give the main address. There should be a big crowd there of natives, as well as Europeans. The school kids of this area are also expected to be present. Our kids have been practicing for several weeks already. I'm surprised how well those youngsters can keep time and remain in step.

We started the Holy Week celebration with the usual blessing of Palms this past Sunday. Because of the large crowd, we passed out the palms beforehand, and blessed them as they held them in their hands. Since our crowd for services is constantly growing, and since the present church is getting worse, we will soon have to build a new church. We actually have plans for an aluminum structure—about 120 feet long and about 30 feet wide. This should be able to accommodate close to 900 people or even more than that the way they jam together. It probably won't be too ornate in appearance from the outside, but we do hope to have a beautiful sanctuary. While plans for this have been drawn up already, it will most likely take us at least three or four months before we can get started. The present church, as you can tell from the pictures I've sent you, is completely of bush material—pit-pit sides and floor, and a grass roof.

One of our big problems in missionary work is learning the language of the natives. We have made good progress in three of the stations. Fr. Benjamin has been working hard on the Mendi language, and by this time, he has translated the Catechism completely into the local language. While he understands a good bit of the local language, he is making a special effort at the present time to become more proficient. For this reason, he had a bush house built by the natives in Kombegibu, and moved up there about ten days ago. All day long, he is surrounded by the natives, and hears nothing but the native talk. Within a couple of months, he should get along fairly well. He is really enjoying his stay among the Kombegibu crowd. That is the place where Kavivi, the boss boy, is in power. Fr. Benjamin says Kavivi lives like a Nero. Whatever he wants, the natives in that area have to do. He now has nine wives, having taken another one just recently. These wives are like servants, or slaves, to him. Fr. Benjamin says Kavivi does nothing but talk all day long. Every once in a while, one of his wives will come along with a hollow bamboo, filled with cold water. Throughout the day, his wives change off bringing him food. He evidently has them well trained. If any of the wives doesn't do what she is supposed to, he just beats her up. With fellows like that in control of their local areas, you can imagine why they would oppose activities on the part of the government, which might curtail their power or authority. Fr. Benjamin came to the mission for a brief visit last Saturday, and he will probably come again for Easter.

Fr. Senan is doing practically the same thing up the Valley. He has settled down at a place called Ekari. He has been there for a few months now. He hears nothing but native talk all day long. He also is doing quite well in the language. Even though he is only about twelve miles from here, that language is entirely different from that which the natives speak right here in Kumin (Kumin, by the way, is actually the name of the place where our Mission is located). Every little area has its own proper name. The place where the government stations of Mendi is located is actually Murumbu.

Yesterday I had a very nice letter from Bede Duz and Francis Kili. Both of these lads are going to school at Mainohana. Francis is in grade 7 and Bede is in 6. Each is right at the top of his class—in a school with a very high standard. In a previous letter, I told Francis his two little sisters had run away from school, but that they were now back again. His comment on that was: "As for my sisters coming back to school for that I am happy. As for their running away, I will deal with them when I come back to Mendi at Christmas time." He'll probably give them a real good talking to. When our Mission first settled down in this area, Francis's father was rather unfriendly, and actually nasty. But he is gradually coming around. Francis in a former letter told me he is praying daily for his father and mother that they will become more friendly towards the Mission, and will become Catholic before they get too old. I feel confident his prayers will be answered.

There are two tribes in this area, Kombegibu and another one about three miles down the valley, who are using every means they can think of in an attempt to buy one of our turkeys. One fellow actually offered twenty Australian pounds sterling, the equivalent of $45, for one. I'm sure we could easily get eight kinas, the ordinary price of a bride. Of course, we would not sell, except in exchange for a bit of land. The sense of value of these natives is really strange. I hope you've had a fine Easter celebration. Hello to all.

Your devoted brother, Msgr. Firmin

[On May 20, 1962, a new plane, a Cessna 185, purchased by the Mission, arrived at Mendi. It had been assembled in Madang and flown to the Mission by SVD Fathers Walachy and Hoff. The Mission's old Cessna would be flown to Australia and sold.]

~~~

5 June 1962

Dear Mary,

As scheduled, I got back to Mendi this morning after a week's visit in Ialibu and the out-stations in that general area. Your two letters, of May 19 and 26, respectively, were waiting for me when I arrived. I don't know when they got here. It was good to hear that you had rain in sufficient quantity to keep the crop going. I hope you had none of the storms that seem to have hit the Midwest last week. According to the international news report, tornadoes hit Emporia, and a few days later a ten-inch downpour flooded north Wichita.—I surely hope Tommy will be able to time his leave right for the harvest.

Thanks for the clipping in reference to Judy's $200 scholarship. I was happy to hear also that Phyllis Ann did so well as to rate a medal at the graduation exercises. In a sense, her honor might be preferred to the other awards. To gain so many credits and at the same time keep up above-average in grades could be a higher achievement than top grades with a minimum of hours or credits. In any case, she certainly deserves hearty congratulations.

So Sister Fidelis was the commencement speaker at Marian High for this year. As far as I know, this is the first time that she has come to Kansas for such a purpose. I have no doubt that she did a good job. I suppose there is a good possibility of her being elected Mother General at the next elections of the Sisters of St. Agnes.

Now to tell you a bit of my week in the bush. It was a rather pleasant week. I spent a couple of days in the Wiru Plateau, a relatively new mission territory. Fr. Gary has charge of that area, and met me at the airstrip when I arrived on our plane. Most of our stations there are in their initial stages, but already some progress is noticeable. It was especially good to see that our schools are well-attended. The teachers we have at most of the stations are not well qualified. However, they do well in teaching the people the catechism, prayers, and even a bit of reading, writing, and arithmetic. At all the stations they keep up the custom of having the rosary and night prayers in common—even in the most recently built stations. At one station, I'm sure there were at least three hundred people present for night prayer—on an ordinary weekday. The station I stayed at the first day has a house for Father, a house for the teacher and a school—all of bush materials. Since that spot is really out in the bush, there was no possibility of getting there except by walking. It was only about a forty-minute walk from the airstrip, but about half of the distance was through swampy area, where frequently one sinks in about eight inches. Fortunately, I had been forewarned and had come prepared, wearing my walking boots.

After a couple of days there at that station we headed for a place called Tindua. We passed a few of our stations along the way. Because of the bad terrain we again had to walk—including a mile or so through swamp. After a walk of about an hour and a half, we hit fairly good road, and could travel by motorcycle, which a government officer had brought there the day before. It was fortunate that we didn't have to walk all the way to Tindua (about ten miles), since it started to rain about three miles from Tindua. This station is quite remarkable for the large number of people it has attracted. The local boss boy, who is a powerful man, being influential both with the government as well as with the natives, is very favorably disposed to us, and thus has talked his people into coming to our Mission, rather than to the Protestants. The station was founded right on the edge of the Wiru Plateau, our first in that general area. A big crowd, including the boss boy (or chief) was on hand to welcome us. I found the people there just about as friendly as the Ialibu people (the friendliest in our Mission). During the rest of the day I met a lot of the local natives.

The next day was Ascension Thursday, and we spread word that I would have Mass there at 9:00 in the morning. Of course, they don't know anything about time. Nine o'clock simply means sometime after sunrise. A few self-appointed (I assume) callers with the strongest voices announced as loud as they could about every fifteen or twenty minutes that I was to have Mass next morning, and all the people should come. They made these announcements from about five in the afternoon until about 10:00 o'clock at night. Their voices, I think, must have carried over a few valleys. Ascension Thursday was bright and clear, and a large crowd began to gather at sunrise—about 6:45. By nine o'clock, the mission's grounds were filled with natives. I would guess there were well over 400 people there for the Mass. Through a translator, I gave a sermon to the people after the Mass. After everything was finished, I went out into the yard and, through translators, spoke with many of them. I guess they would have stayed all day. But Fr. Gary and I pulled ourselves away, ate a quick breakfast, and then started off for Ialibu. Since there was a decent road all the way, I was able to go by motorcycle. It took us less than an hour.

My visit at Ialibu was very pleasant, but it lasted only until Saturday morning, when Fr. Gary and I again headed for the bush. This time we headed in the opposite direction to Orei—eighteen miles from Ialibu. We went to Orei and back all the way on motorcycles. Since it hadn't rained for a couple of days, the roads were quite good. I didn't take a single spill. The people at Orei remembered me from the visit of last year. There were a few hundred on hand to welcome us. I guess I shook hands with almost all of them. I really got a kick out of one fellow by the name of Wama. He is still a pagan but is married to a Catholic girl. As he shook hands with me, he slipped me a threepence (equivalent to about three cents). Fr. Samuel was also at Orei. In fact, he is in charge of that station now that Fr. Gary has taken over the Wiru. The main purpose of my going to Orei was to have Confirmations there. Last year when I was there on a visit, there was no church. A storm had destroyed it a few weeks before, so we had to have Mass outside. Now they have a beautiful bush church. I think it is the nicest church we have in the Mission. It was built entirely by the natives—without any pay. They're surely proud of it now. The dimensions of the church are about thirty feet by seventy feet. In shape it looks like an "A." There are no side walls in the proper sense. The roofs simply come way down to the ground. I took a number of pictures of it, both inside and outside. I hope they turn out well.

The church was well filled for my Mass and the Confirmations that followed. I'm sure there were over 400 people inside the church, and probably over 200 outside. The Catholics are really increasing fast in that area. Ninety-seven went to Communion at my Mass. I forgot to mention that prior to my Mass, I blessed the Church, dedicating it to Christ the King. In their own simple way, these people are really devout. They all participate in saying the prayers at the Mass, and occasionally, they go into a hymn or two. Their volume is out of this world. —Only the Catholics who were baptized a year ago were confirmed. There were twenty-four in all. The forty-one who were baptized this Easter will be confirmed next year.

We had a most unusual guest for the Confirmations—a native dynamic boss boy from a neighboring Catholic Mission, who thinks that all people should become Catholic as soon as possible. He is a most remarkable fellow. I don't know how long he has been a Catholic, but he is really zealous in working for the Church. After the Mass, he asked whether he could speak to all the people. We gave him permission. He gathered the entire crowd around him—about 600 or more—and started to harangue them on being good Catholics, and how to get more of their friends and relatives to come to the catechumenate and to Mass. After about forty-five minutes, following our breakfast, I went outside and noticed he was still talking. When he stopped for a couple of minutes, I walked over and had my picture taken with him. I thought he was finished speaking, but found out differently. He said his first talk is finished. In a few minutes he would begin his second talk. Sure enough, he started again. I think he spoke at least for an hour and a half altogether. The natives of Orei respect him very much, and I know they were impressed with his enthusiasm. In the evening before he left, he told us, after he gets everything straightened out in the neighboring Catholic Mission, he will come to Orei to help make more Catholics. Actually, we found out he is from Orei. He owns ground right near the Mission station. In a few years, I guess he will be coming back to Orei to stay. He will be a terrific help. He really makes a fine appearance. He had a number of medals (of Pius XII, John XXIII, etc.) pinned on his chest. I had heard the Protestant Missions in that area really fear this fellow. I can see why.

Throughout the day I went about meeting people. The day itself was almost like a picnic. From about one o'clock until five-thirty Fr. Samuel had games—shooting arrows, races, etc., for which prizes were given. I'm sure I met and spoke with a couple of hundred people that day.

During the Saturday, Sunday, and Monday morning I was at Orei, five of the seven Sacraments were administered there. On Saturday, Fr. Samuel baptized a little boy, who had been born a couple of days before. The mother of this child was roaming around the mission, just as all the rest. No one would have suspected that she just had a baby less than two days before. In addition to the Sacraments of Confession, Communion, and Confirmation, there was also matrimony on Monday morning. I think you would have gotten a real bang out of that. The two who were married were Felix and Alice. Felix has been a quasi-carpenter for us for about six years. Alice was baptized a year ago and was confirmed on Sunday. I took a picture of the bride and the groom the day before the marriage. If it turns out well, I'll send you a copy. Alice is really a bush girl. The groom is quite sophisticated by comparison. Alice wore a brief grass skirt and a blouse. The bridesmaid, Angela, wore nothing but a very brief grass skirt. Fr. Samuel had regular nuptial Mass.

During the Mass the, bride and the groom were to be kneeling on the pridieus, right outside the sanctuary. However, Alice, the bride, got a little tired, and simply sat down on the kneeler of the pridieu, facing the people. It was a very casual ceremony. Since Felix works at the main station in Ialibu, the bridal couple went to Ialibu that day. The bride carried a bag (about forty pounds) of kau-kau on her back as she walked half of the eighteen miles to Ialibu. How many brides nowadays would carry their own food for their wedding banquet on the day of their marriage? Of course, Alice is rather hefty. She could make a good guard on a professional football team. Alice is really a very fine girl, as is Angela, the bridesmaid. The two were inseparable friends. But I guess they will be separated now. Angela has actually been paid for by another family group in preparation for marriage. But the husband-to-be refuses to take her. The parents are trying to force the marriage. —Incidentally, after the Confirmation ceremonies, I had my picture taken with all those who were confirmed in a group. If that picture turns out well, you will see Angela standing right next to me.

The anniversary of my first Mass and ordination were both spent in the bush. But in our own way we managed to have a bit of a celebration. Fr. Samuel was the cook, and I must say he did a fair job. I tasted a new dish both in the Wiru and at Orei—pit-pit. I used to think that it was nothing else than weeds. But if it is cooked properly with a bit of seasoning, it tastes quite good. Perhaps the country air gave me a good appetite.

While I enjoyed the week immensely, I was happy to get back to Mendi. My trip back was on our new plane. It is really a beaut. The pilot tells me it handles a bit differently than the old Cessna 180, but he is gradually becoming adjusted.

You may enjoy the following incident. On my visit to Ialibu recently (not this time), the wife of one of our workers there complained to me a bit about the food she gets in the highlands. She comes from the coast and has been accustomed to such things as taro, sago, etc. I told her that the other natives from the coast easily become accustomed to our highland kau-kau, etc. She insisted she just couldn't make the adjustment. So, I told her she didn't look like she was starving. She replied: My skin may be big outside, but I'm empty inside." How would you refute such a statement?

I have a few more things to do tonight, so I had better sign off. I hope everything around Catherine is coming along well. Hello to all. Your devoted brother, Msgr. Firmin

∼∼∼

4 July 1962

Dear Mary,

Your letter of June 22 arrived a couple of days ago—on July 2. Thanks a lot. It seems that Sunday June 17 was an unusual day, with the three Solemn Masses. I knew the Schmidt twins were having their Solemn Masses on the 17th, but I had forgotten about Fr. Marion Gross. I suppose there were a number of people who attended the celebrations of both families. For that reason, it surely would have been desirable to have had them divided. I was happy to hear that Severin was able to help out the Catherine choir on the occasion of the Solemn Masses.

This is the 4th of July, but naturally the date has no significance here in New Guinea. However, the Americans who are here make it a bit of a holiday. Two of the Fathers who are working in the bush out of Mendi are in here right now—Frs. Benjamin and Senan. Fr. Senan had gone to the bush on May 19, and didn't get back to Mendi until July 2. During all this time he visited about ten or twelve bush stations. One of them is three day's walk from here. He really loves the bush work. When he comes back to the main station, he becomes restless after a couple of days and heads for the bush again. He wanted to leave today again, but a heavy downpour of rain caused him to postpone until tomorrow morning. He was also caught in a heavy rain when he came in a couple of days ago. I guess he walked about four hours in the rain. –Fr. August of Kagua is also here right now. About two weeks ago, he was given a shot of penicillin for a cut in his leg. After about ten days, a bad reaction resulted from the penicillin. His face started to puff up and swell, and he got a severe skin rash. He came to Mendi to be treated for this strange reaction to penicillin. In a day or two, he recovered and could have returned to Kagua. However, he stayed on for a few days to mimeograph the catechism in his native language.

I had a very fine letter from Sister Eudocia last week. The main reason for her letter is to tell me she had sent some rosaries to our Mission. She was just getting ready to leave for her retreat at Fond du Lac. After the retreat, she is going to visit her people in Altoona. I have to write to her after she returns to her assignment.

I am enclosing a few more photos. Actually, I have a good many more, but I don't want to make the letter too heavy for the regular postage. In the Confirmation picture, the girl standing next to me is Angela Nobia. I have another picture of her, which I will send on later. The picture of the bride and groom—Alice Yapunyo and Felix Walaba—was taken the day before the wedding. They were dressed exactly the same for the wedding, except that Felix had his cap off.

A dentist from Goroka came to Mendi yesterday and set up his office here for a couple of weeks. There is no resident dentist in the Southern Highlands. So, every year or so, a dentist from another area comes in here and sets up shop. The people from the other stations, except Tari, will be brought to Mendi to have their teeth checked. One of our lay missionaries, Bill McQuillan, from Erave, came up this morning. I don't know whether any of the other missionaries are coming. The reason the people from Tari are not brought in is that the dentist will go there with all his equipment for a few days after he finishes here. I also made an appointment for a check-up, even though I have had no trouble of any kind.

We just completed the statistics of our Mission covering the twelve months, July 1, 1961-June 30, 1962. The following are a few facts that may be of interest to you.

Total population in our mission is now estimated at 203,000. This is about 30,000 higher than was previously estimated. The total Catholic population in our Mission is now 737. That is more than double the number when I arrived in 1959. The total number of native Catholics is 691; non-natives: 34; mixed-race: 12. We now have 4,530 catechumens, who come to regular instructions to become Catholics. During the last twelve months, we have had a total of 250 Baptisms. Of these, 148 were solemn Baptisms, and of the 148, there were 103 adults. During the past year, we have had 111 First Communions. The total Communions for the entire year were 28,207. The figure almost doubled during the past year. The total number of pupils in school now is 4,104: of these, 2,482 are boys, and 1,531 are girls. As far as Missionary personnel are concerned, we have 14 priests, three brothers, six lay missionaries, and 89 native teachers. So, you can see the Mission is gradually growing in the statistics that really count. Today, we ran off a sheet of statistics, which will be sent to the Province. I hope to send you a copy one of these days.

I hope everything is coming along well around home. Your brief account of the harvest at the Staabs sounded good. If the rest of the wheat in the general area was comparable, it should have been a good harvest. Hello to everyone around home.

Your devoted brother, Msgr. Firmin

[In mid-July 1962, on behalf of the Capuchin Order, in Pittsburgh, PA, Fr. Don Nally arrives at the Papua New Guinea Mission, with the aim of visiting the Mission stations to observe the progress being made and then reporting back to the Mission Office. Fr. Don visits the various main stations, including Ialibu, Kagua, and others in Papua. In doing so, he is impressed with the progress being made, especially in view of the obstacles the missionaries face, including those related to transportation and shipping. He and Monsignor Firmin then travel to Rabaul, on the island of New Britain, where Fr. Don can see one of the most advanced missions in the territory. Unfortunately, Fr. Don develops an ear infection and is hospitalized for the duration of the visit to Rabaul, while Msgr. Firmin spends time at the mission at Vunapope near Rabaul and then goes to Kavieng, on the Island of New Ireland, for a short visit. Then Msgr. Firmin goes on to Madang on the north coast of the island of New Guinea. Fr. Don must take a boat to Madang to avoid flying in a non-pressurized plane (to avoid damaging his hearing). Msgr. Firmin then flies back to Mendi; however, Fr. Don is delayed in getting back to the Capuchin Mission to complete his visit.]

~~~

31 July 1962

Dear Mary,

Many thanks for your letter of July 21. I received it yesterday, July 30, even though it arrived in Mendi on Saturday. But since the government people here have five-day weeks, it was a couple of days in the Mendi post office. —I was surprised to hear that your rainy weather has been continuing for the greater part of July, at least. The weather here in Mendi, and all of the Southern Highlands, during the last few weeks has been unusually bad, even by New Guinea standards. Today is the first sunny day we have had in about ten or twelve days. I would guess that we had a total of ten or fifteen minutes of sunshine last week. Fr. Don's trip to Tari was postponed by a full week. He wanted to go there on Monday, July 16. Sunday July 29 was the first chance, and it was completely overcast then. For the first seven months of this year, we have had a total of almost 80 inches of rain—an average of over eleven inches per month. And our rains are not the real tropical type, where you get a few inches in an hour. As a rule, they are slow, soaking rains.

Early this afternoon I received a wedding invitation from Wilfric and Alfreda Constance. The invitation was mailed on July 1. I would suspect that the reason it took so long was due to the bad mail service in New Guinea. Even though tomorrow is the day of the wedding, I hope to drop them a line anyway. Fr. Paulinus had mentioned in a recent letter that Wilfric was getting married. I guess that leaves Tusch the only bachelor left of their original crowd.

As you probably know, we have quite a few outstations throughout the Southern Highlands. We try to have a teacher or catechist at each of them. We must have a total of about ninety catechists or teachers in the various outstations. Last week Thursday, at about 9:30 in the evening, a native from the outstation at Pinj (four hours' walk from here) came to Mendi and told us that our native teacher there had drowned. He was trying to wade across the swift Lai River. The river was deeper than he had guessed. Since he was a poor swimmer, he had no chance. This fellow comes from a place called Denglagu—about fifty minutes east from here by plane. This is the second teacher of ours who has been drowned within the last year. A fellow working for us out of Kagua was drowned last August.

School here at Mendi is continuing to come along well. We have some activities for the youngsters, which are not only entertaining for them but also educational. For example, almost every Saturday evening, Brother Claude shows movies. The films are meant to be educational. We don't have a big variety, and therefore we constantly must show the same ones over and over again. We have in fact found out that these natives must see a movie several times before they appreciate it. The more they see them, the better they like them. A number of the movies have sound with them. This is a help for them in their English. A few films have Western songs. They know the words of a number of them, and with these they sing along. Some of the movies are travelogues, which teach them a bit about the rest of the world. Incidentally, most of the films were donated by various companies around Pittsburgh. We loaned some films to the Education Department. They thought very highly of them. Besides this type of film, we have also filmstrips of a religious nature. We hope to use these on a bigger scale next year. We don't allow all the children to come to the movies on Saturdays. Those who misbehaved, or didn't work as they are expected, or need a bit of discipline, are not allowed to attend. It is a good means of making them toe the line. They all love to see the "Pictures."

Besides these movies, the Sister have other forms of entertainment. The latest is square dancing. The Sisters have been teaching the girls and the smaller boys to square dance on Sunday nights. I haven't seen them yet, but according to reports, they are doing well, and seem to like it. It will be an accomplishment to have them switch from their primitive, monotonous dances to something like square dance. On Friday nights they usually have Bingo. The prize for winning is usually a marble. They think it's terrific. Again, good behavior is the requisite for playing bingo. And so, all the nights of the children are taken care of, since all weekday nights they have a study hour.

All the school kids, from the smallest to the biggest, girls as well as boys, have regular work assigned to them every day, unless it is raining too hard. Besides getting firewood they need for cooking their kau-kau, they have to bring sand and stones from the river. Some of them are assigned to take care of the lawns; others work in the garden, etc. We feel it is important for them not only to learn in school, but also outside of school. –I mentioned that we expect the kids to work, unless it is raining too hard. Yesterday, we thought it was raining too hard, so they were excused from work. However, I noticed a good number of them out in the rain, playing marbles. Rain really doesn't keep them from playing their games. They all get soaked, and then build a fire to dry off.

I'm enclosing a few photos again. I'll send as many as will be allowed for the minimum weight of ½ ounce. The one with the little girl carrying a small bag of kau-kau gives you an idea of how young they start teaching their kids to carry a bag. I hope all is coming along well. Hello to all.

Your devoted brother, Msgr. Firmin

〜〜〜

23 September 1962

Dear Mary,

I hope this letter finds you coming along well and improving every day. It was certainly good to receive your letter of September 12, and hear from yourself how well you're recovering [from a hysterectomy]. I think it was most fortunate to have gone to such a competent doctor as you did. When I returned from my visit to Erave (Sept. 21), two letters from Angela were waiting for me, one written the day before the operation. It was surely good news to hear in her second letter that, according to all indications, the operation was a success. Of course, your letter also confirmed that. Please express my thanks to Angela for her faithful letters. I may not be able to write to her for at least a few days. —It was very kind and thoughtful of Fr. Matthew to visit you at the hospital and help you to pass the long hours of waiting. I taught Fr. Matthew one year at Capuchin College, and found him a rather pleasant young man. I think he will make a good missionary. He has a good sense of humor, and that is very important here in the Mission. He is expected to arrive in the Mission around October 4. I suppose his family was not too happy, at first, over the fact that his first assignment is so far from home. They'll get over it, and, in time. will be happy that he has been selected for the Missions.

I would have written sometime last week, but the letter could not have been mailed until tomorrow anyway. In the first place, the mail service out of Erave is not so good. And secondly, the bad weather of last week disrupted all flying schedules. I myself was stranded in Erave until Friday morning.

My visit to Erave was most pleasant. As I mentioned previously, we have our central school for boys there. We certainly have a fine group of lads there. It is always good to see them. The first evening I was there I gave them a talk on their future, especially urging them to plan to do something worthwhile for themselves and their own people. I'm sure a number of them will become teachers for us, and possibly we'll find a few vocations for the priesthood. The highest grade is only the fifth, but I think it's early enough for them to think of the future. The second day I was there I paid a visit to every classroom. The respective teachers had them show off a bit the things they are able to do. It is surprising how well even the third and fourth graders can read. The fifth-grade boys were just completing compositions at the time I visited them. They do quite well. I'm sure the best among them could compete with the average fifth grader in America. I was especially happy to see how faithfully these youngsters are in going to church. They have to attend Mass a few days a week. Even on the days that they don't have to attend, almost all of them attend on their own initiative. And just about all the Catholic boys are daily communicants. I think you would get a kick out of the sacristans. Three of the boys have been appointed to keep the church clean, prepare the altars for Mass, lay out the vestments, and so on. They really are well trained. This time, as on previous visits, I was told by the Father in charge and the teachers, that Firmin Waliba is one of the outstanding boys. Because of his dependability, he is now the time-keeper, and they tell me he is always right on the button. While I was there, however, Firmin Waliba crashed into another boy playing football, and broke the other lad's arm. I brought the boy with the broken arm back to Mendi, where the doctor put it in a cast. He is ready to return to Erave, and probably will go there tomorrow.

The Erave Valley is still very beautiful. In spite of the heavy rains and lack of sunshine in recent weeks, everything looks fresh and green.

Fruit of all types grows in abundance. We loaded the plane with bananas and pineapple coming back to Mendi. Of course, we are still trying to increase the varieties, by constantly getting new types from Australia. Progress in our station is remarkable. I took Fr. Berard down with me to make a survey of hydro-electric possibilities. Fr. Berard is an engineer. According to the initial findings, we should be able to set up a plant that will produce about 15,000 watts. The setting up of the plant will be quite an expense, but once it's set up, we will have almost no expense on it, and at the same time will have electricity there all the time. We are also investigating the hydro-electric potential of other stations. We hope to find at least one or two more that are suitable. – Recently, we also purchased a new sawmill, which we set up at Erave. A big number of high-quality pine is available there, enough to supply all the needs we will have in the future.

Today is only the 23rd, but we are celebrating my Name Day with a big meal tonight. The reason we're celebrating it today is that the Fathers from the bush came in, and they won't be able to stay until Tuesday. Fr. August from Kagua is also here. He came along with Fr. Benjamin. The two left Kagua about two weeks ago, and went through a new area which is still restricted, with the permission of the government, making contact with the people. They arrived in Mendi yesterday morning, after a two-week walk. Fr. Senan is also expected to come in today to join in the celebration.

Today marked the fiftieth consecutive day of measurable rain. While it doesn't rain day and night, as it did in the days of the Flood of the Old Testament, we have an idea how dreary those forty days must have been. I'm sure we're setting all kinds of records on rainfall in the Southern Highlands. While in Erave, I was informed that they had 175 inches of rain last year, and it looks as if they're going to beat that record this year. It's amazing how these Cessna planes are able to land and take off on some of those strips. When we took off at Erave on Friday, there were a couple of inches of water on a good part of the strip, and we didn't have pontoons when we took off.

Hello to all around home. Assuring a special remembrance in my daily prayers and Mass for a quick and complete recovery.

I remain, Your devoted brother, Msgr. Firmin

~~~

Chapter 4

OCT 1962–SEPT 1963
CHURCH AND SCHOOLS FLOURISH,
GOVERNMENT COUNCIL CONVENES,
A SPECIAL INVITATION

2 October 1962

Dear Mary,

I hope this letter finds you recovering well from the operation [a hysterectomy]. Since I haven't heard from you for some time, I presume everything is coming along fine.

As far as I can recall, I wrote to you on the 23rd, the day all the Bush Fathers were in here to help us anticipate the celebration of my Nameday. We really had a delicious meal prepared by the Sisters, who also joined us in the dinner. Right before we started dinner, about eight small girls from the prep class, and first grade, came in and sang "Happy Feast Day to You." They did very well.

Everything here in Mendi is coming along well. Last week a

government inspector came to inspect our school. His report, which was sent to headquarters in Port Moresby was highly favorable. After he had finished the inspection, he told me this was the best Mission School he has ever seen, and he had been in the more advanced area of New Guinea for many years. Almost every aspect of the inspection received the highest rating. He seemed particularly impressed with the prep class conducted by Sister Claver. He said, as far as he knew, the intelligence of the Mendi kids is not supposed to be higher than that of other schools, but he continued, the work of the prep school kids here is by far the best he has seen anywhere. Their English, he said, is better than that of other school kids of a grade or two higher. He also mentioned that this is the first place in the highlands where he found school kids who can sing the scale accurately, and really do justice to a song. Such a report really speaks favorably for the work done by the Sisters here. And they have been working at Mendi for only two years. In a few more years, we really should have a top-quality school.

I think I told you quite some time ago that we have two laywomen as teachers in Ialibu. One, Mary Elizaabeth Rame, is from America, and the other Clair Toohey, is from Australia. They're doing a marvelous job. The two actually balance each other. Miss Rame is small (probably weighs less than 100 lbs.) is very well educated with a Master's degree in music, and is deadly serious in everything she does. Miss Toohey is big and easygoing, with a terrific sense of humor. As might be expected with these contrasting personalities, Miss Rame is in charge of the school. Whenever Miss Toohey has disciplinary problems with the school kids, she sends them to Miss Rame for a "talking to" or a spanking. A few weeks ago, a native man walked into Miss Toohey's classroom and demanded that his boy leave school and return home. Miss Toohey was scared to death. She immediately called Miss Rame to handle the situation—and she really did. According to reports, Miss Rame really laid the old boy out verbally. She ignored all kinds of threats from the old boy, and issued a few threats of her own. The outcome was that the old man left his son in school, having been completely beaten. The next day, the old fellow came to the Mission and expressed his admiration for Miss Rame. As he put in his own language, "she is too strong for me." Miss Rame and the old fellow have been on friendly terms ever since.

Ialibu is rather cold since it is at an altitude of over 6,000 ft. Miss Rame practically freezes to death. She says she uses twelve blankets at night and still is freezing. I ordered a sleeping bag for her. I think this will take care of things. Neither of the two, Rame or Toohey, knows much about cooking. When they first got to Ialibu, Miss Toohey decided to surprise the Fathers by baking an apple pie. She baked the pie without cooking the apples. It turned out to be a raw apple pie. She has been hearing about it ever since then. As soon as these two women started teaching at Ialibu, their enrollment in school more than doubled. At the last report, there were at least forty girls coming to school every day—some walking a couple of hours each way. A third laywoman from Australia, by the name of Mary Fisher, is to join these two in January. Of course, we would prefer to have Sisters for all our stations, but in the meanwhile these laywomen will have to do.

One of our Fathers, Fr. Henry, was sent to Sydney recently because of persistent pains he had been having in the region of the heart. The verdict from the physical examination down there was very favorable. He had been suffering from spondylitis, and the medicine they had been giving him to counteract this caused strange side effects, namely, the pains in the region of the heart. Fr. Henry is still in Sydney. We asked him to stay on until the two new missionaries, Frs. Dunstan and Matthew, arrive. They are scheduled to get to Sydney today. I expect they'll get to Mendi in five or six days.

In my last letter, I mentioned the terrific amount of rain we had been having. The rains haven't let up yet. We have now gone exactly sixty days of rain. August and September together gave us a total of over 37 inches. Since the beginning of January, we have had a total of 116 inches of rain. It would be wonderful to have at least one day without rain.

I hope everything around home is continuing to come along well. Hello to all.

Your devoted brother, Msgr. Firmin

~~~

8 October 1962

Dear Mary,

Your letter of September 25 arrived here a couple of hours after I mailed my last letter to you. It was good to hear that you're continuing to recover so well. Since then, I've had a further confirmation of your recovery from Fr. Matthew.

The two new missionaries, Frs. Dunstan and Matthew arrived here on Saturday (Oct. 6) about noon. Both of them were happy to reach their destination. Fr. Henry accompanied them from Sydney. He had gone to Sydney because of persistent pains in the region of his heart. The physical examination there happily proved that there was no heart condition to worry about. Frs. Matthew and Dunstan arrived in Sydney on the morning of the 2nd. They left the following day and stopped for a visit with Fr. Rudolf in Brisbane. Fr. Rudolf, you may have heard, is a brother of Fr. Cletus. Years ago, he went as a missionary to China. When the Communists forced him out of China, he went to Australia, where he is now working as an assistant in a Capuchin parish. He must be in the seventies by this time.

I remember both of the two new missionaries quite well from Cap. College, where I taught them 1958-59. They're both very fine young priests, and should become good missionaries. Fr. Matt is certainly a delightfully wholesome character. Both are to take their fifth year of theology here in the Mission, beginning next week. So, I'll be doing a bit of teaching again. Fr. Matt mentioned his visits to the hospital and to Joe's. He said his visit with his folks to Felix's farm was one of his most delightful evenings.

Last week, October 3, was a very important historical occasion in the Mendi Valley. The first Local Government Council of the Southern

Highlands was officially established on that day. A Local Government Council is a body of delegates, elected by the natives themselves, for the purpose of taking care of local government needs. In other words, it is a self-governing group that has the obligation of passing laws and enforcing them and, in general, carry out the duties of a local government. There are a good number of such Councils throughout New Guinea, but this is the first in the Southern Highlands. In fact, I was surprised they were able to organize such a council so soon. The Council is composed of forty-two Council members, who were elected by the vote of the people in their respective districts. These forty-two Council members represent about fifteen thousand people of the Upper Mendi Valley. The President of the Council, a local chief of Mulim, by the name of Momei, is a very close friend of our Mission. Every few weeks, he has been bringing children from his area to our school. Now that he is the President of the Upper Mendi Council, he will be able to do even more for us. He is not a Catholic as yet, but he comes regularly to Church when the Father is in that area. The second-in-command (or Vice-President) of the Council seems also to be a good friend of our Mission.

The ceremony of establishing the Council was rather impressive. About eight thousand people from the bush area came to witness it at the Government Station here in Mendi. Since the Council members represent two different language groups, everything had to be translated by two different translators. At one point of the ceremony the people applauded the results of the elections. The bush natives eventually got the message that they too were to express their approval in some way, so they really gave out with a typical tribal yell, or war whoop. Imagine eight thousand giving a war whoop with all the volume they were capable of. Government representatives from Moresby and Goroka seemed a bit surprised, if not shocked at the yelling.

Since a good number of our school children come from the Upper Mendi, where the council is to function, we allowed all the children to attend the ceremony. I guess we had about 200 children there in all. They had a ring-side seat. I had been invited as one of the official guests at the ceremony. The Secretary of the new Council is a native from the Duke of York Island. He is a Catholic and is a very well-educated fellow. His English is perfect. He is known as the best Council organizer in New Guinea.

I don't know whether I told you of the following incident, which happened about two weeks ago. A woman who lies very close to the Mission had a baby two weeks ago Saturday night. Because of the fact that two or three of her babies in the past had died either shortly after the birth, or after a few months, her husband and friends assured her that this baby would also die. As is usual among them, she believed them and thought she ought to do something about it to express her "sorrow." So, within a few hours after the birth of the baby, she (the mother) cut off the baby's little finger. Some of the school girls in that area found out about it and reported it to the Sister. The Sisters went to visit the mother and see the baby. It was bleeding profusely from the cut. The Sisters managed to convince the mother she should bring the child to our Mission. From here, the Sisters went with her to the doctor. The doctor put several stitches in the finger, and told the mother to stay at the hospital with the child. That same evening at about seven o'clock, the mother came to the Sisters' convent and asked to have a place to stay for the night. As usual in such cases, the Sisters took care of her. Next morning early, before sunrise, the mother with the child returned to the hospital so she would be there before the doctor arrived. She has returned to the Sisters regularly. She is doing well, and the baby is as healthy as it could be. As far as I know, the mother is coming to church regularly and is taking instructions. Incidents like this are not too rare in this area.

In my last two or three letters, I mentioned that we had been having a terrific amount of rain. Well, the rains have kept up this past week. Although this is only the eighth of October, we have already had close to six inches since the beginning of the month. We have had rain every day since August 3. I'm sure we're approaching some kind of record.

Please tell Al thanks for his recent letter. I hope to write to Al and Nora shortly. I'm way overdue. I hope everything is continuing to come along well around Catherine.

Your devoted brother, Msgr. Firmin

~~~

24 October 1962

Dear Mary,

Your letter of October 16 arrived a few minutes ago. Thanks a lot. It was good to hear that Severin is coming along well, and that there was no damage to his heart. In this case, I presume he can recover completely in time, without any permanent bad effects, just so he takes it a bit easy. I received his card and note from Wichita sent on the 12th. If I'm not mistaken, you were the one who addressed the letter, or else someone's handwriting is exactly as yours. I wrote to him the very same day. I hope to drop him a line again this evening.

One of the reasons I'm writing today is that I have another First Day cover to send. Severin has a friend who is a collector of such items. That is one of the reasons I'm also writing to him today.

Today is United Nations Day. It is not a national holiday, but the schools in this area observed it with a day of sports. About ten schools took part. Except for the Catholics and Methodists, the rest were all government schools. Our kids came second to the government. They took most of the races in which they were entered, but the government school at Mendi has three higher grades than our school. That is the reason they came in first. In spite of their age advantage, they beat our kids only by five points. The best athletes at the government school are actually Catholic boys. Prizes were given to the winners. I guess our school got as many or more prizes than any other school.

When we first started school here years ago, it was very difficult to convince parents to send their children to school. Frequently the kids had to run away from home, and then the father or mother would come and demand that their boy or girl return home. Things are beginning to change. The parents are beginning to see the reasonableness of their children coming to school. The following is an indication of the trend. A little boy by the name of Musi started school last February. He stayed a couple of months and then ran off. The mother brought him back a month or two later. After a couple more months the youngster ran away again. One of the reasons he ran away was that he had no one from his tribe at the Mendi Mission school. In any case, this time the father really beat up the boy, and the mother brought him back to the Sister again. Only after the Sisters agreed to accept him back again did the mother return to her home area. The little fellow, who is only about six years old, is still here. His brother, Cajetan, is in our central school at Erave. He is in the fifth grade.

As you surely know, last Sunday, October 21, was Mission Sunday. For the first time in our Mission, we took up a collection in all our stations. For a few weeks previous to that date, we told the people what it was all about. Although there isn't too much money in circulation among the local natives, I was surprised at the collection here at Mendi. It amounted to 8.15.3 Australian pounds sterling—equivalent to $20. Most of the money came from the native government employees. These include policemen, teachers, clerks, and all types of workers. I think you would have gotten a kick out of our usher, who took up the collection. He is an old bald-headed native, well over fifty years old. He carried the collection box from one pew to the next, and according to reports, he wouldn't leave until each one had put in something, even though it might have been only three pence. Most of the Catholics gave a shilling, the equivalent to about 12 cents. At one of our other places, where there is a bigger population, the collection amounted to over 18 Australian pounds sterling—over $40. It is very important that we impress early on the people that they must show their appreciation for what they receive from the Church by contributing to the upkeep of the church. It is our aim to keep up this Sunday collection every

Sunday from now on. You might wonder where some of the local natives get any money at all. They get it from selling potatoes, tomatoes, or other garden products. As a rule, they are not interested in getting money for such products, and when they have enough potatoes, they insist on getting a kina shell instead of money. However, in some instances, they don't rate a kina and must settle for a bit of cash. Actually, the government is trying to popularize money as much as possible. I'm sure, however, it will take years before they will abandon the kina. As a rule, the local natives will accept money, knowing that with the money, they will eventually be able to buy a kina.

In about four or five days, I'm slated to go to Tari and Pureni. The latter place is a new main station, and, on November 1, I will bless a new church there. I don't know as yet how long I'll stay in the Tari and Pureni area, but most likely it will be for about a week. Because of my visit to Tari next week, I will probably not be able to write to you next week. I expect to get back to Mendi by November 3 or 5.

I'm enclosing a couple of photos of some of the girls here at Mendi.

[Omitted: a detailed description of the girls in the photo.]

I hope all is coming along well around home. Hello to all.
Your devoted brother, Msgr. Firmin

～

4 November 1962
Dear Mary,
Many thanks for your letter of October 25. I received it upon my return from Tari and Pureni on Friday, November 2. It was certainly good to hear that you are coming along so well since the operation. Even the Doctor says you're ready for work, I think it is wise on your part not to take over the cafeteria for the present. –I hadn't heard that Uncle Eugene had died, until I received your letter. It was good to know that Fr. Paulinus was able to have the funeral, and that so

many of the Schmidt families were able to attend. The old fellow was a unique character.

This is Sunday afternoon and my first chance to write any letters since my return from Tari a couple of days ago. As I had planned, I went to Tari on Monday, October 29. After a two-day visit at Tari and the outstations in that area, I went with Fr. Berard to Pureni on Wednesday morning. Fr. Samuel, who was visiting in Tari went with us. It was a fine trip, except for the crossing of a swift river, which is about 140 feet wide. Since there is no bridge across, we went across on a home-made raft (of logs). It is quite a trick to get across, since the current is so strong. And since we had come on motorcycles, we had to get them across too. With the help of a native catechist, we managed okay. Pureni is a new main station. It is beautifully located—about fifteen miles from Tari and half-way to another of our stations called Koroba. Right in front of the house we have our own private airstrip. Unfortunately, the Commission for airfields had not inspected the field when we went there last week, so we couldn't go in by plane. Since then, we have had it approved and it is ready for use now. Fr. Berard, with a crew of natives, built the strip. This is our only private airstrip. At all our other stations, we use the government airstrip.

The main purpose of my going to Pureni was to bless the new church, which was just completed. Although Fr. Berard designed it and marked it out, the natives did all the work. It is a very fine native church, built in the form of a "T." No one is very far away from the altar. Each of the side wings is as big as the main wing. Each of the three wings would hold about two hundred people. It wasn't quite filled for the dedication on November 1. Besides the natives, we had also the following present: the three Sisters from Tari, Brother Mark, and Ken Olma, our pilot. They all came on a tractor and trailer as far as the river. After taking a ride across on the raft, they walked the rest of the way (about two miles). After the blessing, I had the High Mass for which the Sisters sang. After the Mass, I blessed the airstrip. A lot of pictures were taken of everything. I should get some of them eventually.

Since the completion of the church was a big achievement for the natives, they helped to celebrate the occasion with a sing-sing. Even though there were well over eight hundred or a thousand local natives present for the blessing of the airstrip, only about twenty of them were engaged in singing and dancing. All the rest simply watched. The singers and dancers were completely painted in red and yellow, and all of them had fancy head-dress. It must have taken the greater part of a day to get fixed up as they were. However, the actual dancing lasted only about a half hour. In this matter, those people at Pureni differ a good bit from the people in this area. Here they dance for hours at a time. By about 1:00 o'clock, the people had all dispersed. We ourselves headed back for Tari shortly thereafter. Again, we went by motorcycle—going a long way back, covering about eighteen miles. I'm getting to be quite a motorcyclist. At least I had no trouble of any kind this time. Of course, the roads were in fairly good condition too. –That evening we celebrated the occasion with a delicious turkey dinner, at which the Sisters also joined us. –With Pureni now a main station, we have a total of seven main stations. One of the two new Fathers who just arrived is slated to be assigned to Pureni after the completion of the pastoral training year here in Mendi.

You might be interested in the following incident. For the blessing of the church at Pureni, the catechumenates from three other different places attended. Even though all use the same language, the speed and rhythm in praying is quite different. While attending Fr. Berard's 7:00 am Mass on November 1, Father noticed that while they were all saying the same prayers, they didn't pray together, so he told one of the catechists to practice with them a bit for the following Mass. The catechist took Father very seriously. He kept them all in church for an hour—during which time they "practiced" praying. Actually, I don't think they mind such things too much. They love to chant or sing, and, in praying, they really chant and sing.

After everything was over, Fr. Berard said he was happy that there was no fight. Usually when several tribes get together in that area, they have a few fights. He caught one fellow with a bow and arrow. He had to loosen the string. While they are unfriendly towards each other, they are all most friendly to our missionaries.

We've had unusually fine weather during my visit in the Tari area. In fact, it has been good throughout the Southern Highlands. We have not had a drop of rain for five days now. Even the afternoons and evenings are beautiful. It doesn't seem like New Guinea. I can't recall when we last had a stretch of nice weather like this. Incidentally, for the three months, August, September, and October, we had a total of over fifty-three inches of rain. With two months still to go in '62, we have had 131 inches this year.

I'm enclosing a couple of slides. Both were taken in front of the church here in Mendi. One, with my back towards the camera, was taken after Mass on a Sunday. The two bush fellows in the front are workers here at the Mission. The other slide includes the four who were baptized in July along the sponsors, Mary Ann and Mark. The four newly-baptized are Margaret Tepo, Don Bosco Tomanak, Patrick Osup, and Robert Temo.

We have a new Butoba tape recorder for the school here. We have two speeds for recording: 17/8 and 33/4. I would appreciate it if you could let me know whether either speed is acceptable for any machine that you might be able to use around home. Perhaps Fr. Paulinus could tell you. It is possible that I will be able to make some recordings of the kids' singing at Christmas. Besides the usual Christmas carols, they should have a few in the local language this year.

I hope everything is coming along well with all around home. Hello to all.

Your devoted brother, Msgr. Firmin

~~

2 December 1962

Dear Mary,

As I had cautioned in my last letter, a second week went by since my previous letter to you. I received your letter of November 17 about a week ago. Many thanks. In the meanwhile, I have also heard from Severin. Evidently, he seems to be doing well. According to his letter, he was expecting to start working by the beginning of December. Of course, I don't know much about a heart spasm from a medical angle, but it seems such an attack as Severin had should have no real and permanent effect on the heart itself. If Severin follows the doctor's advice and directions, he should return to the peak of health in a short time.

It looks as if Tommy will spend the winter in a mild climate, if he will stay in Florida. I know very little about the weather conditions in that particular place, but being that far south, it shouldn't get very cold. While there is always danger of war with the constant race in atomic experiments, I don't think such a war will be touched off in Cuba at this time. That matter seems to be fairly well under control—at least under careful observation.

In your letter you mentioned that Mother's 79th birthday occurred on November 17. I didn't remember how old she was, but believe it or not, I remembered that date as her birthday, and had a Mass for her.

Here in Mendi everything is coming along well. All the Capuchin Missionaries in New Guinea, except Fr. Paul, were here for the retreat this past week. Fr. Paul had to stay in Tari to have Mass for the Sisters there. The weather was wonderful, and all the Friars were picked up by our plane according to schedule, and also returned to their respective stations according to schedule. We had quite a big crowd—fifteen Capuchin priests, three brothers, and the retreat master, Fr. Acheson, a Sacred Heart Missionary of Samarai. The new addition to the house here was in use for the first time. I blessed the friary chapel the Friday before the retreat. At the beginning of the retreat, I erected the Stations of the Cross. It was really wonderful to be able to have all our religious exercises in the chapel instead of the church—as we had to do in the previous retreats.

After the retreat on Friday morning, we had our semi-annual Mission Meeting. In the afternoon, as on previous occasions, the

Fathers had a ball game. They beat the government personnel again. This time I didn't play along, since I had a bit of work that had been stacked on my desk during the retreat. –It was great to have all the Missionaries together again. A number of them hadn't seen each other for about six months. As far as I know, this was the biggest meeting of Capuchins in New Guinea in the history of our Mission. Actually, it is about as many as can be handled here at Mendi. In future years, when we have more missionaries, we'll have to divide the retreat into two sections.

Fr. Acheson, the retreat master, is a very fine Priest. He is still with us, and expects to stay until about this coming Wednesday. Their Mission is on the coast (consisting of about a hundred islands), where it gets quite hot every day of the year. I think he is enjoying the cool mountain air. The first night it was a bit too cool for him. He said he almost froze to death—getting very little sleep. Fr. Acheson is an Australian, as are all the Missionaries in their Mission.

During this past week, we received a lot of statues, which had been purchased for our Mission in Spain. The statues include a number of the Blessed Mother (Mother of the Divine Shepherd), the Sacred Heart, St. Joseph, and statues of the patrons of all our main mission stations—including St. Clara for Ialibu, Our Lady of the Angels for Erave, Mary Our Queen for Kagua, and St Francis for Tari. The most beautiful statue is that of the Mother of the Divine Shepherd. We had a number of pictures taken of it. I hope they turn out well. When I selected the Mother of the Divine Shepherd as our Patroness, I had great difficulty in finding a picture or a statue of that title in the States. I knew it was a popular title in Spain, but I didn't have enough time then to procure a painting or a statue from there. The statue of our Patroness will be placed in our new church here in Mendi—whenever we get that constructed.

For the next two Sundays, Dec. 9 and Dec. 16, I will be away from Mendi. On the 9th, I am scheduled to have Confirmations in Kagua, and on the 16th, I'll have Confirmations in Ialibu. I'm having these two

Confirmation dates before Christmas so I won't be too pushed right after Christmas. With a few exceptions, it is desirable for us to have the Confirmations during summer vacation—here in New Guinea, December to January. I'll probably spend about three days at each place.

This week, our school boys from our central school at Erave are walking to their respective stations. Fr. Benjamin will walk back with them as far as Mendi. This walk will take the best part of four days: two days from Erave to Kagua, and two days from Kagua to Mendi. There will be about seventy boys who will make the walk. The smaller lads will be taken by plane. There is always a big shindig whenever the kids get home. By the very fact that these fellows have been away to school, they are sort of heroes to the local crowd.

I hope everything around home is continuing to come along well. Don't work too hard in your preparation for Christmas. Hello to all around home.

Your devoted brother, Msgr. Firmin

~~~

13 January 1963

Dear Mary,

Many thanks for your two letters, of December 31 and January 5, respectively. The first, of Dec. 31 contained the $100 check for Mass stipends. First of all, I should like to say that the Mass stipends are welcome. However, I wish you would get me further information as to the number and type of Masses that are requested: 1) Whether High Masses are requested and how many? 2) Whether Low Masses are requested and how many? As soon as I get this information, I will write to Mr. Delva. You mentioned that he might prefer to have several Gregorian Masses offered. Unfortunately, we are unable to offer Gregorian Masses here. You know, a set of Gregorian Masses means thirty consecutive Masses for the person in question. If there is any break in those thirty, even close to the end, the series would have to start over again. I personally couldn't accept a set of Gregorian Masses, since I have other obligations to fulfill. I am also quite certain that no one else over here would accept a Gregorian obligation because of many uncertainties that could interrupt a series of thirty Masses.

I was surprised to hear of the death of Ed Karlin. You mentioned that Fr. George had come for the funeral. I take it that Fr. Athanasius did not come. I guess he'll never come to Kansas again. As a matter of fact, he seemed rather old when I last saw him in '59—but really not too old to travel. He was always a bit nervous. I guess the death of a number of their family will really shake him up a bit more.

As we had expected, the native Sisters of Nazareth, near Port Moresby, arrived here on January 9. They really are a hit with all the natives, and not only the girls. Yesterday, Fr. Otmar took them to a big sing-sing up the Mendi Valley. Their visit created quite a sensation. The oldest, Sister Mary, has been a religious since 1929. She is 52 years old and is now the Novice Mistress. She has a terrific personality, and speaks perfect English. The other two Sisters are rather young: one, Sr. Carolina, is professed only a few years, and is just beginning Teachers' Training. The other, Sr. Mary Dominic, will take her perpetual vows next year. She had been teaching for a number of years already. The Sisters will stay in our Mission for about two weeks. We hope to take them to the other stations too. Mother Genevieve, a French noblewoman, is their Mother General. She is hoping to send us some native Sisters in about a year. Most of their Sisters have Teacher's Certificates, or are getting them. They have about 100 in their community right now. These native Sisters are currently trying to introduce the saying of the Divine Office in English. Mother Genevieve has asked our Franciscan Sisters to teach them. Quite possibly when the next Franciscan Sisters come from the States, they will stop off at Nazareth to give them a few lessons in praying the Office. I'm happy to see such a friendly relationship.

In a previous letter, I mentioned the possibility of one of our boys, John Iai, entering the seminary. A few days ago, I received a letter from the Head of Fatima College, telling me that John Iai qualifies for the seminary. He is slated to go to Rabaul this week. John Iai will be our first seminarian. We should have a number of boys following him in a couple of years. There are at least five boys here at Mendi who should be ready for the Minor Seminary in a couple of years.

I am sending you a few photos. I'll send some more later on. I don't want to overload the envelope for 2 shillings. I think Agnes and Helen were the first girls who wore veils for their first Holy Communion. On the one photo I indicated that Mary Ann and Agnes are sisters. Actually, they have the same father, but a different mother. Mary Ann's mother died when she was very young. I don't know whether it was after the Catholic Mission came here, or whether she was baptized in danger of death. Their father's name is Tomis, a real crusty old boy. We know the old boy has two wives, but I haven't seen the one for at least a year. His home is just a stone's throw from the Mission. He has been working for the Mission, chopping wood, pumping water, etc., for years, and is quite reliable. He is taking instructions, but whether he'll ever become a Catholic, I can't tell at this time. He has been like a watch-dog for our Mission ever since the Mission settled down here. He knows everything that is going on, and keeps us all informed of the activities of the natives in this area.

I had a very fine letter from Angela Rohr. I was surprised how well she writes, in spite of the fact she had to switch to the left hand. I certainly intend to answer her in the near future.

I had also a very fine letter last week from Fr. Thomas More. He evidently is missing Kansas very much. Among other things, he mentioned how much he misses his occasional visits to the Schmidts at Catherine. He expressed his gratitude for your thoughtfulness in writing to his mother when she was so seriously ill. According to him, it is just a matter of time. He was on the verge of going to L.A. on Christmas, since his sister Mary had called and told him she was critical. However, before he could make the reservation on a plane, he received another call telling him she had made a remarkable recovery.

I hope all is coming along well with all of you around Catherine. With every best wish to all.

I remain, Your devoted brother, Msgr. Firmin

[In a January letter to Mary (not included here) from Msgr. Firmin, he mentions the possibility of his visiting the U.S. later in the year.]

~~~

3 February 1963

Dear Mary,

As I had cautioned in my last letter, a couple of weeks have passed since you last heard from me. In the meanwhile, I received your letter of the 19th January. It was waiting for me when I returned from Tari last Monday, Jan. 28. This past week found me quite busy with a variety of jobs.

My trip to Tari and visit of several days was very pleasant. There were almost eighty people baptized there this past Christmas. A good number of them are fairly old. All of them are thrilled to be Catholics. A few days prior to my coming to Tari, the Catholics asked Father there whether they are now allowed to kiss my ring. Father explained to them that it is proper to do so. Not being acquainted with the technique of kissing a ring, they had quite a time of it. I thought some of them were going to chew off the stone. I don't think any of the Catholics missed me—or the ring. A few of them were a bit awkward. So "those who knew," demonstrated for their benefit.

A number of the Catholics made it a point to see me privately. Each expressed his delight at being now a Catholic. One old crusty fellow by the name of Noah (his Christian name) came to see me privately. I thought he had something real important to discuss. All he wanted was to give me thirteen shillings (about $1.50), which he had saved as a gift for me. I had my picture taken with him, his wife (Lillian Lilli) and their son Henry. In many cases of the Baptisms, whole families were received into the Church at the same time. I would guess that over half of those newly-baptized come to Mass and Communion every day. Whenever the church bell rings, they come to church.

The attendance of Mass and instructions is rising considerably all over our Mission. But it is especially good in the Tari-Pureni area. On Sundays, at six Masses, two at Tari, one each at Pipanda, Hungapo, Pureni, and Iobidia, a total of over 3,000 people attend. Tari itself has usually about 1200 people at the two Masses on Sunday. Here at Mendi, we also have to have two Masses on Sunday to accommodate the people. Today, for the first time, Fr. Otmar went up the valley to Komia (about 18 miles out) and Ekari to have Mass at those places. He left at 7:00 this morning. This will probably be done from now on, since the people have been begging us to have a priest in those and other places on Sundays.

This past Tuesday we had a very impressive little ceremony here at Mendi, when I presented Mission crosses to eight of our new teachers and Catechists. All eight of these boys trained in our schools, and by our Fathers in private classes. These fellows were assigned to definite stations the very next day. All of them will have school for the small children, and they will also teach the grown-ups catechism. In the absence of the priest, they will preside at prayers on Sundays and also during the week. They should do real well, since they all speak the language of the people. One of the boys, Claude Mendil, knows four languages fluently, besides English. A couple of these fellows would be in grade 6 this year. They willingly gave up going to school so they can teach their own people the catechism.

Our school is in full force by this time. The enrollment at Mendi is far greater than we had anticipated. Latest count has the total well over 300. About 160 of these are here for the first time, and must start with prep. More than eighty of the pupils are girls—also many more than we had expected. I'm sure there will be a big drop in the enrollment within a week or two. However, there is no doubt that in a few years we will have more kids interested in school than we can handle.

The Sisters really have their hands full—not only in taking care of the school work, but also in taking care of the kids outside of school. Because of the large number of new girls, Mary Ann Masami is helping to teach prep (kindergarten). Of course, she also goes to school—now in grade 4. She actually would be able to do grade 5. In her spare time, Mary Ann still does some cooking and baking.

In my last letter, I may have mentioned that one of our lads, Francis Kili, had been nominated to go to Australia to see the Queen on her visit. About ten days ago, we received definite word that Francis will go to Australia. The government will pay all expenses. Another Catholic boy from the Southern Highlands by the name of Dominic Mendano of Ialibu will also go. In addition to these boys, Mary Ann Masami had been considered. But since she was only in the fourth grade, she was ineligible. The government officials were going to make an exception in her case, but I guess they were afraid to go through with it, since the Methodists and the government schools have a few girls farther advanced in school. Actually, we did not mention Mary Ann at all to the government officials. We merely sent her with a message to the Director of Education here in Mendi, hoping that he might be impressed with her. He really was.

While I was visiting in Tari, I took a quick trip to Pureni by plane. This is the only place where we have our own private airstrip. At all our other stations, we use the government strip. The strip at Pureni is very good, but a bit short (only 1800 ft.). Because the strip is so short, our pilot will take in only a partial load. Incidentally, Pureni is the place where Fr. Matthew will be stationed by May. Pureni is about four minutes by plane from Tari. It would be about five hours walking.

I am enclosing a few color slides. I hope to have them adequately marked. You might show the one with the altar boys to Fr. Paulinus. He might be interested in showing it to his vocation clubs. The two in black, Pandapis and Nap, are in the second grade now. The one in red, Patrick Osup is in grade 3 at Erave. Patrick is the one who almost died a few years ago when his parents hid him in the bush after a sickness. By threatening imprisonment, we managed to get Patrick to the hospital, and thus save his life. Nap is so short that he cannot reach the missal. The other photo is of Sister Mary—of the native Sisters of Nazareth—and Sr. Claver in front of the church. I had a number of other color slides of the Sisters, but our own Sisters want to use them for propaganda purposes. I have a number of black and white coming. If they turn out well, I'll send you some. Sister Mary is undoubtedly the most outstanding native Sister I have met. She is well read, can handle French, and speaks the finest brand of English. She, as well as the other two Sisters, were tremendously impressed with our Mission. All three were crying when they left Mendi last Monday. We have hopes that they will soon send us three Sisters to stay.

I have not as yet had a chance to write Johnette and Severin since the death of LTJ [Johnette's father]. I hope to write to them in a day or so. I hope all is coming along well.

Your devoted brother, Msgr. Firmin

10 February 1963

Dear Mary,

Many thanks for your letter of January 26. I received it on Feb. 5. Thanks also for the $5 for Masses for L.T. Jones. I'll offer the Masses at my earliest opportunity, and will mention it to Johnette and Severin in my next letter. I had just written to them the day before I received your last letter.

Thanks for the information from Leo Dellva concerning the Mass stipends sent a few weeks previous. As soon as I received your letter, I wrote to Mr. Dellva, thanking him for the stipends and, assuring him that the Masses will be taken care of as requested. I don't think I ever met Mr. Dellva. However, I have a vague recollection that there was a Dellva at St. Joe's around my time.

The Mendi post office went on a new schedule again. Now it closes on Saturday morning at 9:30. Since most of our mail has been coming around Saturday noon, this will delay our mail another two days. With the working hours of the government officers as they are, you would think that Mendi is a big metropolis. As far as I know, the government workers at Port Moresby, Rabaul, Madang, and Lae operate on a five-day week—in imitation of the bigger cities in Australia. The government people at Mendi don't think they should be second to anybody—so it seems. They really can be ridiculous—in a small place like this. As a rule, I used to get the Register on Saturdays. Now I won't get it until Monday at the earliest.

I had a delightful and educational experience this past Wednesday, visiting the local government council in session. I mentioned some time ago that a local government council was organized in the Upper Mendi Valley. A total of forty-two Councilors were elected by the local people representing 15,000 natives in the Bela, Tulum, Map, and Ekari area. They have been functioning as a local government for several months now, collecting taxes, issuing local rules, purchasing equipment like saws, etc. They assemble for a meeting at the Council Hall at Bela every few weeks. This week the District Commissioner took me to Bela (about twelve miles from Mendi) to see the thing in session. I was amazed at what they are doing. As far as I know, there is only one Councilor who can read or write. This one partially-literate fellow had attended one of our schools years ago. Even the President, Momei, and the Vice-President, can neither read nor write. Only a few of the 42 members can speak Pidgin. The rest can only understand their local language. To make matters worse, the council members themselves are divided into two language groups. Yet, in spite of these drawbacks, the Council Meeting (with its two interpreters) was very orderly. The discussions—which were put into Pidgin for our benefit—were rather intelligent. Two outside natives, William, from the Duke of York Island, and Alan, from Yule Island (both Catholics), are the behind-the-scenes directors of the Council. They do very well. To give you an idea of what has been done, and what is planned for this year: They just finished collecting taxes—a total of over 2,000 Australian pounds sterling (close to $5,000). One wonders where they get the money. But they have it. Their budget set up for 1963 calls for 7,200 Australian pounds sterling (about $16,000). Their projects include building schools and roads, putting in gardens for produce to be sold to the government and Mission, building a better (permanent) house for William, and so on. It is almost unbelievable what they are accomplishing with uneducated, backward natives. The Councilors themselves are very presentable fellows. All of them wear trousers and shirts to the meetings. Their hair was trimmed neatly, and all of them were shaved. Their pay, I noticed on the budget sheet, was 7 shillings per month (85 cents) for the ordinary Councilor, and 25 shillings ($2.85) for the President per month. The construction of the Council House was just completed last week, and they really are proud of it. I heard that this Council is the first low-level Council in the Territory. By low-level is meant Councilors who are backward and are almost completely illiterate. If this is successful here, then it is most likely that all of Papua and New Guinea will be organized along these lines, preparing the way for self-government. According to all indications, everything here is succeeding far better than was anticipated.

My trip to the council and back was most pleasant. Mr. Jefferies, the present District Commissioner, took me on a long trip back. I had never been in that area at all, even though we do have a large number of outstations along the way. I met a number of our Catechists at the various stations. The scenery is terrific. The roads seem a bit dangerous in spots. However, we had no mishap. There are sheer cliffs of several hundred feet just a couple of steps from where the road passes. Most of the road, surprisingly enough, is covered with stones. The natives in those areas carried all that stone by hand. I understand there is a total of 78 miles of road in that area that we visited. Fortunately, the particular day we took that trip there was no rain. In fact, it was very dusty. By the time I got back to Mendi, I was as dusty as I used to get working on the tractor on a dry day. While Mendi may be the headquarters of our work in the Valley, I feel confident that the biggest Catholic population will eventually be found in the Bela area that we visited. There is already a big government school at Bela, and Fr. Otmar goes there for Catechism at least once a week. Right now, the natives are putting up a church. Once that is completed, one of the Fathers will be saying Mass there every Sunday.

We're still overrun by school children here at Mendi. I think we still have about 360 kids here at the Mission. The Sisters were happy that over a hundred girls are here for school. I'm sure a good number of these will return to the bush. However, the number is going up gradually. This morning, the Sisters had all the Catholic girls pose for a picture. I was surprised that we have a total of 20 girls here in school who are baptized. With the crowd of 360 here in school, it takes just about a ton of kau-kau (sweet potatoes) to feed them each day. Fortunately, we have been getting almost enough since the beginning of school.

I hope everything is coming along well around home. Hello to all. Your devoted brother, Msgr. Firmin

~~~

10 March 1963

Dear Mary,

Since I have a bit of time this afternoon, I had better have gotten a letter off today. I doubt very much whether I would write later on this week. I hope to spend the greater part of next week in Kagua, and after that I have a number of important tasks to look after here in Mendi.

This past week was one full of activities, as far as we can have them in the Southern Highlands. Among other things, we had a visit by Senator Paltridge of Australia. He is the Minister of Civil Aviation, a post in Australia comparable to membership in the President's Cabinet. The District Commissioner asked me to be at the Government Station for Paltridge's visit. The government officers have been wonderful in this regard. Anytime a person of distinction comes to Mendi, we are the first ones to be informed. Even though the Methodist Mission has been in Mendi four years longer than we, they are rarely informed of the coming of a dignitary. We had a pleasant meeting with Mr. and Mrs. Paltridge and the rest in the party. I managed to have the whole party pay a brief visit to our Mission. They were very favorably impressed with our set-up.

That very same day, Mr. McCarthy, the Director of Native Affairs, came to Mendi. His position in New Guinea is equivalent to the Head of the Department of the Interior in the States. Again, the government officers here in Mendi brought him to our Mission for a visit. To my knowledge, he did not visit any other place during his stay here. Mr. McCarthy is a very influential man in Moresby and is in a position to do us a lot of good.

The biggest celebration of the week was the formal opening of the Council House at Bela. I wrote to you a few weeks ago of a meeting I attended there of a council session. At that time, the Council House was not quite completed. This occasion of the formal opening was a mammoth affair. I went out to Bela with the District Commissioner. The crowd at Bela was tremendous. No one could count the throng very accurately. But a conservative estimate placed the crowd at about 12,000. Besides Mr. McCarthy, who opened the Council House, there were three native members of the legislative body in Moresby. According to these native guests, this was the biggest crowd they had seen for such an occasion. An official photographer from Moresby was on hand. I hope his pictures will be published in some of the papers.

An interesting thing happened when Mr. McCarthy was introduced to the natives. At a sign to clap by the President, Momei, the whole mob of 12,000 burst into their usual war whoop. It took Momei and a few of his helpers about five minutes to quiet them down. After the formal opening, speeches, etc., a very fine lunch was served to the guests.

While we were having lunch, word came that I was wanted outside. When I got out, Momei presented me with a hindquarter of a pig and a live chicken, as a gesture of good will to the Catholic Mission. At the same time, Mr. McCarthy received the same type of gift. Later on, they gave cuts of pig to most of the other European guests. We brought our pork back to the Mission for the school kids. They loved it.

In connection with the opening of the Council House, there was a big sing-sing and a pig-kill. According to the reports that reached me, they killed over 300 pigs, 1 bull, several sheep (I don't know where they got them), and a large number of chickens. All this was sponsored by the Council. However, some of the neighboring chiefs helped along by presenting gifts in the form of pigs, etc. The natives had a great feast that day. Since Momei is very favorable to the Catholic Mission, he saw to it that the Catholic school kids got a big share. The opposition didn't like it too well.

In the course of his speech, Momei expressed a special word of thanks to the Catholic Mission for its work in the Upper Mendi. Fortunately, the translator simply said "Mission" instead of using "Catholic Mission" and eliminating the Methodists. At the Council House opening, it was announced that Momei was going to Australia for a visit to Parliament at Canberra. He is to leave tomorrow. He is thrilled with the whole idea. –Speaking of visiting Australia, Francis Kili, one of our school boys from Mendi, left for a visit to Australia on March 7. He is to stay two weeks, during which time he will meet the Queen. As far as we know, Francis Kili is the only school boy from the Southern Highlands. That is quite a recognition, especially in view of the fact that only 38 school kids throughout the Territory of New Guinea were selected to go. After Francis gets back, it is possible that the government will send him to visit the various stations of the Southern Highlands to give his impressions of Australia.

I paid a brief visit yesterday to a new place called Nipa. This is about 10 minutes flying from Mendi, and two days walking. Fr. Senan went over there about six weeks ago. He is trying to get us a good foothold. I just stopped in to see how things were coming along. He is staying another two or three weeks. In another year or so, Nipa will become a main station.

I had a fine letter from Severin yesterday. He evidently is coming along very well. I hope he can remember that he has to continue to take it easy. In the letter, he explained the circumstances of the death of L.T. Jones, and his funeral.

I am enclosing a few more photos—as many as ½ ounce will allow. I hope all is coming along well around home. Hello to everyone.
Your devoted brother, Msgr. Firmin

~~~

17 March 1963
Dear Mary,

Many thanks for your letter of March 2. I received it on the 13th. That same day I heard also from Angela and received the clipping of Tommy winning first in track driving. I'm sure he is delighted to have his name on his vehicle. That is quite a distinction. I had heard from Tommy recently but have not as yet answered him.

As I mentioned in my last letter, I did go to Kagua on the 11th, and returned two days later. It was a very pleasant visit. I always enjoy spending a few days with Fr. David. He is an avid health food man, favors organic farming, etc. He has, as a matter of fact, a nice supply of fresh vegetables and fruit all the time. For every meal, breakfast, dinner and supper, we had strawberries and raspberries, which they grow right there. They have them so arranged that they can pick them practically every day of the year. As far as vegetables are concerned, they always have turnips, carrots, soy beans, green beans, various types of sweet potatoes, tomatoes, peppers, and almost all types of greens. We have only about fifty acres there, but Fr. David is getting the most out of it. We even have four head of cattle there, including two milking cows. I don't know who does the milking—probably one of the native teachers. We are trying to get another hundred acres or so at Kagua so we can have a bit more extensive farming. Fr. David was fifty-eight years old yesterday, and he says he feels younger than ever. He claims this is the result of his health foods. He may be right. He is completely opposed to canned foods but will eat them when there is nothing else available. At any rate, I always enjoy visiting his place. While we all tease him a lot about his health foods, we all appreciate them.

Fr. Otmar is continuing to do well with his turkeys. We have a good number of fairly big ones, which were hatched here about four or five months ago. Last week another group of nine were hatched—out of ten eggs. That's a fairly good percentage. There are a number to be set again in a day or so. Fr. Omar usually sets the clucks and looks after the baby turkeys and baby chicks. He has been rather successful. Fr. David is also doing well in this line. When I was at Kagua this past week, we had a turkey (10 lbs.) for dinner one evening. It was well prepared. Brother Alfred supervised it.

Everything here in the Mission is continuing to come along well. The school enrollment at Mendi is around 300—almost all boarders. Last week the Sisters started on the cooking part in the Home Economics course. Only the bigger girls are allowed to take this. They are trying to teach them how to cook with the ordinary things available to them. As a special project, we got a bag of wheatmeal for them. With this, they baked cakes, and then, of course, were allowed to eat what they had baked. They certainly are enthusiastic over this. Besides teaching the girls to bake, they teach them to sew, mend, knit, and so on. After a few years with this type of training, I'm sure some of these girls will make good wives for some of the more advanced and better educated natives. I doubt whether many of them are interested in returning to the bush to live with pigs again.

We had a bit of excitement right around noon today. Word was brought that one of our school boys had drowned in a nearby river. Fr. Benjamin and Brother Claude immediately rushed out to the place with the Land/Rover. When they got there, they were told the boy was rescued on time and now was resting in the hospital. This was found to be true. Whenever word like this comes in, we are never really sure what the story is. As a rule, they exaggerate. Drowning could mean almost anything from simply falling into the water to actual drowning. In this case, I guess the boy was on the verge of drowning.

The two young Fathers, Matthew and Dunstan, are slated to leave Mendi this week for a field trip to Ialibu and Tari areas, respectively. After about five or six weeks, both will return to Mendi for another month. After that month, they will receive their permanent assignments. They seem very happy with their stay here in Mendi.

A couple of weeks ago I wrote to Fr. Giles and told him of my tentative plan to visit the States in 1963. So, as far as I'm concerned, there is no need to keep my tentative plans completely secret. In other words, I have no objection to your mentioning to others that I may come around August, unless something causes me to change my plans. Just don't make my visit a certainty.

We heard over the radio a couple of days ago that Fort Hays basketball team was in the post-season play-offs for NAIA Championship. I heard they got to the semifinals, but I heard nothing further. I presume the Cadets are also rated high for post-season tournaments. If you have any clipping of them, I would be happy to see it. For some reason, I have received no Cadet Journal this year. Perhaps they're not publishing it this year.

I hope all is coming along well around home. Hello to all.
Your devoted brother, Msgr. Firmin

~~~

24 March 1963
Dear Mary,

Many thanks for your letter of the 12th. It arrived here on the 20th. Thanks for the information on the photos that I have been sending home. I haven't used a camera much recently, but hope to start using it again when I visit some of the other stations in a month or so. I still have a number of photos on hand here. I'm enclosing some today again. These deal with the making of mats. Actually, the walls of our bush buildings as well as the floors are made out of pit-pit as shown in the photos. These particular photos were taken while the kids were making the last mat for our church. In some of our stations, the natives are able to weave fancy mats. The people around here don't go in for the fancy stuff.

I hadn't heard anything about Fr. Thomas More's brother. I did know John, having met him on a number of occasions. I think he was still living Aliquippa. That family has surely had its share of setbacks in recent months.

Everything here in the Mission is still coming along quite well. Our school enrollment at Mendi is staying around 310. That is unusually good. We have found that we lost almost none of the kids who have been here a year or more. Those who dropped out since the beginning of the year were almost entirely from the prep or kindergarten group. That certainly speaks well for the school since the people here generally are unstable.

A few weeks ago, I told you of the older girls here learning how to cook with the things available to them. They are doing very well. This past Wednesday, they made a kind of meal biscuit. As a preparation, they made their own yeast from corn. How they prepared it I don't know. In any case, it worked. They sent me a sample of their biscuits. It really was delicious. It could have been accepted as a genuine biscuit, or cookies, as we call them in America. The younger girls are eager for the time that they will be allowed to learn this type of cooking.

If you remember from last year or the year before, I mentioned that the seven Fridays of Lent are the only fast and abstinence days here in New Guinea. Even though the natives don't have much in the way of meat, it is not easy for them to remember not to eat whatever meat they get a hold of. One of the delicacies for the kids is the cicada. I guess it is known as locusts in some places. Anyway, the kids go around at night catching them. After they get a few, they cook them or roast them. They seem to like them. This past Friday, one of the bigger girls brought one of the smaller girls to our house and told us that the youngster, who is a Catholic, ate a locust, and hence she violated the Friday abstinence. Of course, we found out that the young girl had forgotten all about this being Friday of Lent. I imagine about one hundred percent of the kids in the States wouldn't even think of eating locusts as a penance. And here it is a penance not to eat them. Conditions surely are different from one part of the world to another. I only wish some of your kids in school could eat with, or simply watch, the Papuan children at their meals. Some of them would probably lose their appetite for a month.

Our rainy season continues. Today was the thirty-fifth consecutive day of measurable rain. During this time, we have had about twenty inches. This past Wednesday, we had over three and a half inches in one day. According to the radio, we seem to be getting the effects of the monsoons in some parts of the Pacific. As far as I know, we are not actually in the monsoon paths.

Have you heard anything yet of the Sisters from Catherine, whether they are planning to come out West this coming summer? I refer especially to Sisters Judith, Stella, and Clareann. No matter what their schedule, as a matter of fact, I simply cannot come earlier [to the United States] than about August 12. I just hope I'll be able to make it by then.

This past week one of the government officers, Alan C. Jefferies, came to our Mission to show us some of the movies he took on his patrols in areas that are part of our Mission, both in the Gulf Area as well as here in the Southern Highlands. These patrols were made when the natives were still quite wild, and eager to fight at a moment's notice. The movies were most interesting. On a few occasions, Jefferies' patrol was actually attacked by the natives. However, as was proved repeatedly, these people are cowards in the face of superior power. All Jefferies had to do was to fire a gun in the air, and they all ran. Incidentally, two of our Fathers went through an area just a few days before the natives of that place attacked the government patrol. Of course, this is not unusual. We have always found that the natives are very friendly with us, in spite of their occasional hostility towards the government.

Our two young Fathers, Matthew and Dunstan, left Mendi this week, Fr. Matthew going to the Ialibu-Pangia area and Fr. Dunstan to the Tari-Pureni area. Both will get back to Mendi for another session of classes during May. The day before they left, they took a trip to a place called Ekari, about sixteen miles up the valley, going by motorcycles. They had quite a time of it. Both had troubles finding the place. They managed to get back to Mendi at about 4:30 in the afternoon, completely soaked by a heavy downpour of rain. Naturally, no one expects not to get caught in the rain if he goes any distance at all. Fr. Otmar went up the valley for Mass today, as he does every Sunday. He returned at 5:30 and was completely drenched.

I hope everything is coming along well around home. Hello to everyone.

Your devoted brother, Msgr. Firmin

~~~

25 April 1963

Dear Mary,

A bit more time has passed than usual since my last letter. And I think from now on you can continue to expect that, since I will be cutting my correspondence to a minimum for the next few months. I hope you received the tentative time schedule for attempts of establishing contact via ham radio with Charlie Polifka. The first date I set, namely this afternoon, 1:30pm, New Guinea time, or 9:30pm Wednesday, Hays time, didn't prove successful. We contacted a fellow from Arizona, but could not get to Kansas. We did hear a WO- on top of one of the stations but couldn't establish a true contact. As far as I know, WO is in the Kansas area. Unfortunately, I don't have the exact call numbers of Charlie. We hope to try again tomorrow afternoon. I hope we can get through one of these days.

Today is Anzac Day in New Guinea, as well as in all Commonwealth countries. Anzac, in case you don't remember, is equivalent to our Memorial Day. As in the past, I gave the main address here in the Mendi celebration. This is the fourth Anzac Day I have celebrated in New Guinea. The celebration we had here was rather brief but fairly well arranged. The crowd today wasn't as large as usual—due to unsettled weather conditions. It rained early this morning, and was still cloudy at the beginning of the celebration. And right as we finished, it started to rain again. Besides the government employees and a few local people, all the school children within a five-mile radius were present. Ours were by far the neatest group as well as the largest. In fact, our total number of children in the parade surpassed the total number of all the other schools combined. We had 330 in the group. They were all dressed in bright red—the boys wearing red lap-laps, and the girls red blouses. It was an impressive sight. Not only did we have the largest and neatest group, they also marched the best. They came into the parade ground almost in perfect step. The government police were particularly proud of these. The (about five policemen) had been coming to our Mission every morning for about two weeks, teaching the children how to march. Today, as our crowd came on to the parade ground, the policemen became quite excited. They were naturally proud of their achievement, and they didn't fail to tell everyone that the Catholic Mission is the best. I mentioned that the girls were wearing red blouses. At least half of them did their own sewing. Even little kids like Agnes Porkiami, managed to do their sewing. I'm not sure whether little Lumi did any work on her blouse.

Today is also the fourth anniversary of my receiving notice of my appointment as Prefect Apostolic. The appointment actually is dated April 3. However, the notice traveled by way of the Apostolic Delegate in Sydney. It hardly seems that a full four years have passed by since then.

Our pre-fab aluminum Church for Mendi arrived here last Friday and Saturday. It required a total of six Otter charters. An Otter carries a load of 2,500 lbs. Some to the crates weighed over 800 lbs. They were rather awkward to handle. Brother Claude and his helpers have been working for four days now, sorting all the parts, and starting to bolt them together. I heard that there was a total of 17,500 bolts just of one type. I don't think the Church will be anything fancy. But it should be neat and practical. And this is all that counts in the Highlands.

The weather here has been terrible, from the pilot's point of view. On Tuesday and Wednesday, our pilot tried to go to Tari from Madang. Both times he couldn't get through. Fortunately, he managed to find his way into Mendi. Because of the bad weather, I told Ken (our pilot) to remain here in Mendi yesterday, and attempt a trip to Tari this morning. Again, the weather did not permit any flying in the Tari direction. After one unsuccessful attempt, he finally got out of Mendi to Madang after dinner. He had to take Fr. Gregory down there to catch a plane tomorrow for Rabaul. He is going to Rabaul for the education course, which I mentioned previously. Fr. Gregory said Fr. Matthew seems to be doing quite well at Erave. He seems happy with this temporary appointment of his. I guess he would like it anywhere in New Guinea.

This is sing-sing time in Kombegibu. They're planning a big pig-kill and a cassowary-kill in the area. We heard they will kill a hundred cassowaries and a few pigs. They have been preparing for this for months. Now that they're getting closer, they're beginning to sing-sing during the night. A couple of nights ago they started their singing and dancing at about 2:00am. According to reports, these preliminary sing-sings are actually classified as practices for the real thing. I personally can't see why they need any practice at all. It seems no one ever gets any better at it.

Tomorrow Fr. August is to come to Mendi in preparation for his trip to the States for his six-month vacation. He came to New Guinea in 1958. As far as I know, he is to come through Kansas. Most likely he'll stop there for several days. He is quite a young fellow, and looks even younger than his age. He is a very hard worker, and has done excellent work in the bush. He comes from Pittsburgh. As with most of the Missionaries here in New Guinea, I taught him at Capuchin College.

I had a letter from Fr. Giles a few days ago. He mentioned that he was leaving for Kansas for Visitation. He said he would stop at Catherine if he could find the time. He has to get back to Pittsburgh by May 12 for the departure ceremony of the two next missionaries,

Frs. Colman Studeny and Brian Newman. Both of them were in Fr. Matthew's class. But instead of coming to New Guinea for the fifth year of theology, they took it in Pittsburgh.

I hope this letter finds you all coming along well. Hello to everyone around home.

Your devoted brother, Msgr. Firmin, O.F.M. Cap.

~~~

19 May 1963

Dear Mary,

Your letter of May 11, arrived here on the 17th. Many thanks. Realizing that we're practically a day ahead of you, that was really good mail service—five days from Catherine to Mendi. I was happy to hear that Fr. Giles stopped in at Catherine. I have not heard from him since he visited in Kansas.

As to the suggestion that I go to Seattle from Honolulu [in Msgr's planned trip to the U.S.], I really haven't given any thought to that. It may be worth investigating, although as far as I can recall, I have no relative or friend that I would want to see in the State of Washington. My main objective I suppose will be Portland, for the purpose of visiting Brother Francis. This may require that I go either to San Francisco or Seattle. Whatever is the best way to go according to the airline schedule will be acceptable to me. I hope to pass through San Francisco, either going to, or returning from, Portland. It is possible that I'll have to go by way of Los Angeles to Tucson. If I do, I may stop a day there also. Otherwise, I'll aim to stop there on the way back. It is possible that Isabel or Teckla will be in Kansas anyway during August. At least, they used to be there while their mother was still living.

I hadn't realized that Severin and Johnette have been married twenty-five years already. Time surely passes quickly. I can even remember that I was best man at their wedding.

It is still sing-sing time here in the Mendi area. For some reason or other, the native boss boys found reason to extend the celebration for another week. A lot of our local boys, including our cook boys are all worked up over the sing-sing. Believe it or not, most of the boys had their hair fixed up for the occasion. It takes the greater part of a day to have the job done—matting in all kinds of grass, sticks, etc. I asked one boy by the name of Fundiap how much he had to pay to have his hair fixed up. He said it cost him two shillings (about 25 cents). There is no beauty about their type of hairdo, but I guess it's part of the ceremony.

One of the reasons that the main part of the sing-sing was postponed until the middle of this week is the Hagen Show. A lot of our people went over for it. According to the estimate of last Friday, at least 2,000 people from our area went to Mt. Hagen. With so many outsiders, one wonders how they're going to provide accommodations and food for all. I have heard that they did build a number of longhouses. One house is reported to be 2,250 feet long. I also heard that several hundred tons of kau-kau (sweet potatoes) were gotten for the occasion. The last time they had the Hagen Show, there were close to 200,000 natives present. I suppose there will be that many again this time. There are also a good number of Europeans—from all over the territory. One of the airline pilots who stopped at Mendi yesterday said there were thirty-seven planes parked on the Hagen airstrip.

Our school girls entered a number of items in the Hagen Show. One girl by the name of Eleanor Kipa knit a sweater all by herself and sent it over as part of the Mendi exhibit. Two other school girls made a blouse and skirt. What is interesting in the presentation of their items, is that they have the "old" in contrast with the "new" as part of the exhibit. For example, side-by-side with the blouse and skirt, they have a native grass skirt—to emphasize the contrast between the old "grass dress" and the new blouse and skirt. Besides these items, some of the girls, including Mary Ann Masame, baked bread, scones, and biscuits. I'm sure the exhibit of our school will attract wide attention. Speaking of knitting, a number of the girls have knitted sweaters for themselves. They usually wear them in the morning for the Mass, when it is usually quite cool.

Mary Ann Masame is really being kept busy with all kinds of work around here. She doesn't have much time any more for baking and cooking. She spends every morning and part of the afternoons teaching the prep girls. After these classes are finished, she takes special classes from Sister covering Grades 5 and 6 material—afternoons and evenings. Three afternoons each week, she takes an hour off to give catechism instruction in the native language to about forty local women. She is a very talented girl, and we would like to have her talents developed as much as possible. If she can pass the government grade 6 examination at the end of this year, we may send her to a more advanced school on the coast.

Almost all of last week was taken up as far as I was concerned, with preparation for our Mission Meeting, which begins Sunday, May 26. The two new missionaries, Frs. Brian Newman and Colman Studeny, are to arrive during the meeting. Because of the fact that we will begin our meeting already next Sunday, and will extend until June 1, you will probably not hear from me again for at least two weeks.

Our weather has been unusually good during the last week or ten days. I don't think we've ever had a stretch of more beautiful weather. It was very fortunate too, since Brother Claude and his helpers were working on the new church. The shell is almost complete. It is beginning to look very good.

I hope you received the rain you needed for the crop. I have been listening to the news from Armed Forces Radio Service, but nothing was mentioned about the weather in the last week or so.

I was sorry to hear that Fr. Francis Staab suffered a stroke or two. Obviously, they were quite severe. —Please extend my best regards to all around home.
Your devoted brother, Msgr. Firmin

~~~

9 June 1963
Dear Mary,
Close to two weeks have passed by since you last heard from me. In

the meanwhile, I received your letter of May 25. I think it arrived here on June 1. Thanks a lot.

Before I say anything else, I want to pass on to you some important news. I received a special invitation to the Second Vatican Council. Although the invitation was signed by the Secretary of the Council, it was ordered by Pope John XXIII. It was evidently one of the last things that Pope John did. If you remember, it was on May 21 that the Pope was ordered to go into retirement to his apartments—obviously because of his health. The invitation was dated May22. The invitation mentioned that Pope John XXIII had ordered that this privilege—of taking part in the Council—be extended to me.

Naturally, I am delighted with the invitation. Next to my appointment as Prefect Apostolic, this is the biggest privilege I could have received. I presume that, in spite of the death of Pope John, the invitation will be honored by the next Pope. In any case, I am planning on going to Rome to take part in the Council, no matter when the next session begins. As you might guess, this puts me in a dilemma. Since I can't get away from here until the end of July, and since the next session of the Council was scheduled to open on September 8, I would have only about two or three weeks in the States if I would follow my original tentative schedule. You see, I would want to be in Rome about a week before the opening of the Council. On the other hand, since Pope John died, the new Pope will have to re-convene the Council and also set the date. It is entirely up to him to decide both of these points—actual re-convening and the date. It is my opinion that if the original date of the next session, Sept. 8, is retained, it would be unwise for me to visit the States first, since it would allow me only about two weeks there. But if the new Pope postpones the session, let's say for a month or more, it still might be reasonable for me to keep my schedule in visiting the States in August. However, at this time I can make no definite decision. Here is what I am going to do today or tomorrow. I will write to the Travel Agency and ask them to keep my schedule to the States as tentative (leaving Sydney August 2, etc.) until we have a new Pope, and he makes known his plans for the Council. At the same time, I will draw up a tentative schedule for a trip to Rome, if the Council goes into session on September 8. I should have definite word one way or another by the beginning of July. I will notify you as quickly as possible, as soon as I know what the Pope is planning.

If I go to Rome first, I would naturally come to the States at the end of the Council, which would be after December 8, thus permitting me to be home over Christmas. To be sure, I would stay more than a few weeks.

If I will go to Rome at the end of August instead of the States, it may be a bit of a disappointment to some in the family. Of course, from one angle, it would also be a disappointment to me. However, that disappointment is far outweighed by the extraordinary privilege of being a member of the Ecumenical Council, and of having all the rights in that Council as any other Bishop, Archbishop, or Cardinal in the Church. This would be the first time that any Capuchin from our Province was given such an honor. And my taking part in the Council would also be an honor for the family. Certainly, I wouldn't want to pass up such a privilege for anything in the world.

While there may be a bit of disappointment if I can't come to the States this July, I think you all can readily see that it would be unwise to come for a visit of only two weeks. It is just one of those things that one couldn't foresee. I would appreciate it if you would notify all in our family about my invitation to the Council and the consequent possibility of not coming to the States this August. Also, please tell Fr. Paulinus about it. I will write to Fr. Giles today and notify him. I would suggest also that you drop a note to Sister Stella and Sister Judith. I don't think either of them should change their schedule, or suspend it, until my schedule is known. If they make their visit to Kansas as planned, I certainly would try to visit them (and also Sister Clareann) when I finally do come to the States. By the way, I have not as yet written to Fr. Raphael. I wish you would bring him up-to-date in this matter, if it is convenient.

I hope I have made everything clear. To repeat: 1) If the Council opens on September 8, or shortly thereafter, I will go to Rome first and then to the States at the end of the Council; 2) If the Council is postponed by the new Pope for more than a month, I probably would retain my original schedule—to arrive for my visit about August 12; 3) a definite decision can be made only after I know of the new Pope's plans for the Council—presumably by July 1.

We had a delightful meeting here of our Missionaries June 2-8. There were eighteen Friars here altogether. We were busy with the meetings every day from early morning until about 4:30pm. On two afternoons, after 4:30, the Fathers challenged the government personnel to a softball game and a volleyball match, respectively. We clobbered them badly in both. On one of the evenings, we had a Holy Hour, during which I gave the sermon. The weather for our meeting was delightful. We had rain several evenings, but the days were beautiful. Yesterday morning, eight of the Friars were taken back to their Stations. The rest will leave tomorrow. Such meetings have been very good, not only for solving some of our mission problems but also for a bit of relaxation.

On Friday, the Tari Sisters were brought here for their annual spiritual retreat. The retreat will be given by a Negro Priest from Madang. He is originally from the States and was assigned to Madang last year to teach philosophy to the New Guinea Seminarians. The name of this Priest is Fr. Raymond Caesar. In appearance, he looks very much like Sonny Liston. I think he is at least as heavy. He evidently has a fairly good education. He has been a big hit among the natives here. I guess this is the first dark-skinned Priest most of these natives have seen. If possible, I will have him taken to our Central School at Erave before he goes back to Madang.

Thanks for Mrs. Cyrilla Bloss' address. If there is need, I will contact her prior to my arriving there. I hope all is coming along well. Hello to all.

Your devoted brother, Msg. Firmin

~~~

19 June 1963

Dear Mary,

This is Wednesday evening. Even if I had written last Sunday, you would not have gotten the letter earlier than this. The reason is that, except for our own plane, not a single plane has moved in or out of Mendi since last Sunday. Our plane got to Madang on Monday morning. However, since then, the clouds have been hanging right on the ridges with almost continuous rain. It stopped a couple of hours ago. But I suspect by morning we'll be clouded in again. Naturally, our plane has not been in the Highlands since Monday.

Thanks for your letter of June 1. It arrived last Saturday noon. I was happy to hear that Tommy is getting out of the service in September. I'm sure he is counting the days already. –You apparently had quite an outing, celebrating the end of the school year. I enjoyed your description of the softball abilities of Srs. Hilda and Eloise. You ought to see our Sisters here play ball. One of them, Sister Martine, is as good as a man playing almost any kind of sports. She throws the ball as hard as a man and fields just as well. Before she entered the convent, she used to play on a championship ball club in Indiana. She is only about 26 years old now. I think she was also outstanding in basketball. A couple of the other Sisters are also quite good, but not as good as Sister Martine. –Speaking of the Sisters, the Tari Sisters are still here. They completed their annual Spiritual Retreat last Saturday. This week, they're enjoying a bit of relaxation. Fr. Otmar took all six up the road on Monday for an outing at Lake Ekari. They came back in a downpour of rain. Four of them, seated in the back of the Jeep, were soaking wet. They seemed to enjoy the rain as much as our native kids.

I still haven't heard anything further on my invitation to the Council. Naturally, I don't expect to have definite word until after the election of the new Pope. Besides having the Travel Agency arrange tentative schedules for me, I also applied for a new Passport. My old one ran out a couple of years ago. I'll keep you posted on developments. I have already written to one of my contacts in Rome to make reservations for me to stay there for the duration of the Council.

In all probability, you won't hear from me for about two weeks. This Friday, June 21, our pilot will take me to a place called Tambul. There, Fr. Samuel, who works the outstations out of Ialibu will pick me up either with a Jeep or a motorcycle. The first night we will spend at Togomagob, where Fr. Samuel baptized about fifty around Easter. Togomagob is about thirty-six miles from Ialibu. From there, we will move on to Orei on Saturday, where I will have Confirmations on Sunday, June 23. On Monday, I hope to get to Ialibu, where I intend to spend a day or so. On Tuesday or Wednesday (June 25 or 26), I will go to Madang to conduct a week-long retreat for the S.V.D. Fathers, beginning Wednesday. I won't finish until July 3. On that day, I hope to get back to Mendi for a week between retreats. I will be quite busy during the retreats, but I may find time to drop you a note sometime.

Your asked how the kids made out in the Mt. Hagen show. As a matter of fact, their exhibits were not entered into competition, since notification came too late. We merely presented the various items with the general Mendi exhibit. There is no doubt that the sweater, skirts, and blouses were excellent and surely could have rated with the best. I don't know whether I mentioned to you before that one of my photos was also on exhibition at the Hagen Show. It was an aerial view of Mendi. The government officials had it enlarged to 20" X 15." I had sent a copy of it, I think, to you about three months ago.

Fr. Colman received his transparent photos which he had taken on the occasion of his visit to Kansas. I took four of them and will enclose them, if they can be included in the envelope for one-half ounce or less.

As part of our instructions to the natives, we tell them of the importance of calling a priest in case of serious sickness or in danger of death. They really take this seriously. Since Sunday, we were called to the hospital three times, each time baptizing a child who seemed close to death. Once I was called—on Monday—only to find out after I got there that the child had already been baptized. They explained to me that they merely wanted me to give the child a blessing. This particular child couldn't be more than a year old. We have a number of Catholics working at the hospital now, and they keep us alerted in case a child from an unknown area comes in. Of course, we also have baptized a number of adults in danger of death. I feel certain that all of the natives who have come to regular instructions for even a short time, would come running quickly whenever one of their friends is seriously ill.

By the time you get this letter, I suppose you are in the midst of harvest. I hope everything is turning out well. I'm sure you can use it. Hello to everyone around home.

With every best wish, I remain, Your devoted brother, Msgr. Firmin, O.F.M. Cap.

[In Madang, Monsignor learns that the Council will begin on September 29.]

∽

9 July 1963

Dear Mary,

I'll be leaving tomorrow morning for Madang and my next retreat for the Society of the Divine Word Fathers, so I had better have gotten off a letter to you today. Thanks for your letter of June 29. It arrived yesterday. Thank also for the clipping from the Register. Evidently, Fr. Paulinus went all out in publicity on my invitation to the Council. The article you enclosed was very well done and accurate. Please tell Fr. Paulinus that I thought he did an A-1 job. If I find time in Madang, I may drop him a line.

It was good to hear that the harvest turned out fairly well—after that dry spring. I'm sure with the ever-mounting expenses, the entire crop is already accounted for, especially in view of the fact that the price on wheat sagged somewhat, or will sag.

I had good news from Rome yesterday. As soon as I received the invitation to the Council, I contacted one of our Mission secretaries in Rome, concerning the Council, reservations, and so on. His letter yesterday assured me that he is taking care of everything. He also confirmed the fact that in spite of a change of Popes, the invitation holds. He told me that while I could arrive anytime at all in Rome, my reservation begins on September 26. So that will be the date I will plan to arrive in Rome. I haven't had a chance as yet to make up my itinerary. I certainly intend to make the most of this opportunity. I mentioned that Hong Kong and Jerusalem will mean several-day stopovers each. In addition, I may spend a few days in Manilla, Singapore, and possibly Bangkok and New Delhi. I inspected a map of that part of the world last night, but did not come to any definite conclusion. I have some friends, formerly from Washington, D.C., in Thailand, so I may stay a few days there.

As scheduled, I ended the first retreat at Madang on July 3, and came back to Mendi that same day. It was quite a trip. About a half hour out of Madang, we met a wall of cloud and rain. We climbed to an altitude of 13,500 ft. and headed in the general direction of Mendi. We saw nothing but clouds. Even the mountain peaks were covered. Since we couldn't find an opening in the Mendi valley from the northern approach, we diverted and headed south. Right at the edge of the Ialibu Basin, we spotted an opening in the clouds. After circling the opening for a few minutes, the pilot (Ken Olma) recognized the area. We quickly dove down and within a couple of minutes found an approach to a gorge. Ken knew this gorge well. We flew in the gorge and followed it into Mendi. It certainly is good to have a pilot who can recognize even the most inconspicuous marks on the ground. Such a trip as this would be nerve-wracking for someone who is inexperienced. Ken is a very careful pilot. He refuses to fly into a cloud. This is an important rule over here. He always wants to see where he is going. And that rule is also most important here.

Last Sunday evening, while I was in Madang, the Rector of the Major Seminary invited me to give a talk to the Seminarians—Philosophers and Theologians. I think there are twenty-two in all. I found these fellows quite alert. According to the Rector and the other Priests who are Professors, these fellows would compare favorably with seminarians in Australia or America. After my talk, the Fr. Rector said that a few of the fellows would like to spend their Christmas vacation in our Mission. Of course, I told him they were most welcome. Their visit here, I hope, will stir up a bit more interest in the priesthood among our boys. We have a good number interested already, and we surely want to keep up their interest.

The two new Fathers, Colman and Brian, are gradually getting adjusted to New Guinea. One of the first things they have to learn is to ride a motorcycle. Both are doing quite well by this time. Today, one of them went out about twelve miles to teach catechism in one of the government schools. Fr. Otmar still covers over a hundred miles by motorcycle every week. He usually covers about fifty miles just on Sunday. When the roads are good, there isn't much of a problem.

We received word yesterday that the two new Missionaries, Frs. Malachy Mcbride and Cyril Repko, will arrive here in the Mission on August 28. Both have to complete their fifth year of theology here in the Mission. Since I will be absent for just about all the time, we haven't figured out as yet how we'll make that up. By the time I get back from Rome and the States, their fifth year of theology will be completed. These two Fathers are the first that I haven't taught at Cap. College. They will be complete strangers to me.

I hope all of you are coming along as well as ever. Hello to everyone around home.

Your devoted brother, Msgr. Firmin

~~~

Port Moresby, New Guinea
8 August 1963 (handwritten)
Dear Mary,

I'm writing this letter from Port Moresby. I came here yesterday and will be returning to Mendi early tomorrow morning. I came to Moresby to see through our application for another 157 acres of land at Erave. Because it is such a large piece, the Director of Lands called me on Monday afternoon at Mendi and advised me to be present when the Land Board met to consider my application this Thursday. The Director of Lands is a very good friend of mine. While he was favorably disposed all along, he was afraid one of the members of the Board might object to our getting such a big piece of property. Fortunately, I managed to convince everyone on the Board that we should have the lease. They all voted in favor. So my trip, even though short, was successful. With this new piece of land, we will have over 300 acres at Erave. The head of the Lands Department told me this evening that it was quite possible that if I had not been here, our application would have been unsuccessful. Incidentally, this Director of Lands is equivalent to a member of the Cabinet in the States.

I had a very fine trip down. First, our pilot took me to Madang. From there, I caught a plane to Goroka, where I stayed overnight. When I got to the Catholic Mission at Goroka, I found it deserted. Fortunately, I ran into the Sisters, and they happened to have the keys to the Father's house. So I took right over and made myself feel at home. Since there was absolutely nobody around, not even a cook, I took care of my own supper—and it was a delicious one. At about 9:00pm, while I was reading, a car drove up. It was the Father who is in charge of Goroka. I guess he was a bit surprised to find me there, but the fact that I helped myself, of course, was taken for granted. The Missionaries do this all over the Island. Everybody feels he is welcome at any Catholic Missionary's station.

According to my schedule, I am to get to Madang around noon tomorrow (Aug. 9). If the weather is reasonable, on Saturday, I'll go to Tari for a couple of days. Actually, I was supposed to get to Tari today, but this call from Moresby caused me to revise my plans. At any rate, I hope to be back in Mendi for August 15, when we will have Baptisms. The following Monday, August 19, I hope to go to Kagua for a two-day visit. These visits to these various stations are intended mainly to say goodbye before my departure. Fr. David assured me we will have a turkey dinner on this occasion.

This past Monday, August 5, I took the three Sisters and three native teachers about twelve miles up the valley by Land/Rover to a place called Kundago, where Fr. Senan had some Baptisms. It was a very fine celebration. People from all over that area came to witness those first Baptisms at that station. With the help of a translator, I explained the ceremonies to the large crowd of bush natives. Since Kundago is right at the foot of Mr. Giluwe, rains can be expected at almost any time of the day! This day it started to rain at 11:00 o'clock—right after we had completed the Baptisms. After everything was over, we fried hamburgers over the open stove in Fr. Senan's house. It was a little smoky in the house, but it was better than getting soaked in the rain. In the afternoon, after we got back to Mendi, I got my final two shots: typhus and paratyphoid. My arms were as sore as anything, and in addition, I felt a little dopey. By the following morning, I was okay and had no further ill effects—not even in the plane.

In a recent letter, Al and also Severin mentioned that Sister Judith was coming home earlier than originally expected. I presume by this time her visit is a thing of the past.

I hope all is coming along well.

Your devoted brother, Msgr. Firmin

~~~

14 August 1963

Dear Mary,

The main reason I'm writing at this time is to send you a first-day cover of the new stamps. I have only a few minutes to dash off a brief note, or else I'll miss the first-day postal mark.

As scheduled, I returned to Mendi last Friday. I was surprised that I got all the way back to Mendi in one day. I left Moresby at about 7am, going by the way of Lae and Goroka. As soon as I got to Madang,

I called the Catholic Mission Hangar, and found that Ken, our pilot, was just getting ready to leave for Ialibu. So, I went along with him and arrived in Mendi at 2:00 pm, in a heavy rain. The following morning, I went to Tari for a brief visit. I also managed to stop briefly at Pureni on Saturday. On Monday, I returned to Mendi again. Except for another brief visit to Kagua, I hope to spend the rest of my next four weeks cleaning up my work here, and preparing for my trip to Rome.

We just completed our statistics for the past year, and I think they are indicative of genuine progress. I'll give you a few figures. We now have 115 schools throughout our Mission.

Catholic boys in school	————	114
Catholic girls "	————	29
Non-Catholic boys "	————	3,163
Non-Catholic girls "	————	1,861
Total school kids	————	5,167

We have 42 native teachers, and 115 Catechists. Our total Catholic population is 1,412. That is almost double the Catholic population of last year. The total number of Catechumens now preparing for Baptism is 7,956. During the past year, July 1, 1962-June 30, 1963, we had over 600 Baptisms. Almost 200 of these were in danger of death. Eighty-nine of those baptized in danger of death actually died shortly after Baptism. During the year we also had a total of 56,626 Communions. That practically doubled last year's number. These figures, all of them, should rise considerably during the next year and thereafter.

I haven't heard from anyone around home since Sr. Judith was expected for a visit. I presume everyone enjoyed her stay in Kansas. I haven't heard anything yet about Sister Stella and Sister Clareann. I presume they retained their original schedule, and came during August.

Tomorrow will be another big day in a number of our Mission stations. Here at Mendi, we will have about nine baptized. At Pureni, about fifty will be baptized. And in another outstation very close to

Tari, there will be another fifty received into the Church. There will actually be Baptisms at just about all of our main stations and also in a number of outstations sometime this week.

I hope to write more later on, since I have to get this up to the post office within a few minutes.

Your devoted brother, Msgr. Firmin, O.F.M., Cap

~~~

2 September 1963

Dear Mary,

I am quite busy, clearing things away before my departure, a week from today. I must take a few minutes to write at least a short message. First of all, thanks a lot for your letter of August 22, and the ten dollars. I'll use the money on my trip. Thanks also for the photo, which I am now returning. I'm surprised that you're still as good looking as you used to be. I suppose by the time I get home, people will think I'm one of the older members in the family—by contrast with yourself. –Speaking of age or aging, I always thought I was still quite young, until about two months ago, when one of my former students in Washington, Fr. Dunstan Jones (now a Missionary here) deflated me. He said he always thought I was about Fr. Alfred's age. Then, last week, I visited all the classrooms here in Mendi. The Prep class was just learning colors. So, I quizzed them by pointing to a few objects. They had no trouble until I pointed to my hair. There was a strange silence. Finally, one bright youngster hollered "white." I don't think I'm completely white, but I was a bit flattered to know I have enough hair that the color was recognized. On my passport application, I stated the color of my hair was brown. I guess I'm accustomed to that answer.

Almost everything is prepared now as far as my trip is concerned. I got my ticket, passport, visas, etc., last Friday. I will leave just a week from today. I hope to drop you cards or short letters along the way, but don't count on it. You need not write to me until you hear from me in Rome after September 26. I already have my reservation in

Rome. Just a couple of days ago, I received a letter from the Secretary of the Council, informing me that I will stay at Hotel Derby, Largo Settechiese, in Rome. This reservation is good for the duration of the Council. It is taken care of by the Vatican Council itself. A few days ago, I also received a notice that the Session of the Council is to end on December 4. If this schedule is kept, I will be in Kansas in plenty of time before Christmas. According to my present intentions, I will leave Rome for the U.S. as soon after the Council as possible. I will probably spend a week or ten days in Pittsburgh before coming to Kansas about a week or so before Christmas.

A few days ago, the Sisters gave me a tape-recording which they had been making for me over the greater part of the year. Besides having a number of recordings of last year's Christmas caroling, they have a number of other hymns and songs, along with samples of how they teach: Prep, Grade 1, Grade 2, and Grade 3. I think the whole thing is excellent. I am bringing it along, rather than send it.

Within the next few days, I will probably send a number of transparencies. I have not definitely decided on these as yet. I may carry some of them with me. However, most likely, I'll send them airmail. Please keep them until I get to Kansas. I haven't classified them very well as yet and may not get the time to classify them before I send them off. In my last letter, I quoted some statistics. I think I covered most of them. However, I decided to send you a copy of the complete statistics we compiled recently. I think you might be interested in a few facts I may have omitted.

We have been having quite a bit of a distraction here in recent weeks. The biggest probably is the death of Lumi's mother and the adoption of Lumi's little sister. Lumi's mother had a baby about a month ago. About a week or so after the child was born, Fr. Otmar was called to the bush, where the mother was staying, with the report that she was dying. Fr. Otmar found she was quite sick but wasn't actually dying at the time. He managed to have her brought to the hospital. At the hospital, they found the mother had tetanus. She responded well to the treatment.

However, one morning the report came that she was dying. Fr. Otmar rushed to the hospital and baptized her. She died that same day and was buried here the next day. The baby, less than a month old, was kept at the hospital. Because of some misunderstanding and confusion of some kind, the baby disappeared from the hospital. Because someone of the natives feared for the life of the child, she was brought to the Sisters. The Sisters have been taking care of the baby ever since. The youngster was almost starved when the Sisters took the child in. She is coming along fine now. The Sisters change off in taking care of the baby at night. The first night, Sister Martine and Sister Lorraine practically got no sleep. But she has been better since. During the daytime, some of the bigger girls around the Station look after the youngster. We don't know as yet whether the Sisters will adopt the child or not. That will depend somewhat on the Government Social Worker who is expected to come to Mendi shortly. The Sisters are happy to take care of the child. –In the meanwhile, the second wife of Lumi's father also had a baby, and the baby got sick. The mother brought the child to the Mission. Fr. baptized the youngster, giving him the name of Eugene, and then took the mother and child to the hospital, for treatment. Within a couple of hours, the mother returned again to the bush with the child. I doubt very much whether the child will live unless he can be found again for proper medical attention. –As far as Lumi's sister is concerned, the hospital authorities here are delighted that the Sisters are looking out after her. Incidentally, the Sisters have done many similar things, which make them very popular with the natives.

I told you in a previous letter about my getting a suit from Ah Chuk in Hong Kong. I don't know whether I mentioned the letter I received in return from Ah Chuk. He wrote that I should contact him immediately when I reach Hong Kong. And he said his car will pick me up immediately. Furthermore, he said he will give me his chauffeur and one of his cars for the duration of my stay in Hong Kong. I probably will take him up on that.

I hope this letter finds you and everyone around home coming along as well as ever. I may drop you a card or a short letter before I leave the Territory. Hello to all.

Your devoted brother, Msgr. Firmin.

P.S. You can tell Pia and Roseann that they also look very fine in the photo. And of course, little Donna Marie looks very good.

~~~

[Following are excerpts from a letter, handwritten the day after Monsignor Firmin left the Mendi Mission, heading for Madang, on his way to the Second Vatican Council in Rome.]

9 September 1963

Dear Mary,

As you can see, I'm on my way. . . .

The school kids of Mendi gave me quite a send-off. Last might at about 8:30, the whole crowd, well over 200, came to the door and sang a very beautiful farewell song, composed by one of the Sisters. I wish I could have recorded it. After they were finished with the singing, they gave me a spiritual bouquet of 2000 rosaries. This morning they were all on hand again as I left the Mission. After we took off, Ken buzzed the Mission. They were all out in the yard waving. Right before I left, one of the Sisters told me that little Eleanor Kipa (third-grade girl) offered her prayers yesterday and today that we would have bad weather so I would stay in Mendi

. . . .

I forgot to mention the farewell dinner the Sisters had for me. The Sisters, including the three from Tari, who were in Mendi for an Educational Meeting, prepared two medium-size turkeys, with the usual trimmings. It was most delicious. There were eleven of us for the dinner, including the six Sisters. . . . I hope this letter finds you coming along as well as ever.

Your devoted brother, Msgr. Firmin

~~~

Appendix A.

———✦———

FOUNDING OF THE
CAPUCHIN MISSION
AND APPOINTMENT OF ITS HEAD

ACCORDING TO THE book *Only the Beginnings: Commemorating the Coming of the Capuchins and Their Co-Workers to the Southern Highlands of Papua New Guinea,* by Fr. Blaine Burkey, O.F.M., Cap., long before the Franciscan Order of Friars Minor, Capuchin (O.F.M., Cap.), arrived in Papua New Guinea, Christian missionary activity had been carried on for several centuries in Oceania. It had begun in earnest in the late eighteenth century when Protestant missionaries established stations on various islands there. Beginning in the nineteenth century, Catholic missionaries, including those from the Society of Mary, or Marist Fathers and Brothers, started missions in the South Pacific islands, but with little success. Later, in the 1880s and 1890s, other Catholic congregations, including the French Missionaries of the Sacred Heart (MSC), founded a mission on the island of New Britain and, ultimately, on Yule Island, northwest of Port Moresby. In addition, the Society of the Divine Word (SVD) missionaries established a mission on the north coast of New Guinea, near Madang.[10]

Christian missionary work continued in New Guinea, intermittently, throughout the early to mid–twentieth century, until World War II, when Australia halted missionary activity when Japan entered the war. After the war, missionaries were once again allowed by Australia onto the island to continue their efforts to convert the natives to Christianity. In fact, by the time the Capuchin Franciscan mission was founded in the Highlands in the mid-1950s, other Protestant missionaries—namely, Methodist missionaries and the Unevangelized Fields Mission—had already preceded Catholic missionaries into the area near Mendi.

Starting after World War II, individuals in Rome at the Holy See, the headquarters of the global Catholic Church, were eager to seek missionaries to minister to the peoples of the vast territory of Papua. Three different high-ranking members of the clergy in the Pacific Islands and Australia, in their separate and combined efforts, sought to secure the commitment of religious congregations to establish missions in Papua New Guinea. The three prelates were the following: Andre Sorin (MSC), Bishop of the newly-created prefecture of Samarai, constituting one-fifth of Papua on the east; Archbishop Romolo Carboni, Papal Apostolic Delegate to Australia, New Zealand, and the Pacific Islands; and Fr. Pierre Guichet, Superior of the French Missionaries of the Sacred Heart, serving in Australia and the Pacific Islands. Through 1953 and 1954, their efforts to secure more missionaries in the South Pacific, including Papua, paralleled proposals and deliberations among the international Capuchin Franciscan religious congregations in Italy and the United States. The intended goal was to identify a religious group that might realistically be able to take on and support a new mission.

In September 1954, Fr. Guichet decided to send several veteran Sacred Heart missionaries, Fr. Alexis Michellod and Brother Jean

---

10   The information provided in Appendix A is from Fr. Blaine Burkey's book, pp. 20–135.

Delabarre, to make first contact in Papua New Guinea. Allowed only a month to make contacts, Fr. Michellod and Br. Delabarre flew to Mendi, in the Southern Highlands, in September. They met with Australian government officials, who introduced them to local headmen in the Mendi area as well as later in Tari and Kubari. Then, at the end of the month, preparing to leave Mendi, Fr. Alex received unexpected word by telegram that they should stay and that further help would be arriving. Thus, Fr. Michellod and Br. Delabarre continued to travel through the area around Mendi, trying to identify possible future mission stations in Papua. Meanwhile, Archbishop Carboni contacted Fr. Anastase Paoletti, the superior of the small group of Capuchins in Australia, to ask whether that group could take over the mission. Unfortunately, after deliberating, the Capuchins in Australia decided their numbers were not sufficient to take on the commitment of a mission in Papua.

Then, in November 1954, Fr. Guichet, Fr. Michellod's superior, and Fr. Paoletti arrived by plane in Port Moresby, Papua New Guinea. They learned from religious superiors and several bishops meeting there of the extreme difficulties and high financial costs of undertaking a mission in the New Guinea Southern Highlands. Nevertheless, Frs. Paoletti and Guichet traveled on to the Southern Highlands, arriving at Mendi on December 1. After staying in Mendi for several days and conferring with Fr. Michellod, the priests traveled to Alexishafen, near Madang, on the north coast of Papua. There they met with Bishop Adolph Noser, of the Society of the Divine Word Mission (SVD), who strongly urged Fr. Paoletti to seek American Capuchins to take the mission both because of the need for English speakers and the likelihood that Americans could support the high financial cost to establish and maintain a mission. Accordingly, when Fr. Paoletti returned to Sydney, he sent his report of the visit to the Southern Highlands to the Minister General of the Friars Minor, Capuchin, in Rome.

Next, Catholic Church officials in Rome made a request of a religious congregation in the United States to accept the challenge of founding a mission in Papua. Thus, near the end of January 1955, Fr. Victor Green, the Superior General of the Pittsburgh, Pennsylvania, Province of Friars Minor, Capuchin, received a letter from Fr. Conrad O'Donovan, General Definitor of the English-speaking Capuchins in Rome. The letter asked the Pennsylvania Province to consider taking on the mission in Papua. Two weeks later, after consultation with his advisors, Fr. Victor accepted the mission on behalf of the Pittsburgh Province. In short, in 1955, in spite of the certain difficulties that the Southern Highlands posed, the Capuchin friars of the St. Augustine Province of Pittsburgh, Pennsylvania, undertook to establish a mission and bring the Catholic faith to the people of the Southern Highlands of Papua New Guinea.

When the call went out within the Capuchin congregation for volunteers to become missionaries in Papua, twenty-six friars of the congregation stepped up. Ultimately, six friars ranging in age from 28 to 43 were chosen to become missionaries in New Guinea. These individuals variously possessed prior mission experiences, specific engineering and carpentry skills, and personal traits that could serve them well in the remote and difficult circumstances they would encounter.

As mentioned above, the members chosen for the Capuchin Mission had had varied experiences and possessed skills that would help significantly in building the mission. Specifically, Fr. Otmar and Fr. Stanley had served in the Capuchins' Puerto Rico mission. Fr. Otmar had held multiple posts throughout seven years, including the administrative posts of associate pastor and later pastor of a parish in Utuado. He had also served as chaplain of a tuberculosis sanatorium in Ponce and at other posts in Puerto Rico. Fr. Stanley had served in a variety of assignments in Rio Piedras and Utuado for eight years. Two other members of the mission had served Stateside. For four years, Fr. Paul had been associate pastor at St. Augustine's Church in Pittsburgh. Brother Mark, the youngest of the group of missionaries, had trained in the program for lay brothers in Cumberland, Maryland, and had served in several positions, including as an engineer at Capuchin

College in Washington, D.C. Fr. Henry had already been in Australia for seven years and was religious superior in Melbourne and pastor in the Leichhardt sector of Sydney. In fact, it was Fr. Henry who was the first of the Pittsburgh Capuchins to go to Papua. He reported back to and advised the Superior General, Fr. Victor Green, about conditions there. Finally, Fr. Berard had graduated from Carnegie Institute of Technology, in Pittsburgh, and had been a Sea Bee engineer with the 78th U.S. Naval Construction Battalion in World War II before he had joined the Capuchins. He had served in the South Pacific, including on the New Guinea mainland.

After the friars received their mission crosses in August 1955, Frs. Paul, Stanley, and Berard and Br. Mark headed for San Francisco to depart the U.S. on the ship *S.S. Orcades* of the Oriental Line on September 10. Along with the friars and other passengers, the ship also carried over ten tons of equipment needed for the mission. These supplies and equipment had been ordered and shipped to San Francisco by the Capuchin Province Mission Office.

On October 1, 1955, when the ship docked at Sydney Harbor, the friars were met by Frs. Otmar and Henry, who had arrived by plane on September 29. As the Capuchin friars waited in Sydney for a ship to take them to Madang, on New Guinea's northern coast, they boarded in a house supplied by the Leichhardt parish.

The month spent in Sydney was productive; they learned much about Papua and information about building a mission. They consulted with New Guinea experts on tropical diseases and other matters, met with Archbishop Carboni (who presented them again with missionary crosses), and visited with other Church officials and missionaries who had been in the Southern Highlands. In addition, they participated in a variety of apostolic activities in local churches and viewed films taken by visitors to the New Guinea Highlands. In short, they learned everything they could about their future home in the difficult, mountainous terrain that was the Southern Highlands.

On October 28, the friars boarded a ship that took them to

Port Moresby, arriving on November 6. As they waited for the ship to Madang, they faced several delays. The ship left Port Moresby on November 9. Unfortunately, Fr. Paul had become sick with what was thought to be appendicitis, and the ship had to sail to Samarai, an island off the southeastern tip of New Guinea, where Fr. Paul faced medical complications and had surgery. Besides the delay regarding Fr. Paul's health, a huge downpour at Madang, the friars' destination, had flooded its airstrip. The flooding would prevent larger planes from taking off to deliver to the Highlands the cargo brought by their ship. Fr. Berard stayed with Fr. Paul on Samarai as he recuperated from surgery, and the rest of the friars finally arrived by ship at Madang on November 15. The Society of the Divine Word missionaries at Alexishafen, near Madang, then hosted the Capuchins as they waited to proceed into the Highlands (Fr. Paul was well enough to leave Samarai Island only by the middle of December).

Over the course of weeks, the friars flew into the Highlands. On November 23, 1955, Fr. Otmar Gallagher, OFM Cap., appointed the superior of the Capuchin missionaries, joined Fr. Alexis Michellod at Tari. The other members of the missionary team—that is, Fr. Berard Tomasetti, OFM Cap.; Fr. Stanley Miltenberger, OFM Cap.; Br. Mark Bollinger, OFM Cap.; Fr. Henry Kusnerik, OFM Cap.; and Fr. Paul Farkas, OFM Cap.—all arrived at Tari by December 22, 1955.

It is important to remember that before the Capuchins arrived in the Southern Highlands in December 1955, during 1954–55, Frs. Michellod, Alphonse Rinn, Louis Van Campenhoudt, MSC (who, at 66 years of age, had been a missionary in Papua for 33 years), and Br. Delabarre, MSC, carried out significant work toward founding the Mission. In October 1954, at Kumin, where the Mendi Mission would be located, Fr. Michellod opened the first Catholic school in the Southern Highlands, besides building a church and other structures. Also, Frs. Michellod and Rinn visited Tari, where the mission was progressing, and went to Ialibu, where Fr. Rinn started the first Catholic mission in August 1955. Further, Fr. Michellod's great facility with languages resulted in his creating dictionaries and translating prayers and catechisms into the Huli and Mendi languages. Additionally, Fr. Michellod was especially helpful to government officials in surveying land and working with them on patrols to chart new roads. One of these was a key road for motor traffic from Mendi to Tari. Further, Fr. Van Campenhoudt spent months at Kumin, near Mendi, taking care of the Mission.

In short, throughout 1954 and 1955, much significant ground-work was carried out by the Missionaries of the Sacred Heart to pre-pare the way for the coming of the Capuchin Franciscans. Calling Fr. Michellod the "father of the Mendi and Tari missions" in his book, Fr. Blaine Burkey praises Fr. Michellod and his fellow MSC Fathers. In the course of 1956, the Capuchins, Frs. Alexis Michellod and Alphonse Rinn, and other MSC priests continued to make notable progress in contacting as many peoples of the Southern Highlands as they could, including establishing out stations as areas were opened up by the gov-ernment. Then, as had been planned, when the Capuchins settled in, the MSC priests made arrangements to depart the Highlands. By the beginning of 1957, the MSC clergy returned to their headquarters at Yule Island. Naturally, when the MSC priests left, additional staff from the Pittsburgh Province was assigned to the Capuchin Mission. Those assigned to the Mendi Mission were Frs. Gary Stakem and Gregory Smith, and Br. Claude Mattingly. At that point, the Mission was fully recognized as the Capuchin Mission.

In addition, throughout 1956, Fr. Otmar Gallagher, Religious Superior and Procurator of the Capuchin missionaries, continued to work with Fr. Alexis Michellod, MSC. Fr. Michellod, as Bishop Sorin's vicar delegate, had been put in charge of all the missionaries in the Highlands. At first, Tari had been identified as the main mission lo-cation, with the following missionaries stationed there: Fr. Otmar, as Superior; Fr. Paul, as a teacher; and Brother Mark, as the builder and mechanic. Two other stations, one at Mendi, the other at Ialibu, were staffed by both Capuchins and MSC clergy. In spring of 1956, in a second visit to the Southern Highlands to confer with the clergy there, Bishop Sorin determined that Mendi would be the Catholic headquarters of the Southern Highlands (since it had already been designated the government headquarters of the area). Indeed, it also had been decided that Mendi would be the headquarters of the Capuchin Mission because the Mendi Valley had already been opened by the government, whereas the areas around Ialibu and Tari were still restricted, preventing the missionaries from carrying out their work there.

Besides beginning their work in 1956, the Capuchins also made key purchases that were critical to carrying out their mission. Through the efforts of Fr. Otmar, the Mission purchased an airplane, a new Cessna 180—essential to moving supplies and people from the coast to the Highlands. The plane first arrived in parts on a ship at Port Moresby, then was sent on to Madang, where it was assembled in November. It was flown into Mendi for the first time at the end of December by Fr. Henry Hoff, SVD, who had led its assembly. On board also were Fr. Stanley Miltenberger; Fr. Stanley's brother, Fidelis Miltenberger, hired as a pilot for the mission; and his fiancée Josephine Coleman. Also, the mission secured a vehicle for land travel: a Land Rover, brought in parts over the mountains (along with a second one for the government station) and then reassembled.

While the Capuchins were establishing their presence in the Highlands, the skills of the various friars helped advance the progress of the mission. For example, Fr. Paul, an experienced teacher, took on the task of forming a school at Tari and later taught at Guluanda for a number of years. Brother Paul put his carpentry and engineering skills to work at Tari. Fr. Berard, being a civil engineer, was of great service to Australian government officials as areas were de-restricted. Bridges over rivers were needed, and, as he planned the building of bridges, Fr. Berard's skills allowed the Capuchins to be the first missionaries to make contact with native groups and to come to agreements with them about setting up missions. This occurred, for example, when Fr. Berard designed a wire suspension bridge over the Tagari River. The bridge was completed in 1957 and was the first of its kind in the Southern Highlands. Fr. Berard also took on other tasks such as resurveying the airstrip at Guluanda, to make drainage better, and surveying the hospital grounds at Rumu to build a possible water system.

In the next three years, the Capuchins achieved numerous successes in expanding and improving their missions. To offer three examples, in 1957, they established the Catholic mission in the Ialibu Basin with the help of a group of native Simbu catechists. The catechists had been recommended by Fr. Alphons Schaefer, SVD, who had been in the Highlands since the 1930s. Then, in 1958, Fr. Henry Kusnerik, with Br. Paul Idomaka and Br. Mark Bollinger, set up a sawmill at Amburugi. Making further progress, Fr. Stanley Miltenberger was "the first Capuchin to open a main station in the Catholic Mission to the Southern Highlands." With native catechists and other workers, he established a mission in the Kagua Valley. At Karia, they built a church by mid-August and then continued to build a teachers' house, dormitories, and other buildings to improve the mission.

Along with their successes in expanding the Capuchin Mission, the missionaries faced numerous challenges in setting up outstations in the primitive conditions of the bush. For example, in the beginning, before the mission purchased a plane, there were difficulties in obtaining needed supplies from the coast for the various mission stations. Also, as mentioned above, Christian missionaries were limited to restricted areas—that is, only those areas that had been "pacified" by Australian government officers. Additionally, Protestant missionaries competed with the Capuchins. For example, in the Kagua Valley, where Lutheran catechists had arrived first, they used a variety of tactics (without success) to make the Catholics "move on." Further, in order to set up a mission in a particular location, the Capuchin missionaries would negotiate and make agreements with native headmen in charge of certain lines of descent among the people of an area. However, sometimes the natives would prove themselves capricious and acquisitive. The natives would renege on their agreements with the Capuchins and welcome missionaries of other denominations because they offered the natives axes or knives as gifts for their willingness to accept the missions the Protestant missionaries wanted to build. Finally, because the Capuchin Mission consisted of only male clergy, who naturally set up schools for boys, there remained the necessity to reach out to and educate native girls and women. Accordingly, from the beginnings of the mission, there was a concerted effort to secure an order of religious Sisters to commit to serve the missions in Papua.

Even though the Capuchins had begun a new mission in the Southern Highlands, more clergy to help with missionary work was needed. From 1955 onward, Archbishop Romolo Carboni, along with higher clergy in Rome, continued to search for an additional religious congregation to set up another mission west of the territory served by the Capuchins. For instance, in 1957, the Capuchin Fathers of Parma, Italy, were asked to assume a part of the Papua Highlands mission. However, the Parma Capuchins declined the proposal. In short, over the course of three years, efforts to secure a religious community to aid the Capuchin Mission did not succeed.

CAPUCHIN MISSION DECLARED AN INDEPENDENT APOSTOLIC PREFECTURE AND FR. FIRMIN SCHMIDT APPOINTED HEAD

Meanwhile, Archbishop Carboni took steps to expedite the process for the current Capuchin Mission to become independent. The result was that Fr. Benignus, the Capuchin General Minister in Rome, wrote the following to Fr. Otmar on May 26, 1958: "'The erection of your Mission into an independent Prefecture Apostolic does seem imminent. The Sacred Congregation of Propaganda Fide recently approached us on the matter and it would seem that an announcement should be made shortly. We shall just have to wait until they think it opportune.'"

What followed were changes that significantly affected the status of the Capuchin Mission in the Papuan Highlands. In the interim, Fr. Clement Neubauer of Milwaukee succeeded to the position of

Capuchin General Minister in Rome, following Fr. Benignus, whose term had ended. Pope Pius XII authorized the establishment of the "Apostolic Prefecture of Kikori." (The Capuchins subsequently requested that the prefecture be changed to Mendi because their mission work had little to do with the area around Kikori. This request was granted.) Then, unexpectedly, Pope Pius XII died. This unfortunate event required that the request to erect a prefecture would have to be resubmitted to a new pope. Pope Pius XII's successor, Pope John XXIII, was elected on October 28 and crowned on November 4, 1958. Then, acting most expeditiously, Pope John XXIII "erected the Prefecture of Mendi, on Nov. 13, 1958."

Anticipating the erection of the prefecture, the Capuchins were at work to name a prefect. The Provincial Minister and his advisors asked the eight missionaries in Papua to choose three priests of the Capuchin Congregation whom they thought could be successful as its head. They were to list them "in order of preference." The Provincial Minister, Fr. Claude, and his advisors also each voted for and ranked three priests on the list provided by the missionaries. In the case of both sets of votes, the outcome was the same: Father Firmin Schmidt was at the top. Although at the time Fr. Firmin served as one of the definitors (advisors to the Provincial Minister), at no time did he advocate for himself. He simply stated that he would accept the outcome of the votes.

In April 1959, Fr. Firmin Schmidt was appointed by Pope John XXIII as Prefect Apostolic of Mendi. In September, Right Reverend Monsignor Firmin, with new missionary Fr. David Dressman, left the United States, arriving in Sydney, Australia. Then, with Archbishop Carboni present, he completed the formalities of his appointment to the prefecture, with documents verifying the proceedings being sent to the Holy See in Rome. Monsignor Firmin arrived in Mendi on October 20, 1959. On the next day, October 21, in the bush chapel at Mendi, Monsignor Firmin conducted ceremonies and "took possession of the prefecture, . . . consecrated [it] to the Sacred Heart, and dedicated it to . . . Mary, Mother of the Good Shepherd." From his appointment as Right Reverend Monsignor in 1959 to his ordination as a bishop in 1965, Monsignor Firmin "had all the powers of a diocesan bishop" except those that would allow him to ordain priests.

Appendix B.

───── ❦ ─────

PAPUA SOUTHERN HIGHLANDS SOCIETY IN THE 1950S

BELIEFS OF THE PEOPLE OF THE HIGHLANDS

IN THE 1930s and earlier, anthropologists from Australia and elsewhere carried out limited field studies to learn what they could about the native peoples of the Central and Southern Highlands. Yet because of World War II, significant anthropological study ceased and began again in earnest only after 1945. Even by 1950, the Central Highlands District "had not been systematically explored by Europeans."[11] Through the 1950s and 1960s, anthropologists such as Peter Lawrence, Mervyn J. Meggitt, Robert M. Glasse, D'arcy Ryan, and others, carried out field studies on the peoples living in the Highlands. While doing so, they encountered peoples who had had little exposure to Westernized ways and whose lives and beliefs had been little affected by Western culture.

---

11   John Dademo Waiko. *A Short History of Papua New Guinea.* 2nd. Ed. (South Melbourne: Oxford, 2007), 108.

In their collection of essays *Gods Ghosts and Men in Melanesia*, Lawrence and Meggitt identify and include discussions of the religious beliefs among the inhabitants of the Papuan Highlands. The authors also provide a definition of the term *religion*: "the total cosmic order that a people believes to exist."[12] The studies carried out by these anthropologists found that throughout Melanesia, including Papua, native belief systems varied a great deal and exhibited little consistency across geographical areas.

In Melanesia, the people's worldview had two parts: 1) the natural world, including material resources, animals, and humans and 2) the supernatural world, including spirit beings and supernatural forces. In this view, humans interacted within three interconnected systems—that is, with the natural world and the economic resources available; with other humans within society; and with spirit beings and impersonal supernatural forces. Religion functioned in the whole cosmic order "to explain and validate through myths the origin and existence of the physical world, its economic resources and the means of exploiting them, and the socio-political structure." Also, it gave humans "the assurance that . . . [they could] control the cosmic order by performing ritual."[13]

Although belief systems varied randomly, almost all groups of the Southern and Central Highlands concerned themselves with the influence of ghosts on the living, and they held pervasive beliefs about the spirits of the dead. Most of the Melanesian belief systems held that the spiritual, or nonempirical, realm was closely related to the physical world. Ghosts and other supernatural beings were believed to live near the places where people settled, even at times taking human form.[14] Besides believing in spirit beings, almost all Melanesian people be-

---

12 Peter Lawrence and Mervyn J. Meggitt, eds., "Introduction," in *Gods Ghosts and Men: Some Religions of Australian New Guinea and the New Hebrides.* (Melbourne: Oxford University Press, 1965), 1-26.

13 Lawrence and Meggitt, 7.

14 Lawrence and Meggitt, 9.

lieved to some degree in sympathetic magic (rituals employing actions that might bring about a large-scale effect).[15] Natives of the Papuan Highlands, like other Melanesian peoples, had strong beliefs about the attitudes and importance of recently deceased individuals (spirits of the dead) in contrast to those of the remote dead (ancestors or ancestral ghosts). Just as living humans used the strategies of bargaining and bribery to influence rivals in life, so too did they use the same strategies to try to control and placate the spirits of the dead.[16]

According to Lawrence and Meggitt, spirit beings were generally of three types: 1) deities, some who could control and regulate nature and some who involved themselves in human matters; 2) independent spirit beings such as tricksters or demons, who annoyed or harmed people; and 3) the spirits of the dead, recent or distant (ancestral ghosts). Rituals, supported by taboos, might involve the following: a) prayers or offerings to appease a deity; b) presenting offerings as a way to bargain with the deity or remote dead, including, attempting to create a reciprocal relationship with a deity through a spell (using sympathetic magic), in order to control the occult being and thus obtain material benefits; and c) sorcery, a ritual that is harmful or fatal to human beings.[17]

Anthropologist, Robert M. Glasse studied specific beliefs held by the Huli of the Southern Highlands and found that four ideas accounted for their religious behavior: *dinini, dama, gamu,* and Datagaliwabe. *Dinini* refers to the "immaterial essence of human personality," a vital essence, or soul, that lives on as a ghost after the individual dies, that may affect the behavior of people still alive, and that possibly affects dama; *Dama* were considered powerful gods who could control nature and who involved themselves in the actions of humans; *Gamu* was "a special form of behavior," including oaths taken or offerings made, that could sway the deities and ghosts to bring about a desired result or keep

---

15   Lawrence and Meggitt, 10.

16   Lawrence and Meggitt, 14.

17   Lawrence and Meggitt, 8–10.

an unwanted event from happening. Finally, Datagaliwabe was a deity whose only function with regard to humans was "punishing breaches of kinship rules."[18]

The Huli held strong beliefs about ghosts affecting those still living. For that reason, it will be useful to focus on *dinini*, understood as a vital essence or soul. Among the Huli, there was little interest in what happens to the soul after death. They did not believe that a person is judged in the afterlife according to the individual's actions and character in life. Many believed that the soul of a person remains on earth after death, dwelling among and still interested in the lives and actions of the living. In believing that the soul persists after the death of the body, the Huli emphasized "continuity rather than eternity" and took a strong interest in the "fate of ghosts."[19]

The peoples of the Highlands often regarded the spirits of the recently deceased as vengeful and desiring to punish any perceived slight against them by the living. Interestingly, male ghosts were seen as having a kindly and protective interest in the affairs of their children and grandchildren. However, female ghosts were believed to be threatening to their other descendants, with the living attributing to them excessive greediness and other negative attributes (see below comments about the subordinate status of women in Highlands culture). Female ghosts were said to cause sickness in order to get people to sacrifice pigs for them. They were also viewed as causing infertility in women and in pigs.[20] As mentioned above, Highlanders tended to emphasize bargaining and bribery, in their efforts to placate angered ghosts, the same techniques used to manipulate fellow native rivals.

Religious rituals functioned as an important means of reinforcing society's welfare by strengthening social bonds and fostering fertility among its members. Honoring the dead through ceremonies of formal

---

18 Robert M. Glasse, "The Huli of the Southern Highlands," in Lawrence and Meggitt, *Gods Ghosts and Men*, 27-49.

19 Glasse, "The Huli of the Southern Highlands," 30-31.

20 Glasse, "The Huli of the Southern Highlands," 30-31.

gift exchange on the occasions of birth, marriage, and death reinforced clan unity. At the same time, the gift exchange placed pressure on members to come up with the wealth that would be distributed at the feasts. The ceremonies strengthened kinship bonds, acknowledged the mutual dependence between men and women, and highlighted the sexes' differences in social functions and status.[21]

Funerary ceremonies and customs among the Kyaka and Mae Enga of the Western Highlands illustrate the importance of kinship. The feast held at the funeral of an important man would involve his entire clan, with immediate relatives making a sacrifice at their home while other groups in the clan would also make sacrifices at their own homes and bring cooked meat to the site of the feast. With funeral feasts never being solitary affairs, pigs were contributed by brothers, their sons, and fraternal nephews. The man holding the feast for the individual who died expected all his domestic kin, including married sisters with their children, to attend the feast for the deceased.[22] In groups like the Mae Enga, close relatives were expected to show their grief and pacify the ghost of the deceased by cutting part of their earlobes or cutting off finger joints.[23]

The size of the gift exchange was determined by the status of the deceased. The funeral feast of an unimportant person was much smaller in scale and was perhaps even delayed and carried out after further deaths of less important people. Usually, the body of the deceased was buried in a shallow pit near the person's residence.[24]

Finally, sorcery was used, but it varied from region to region, with some forms employing the power of deities and ghosts and others using sympathetic magic. Accusations of sorcery often occurred against

---

21   Lawrence and Meggitt, *Gods Ghosts and Men in Melanesia,* 14–15.

22   Ralph Neville Hermon Bulmer, "The Kyaka of the Western Highlands," in Lawrence and Meggitt, *Gods Ghosts and Men,* 132–161.

23   Mervin J. Meggitt, "The Mae Enga of the Western Highlands," in Lawrence and Meggitt, *Gods Ghosts and Men in Melanesia,* 105–131.

24   Bulmer, "The Kyaka of the Western Highlands," 144.

people who did not have secure membership in firmly established clans or groups. Accusations might also occur among firmly settled groups in which feelings of rivalry or resentment had risen, and thus the accusations were an excuse for starting warfare.[25]

PAPUAN SOCIETY AND CULTURE

Sociologists classifying human societies often determine groups according to population size, to what extent political organization is centralized, and whether people are grouped into social hierarchies, based on income, wealth, status, etc. According to these considerations, the Mendi would be considered a "tribe," like other groups in the Highlands. Each local group had approximately several hundred members, little economic specialization, lacked strong leaders, and made decisions in face-to-face meetings.[26] Groups were also autonomous, with local clans not seeking further territory than was traditionally defined.[27]

In the mid-1950s, anthropologists D'arcy Ryan and Robert M. Glasse spent time among the Mendi and the Huli, respectively (as mentioned above). Ryan observed that the Mendi and other peoples of the Southern Highlands were typically short in stature (around five feet tall), well-proportioned, and muscular, with their skin color varying from darker brown to olive.

As subsistence farmers, the Mendi used slash-and-burn techniques to clear land, and also practiced fallow farming. They grew primarily sweet potatoes, taro, beans, leafy vegetables, bananas, and sugar cane. They also raised pigs, which were important economically.[28]

The sweet potato is the primary food crop of the natives of the Highlands. The history of the sweet potato's introduction to New

---

25 Lawrence and Meggitt, *Gods Ghosts and Men in Melanesia,* 17.

26 Diamond, 15.

27 Waiko, *A Short History of Papua New Guinea,* 30.

28 D'Arcy Ryan, "Marriage in Mendi," in *Pigs, Pearlshells, and Women: Marriage in the New Guinea Highlands,* ed. Robert M. Glasse and Mervyn J. Meggitt (Englewood Cliffs, NJ: Prentice-Hall, 1969), 159-175.

Guinea is complex, but it likely took place at least several hundred years ago. It was more productive than other crops, could be grown in poor soil, and could be grown at higher elevations. Green vegetables were grown as a source of protein for the native inhabitants, and pigs replaced wild animals; because the pigs' ability to forage was limited by land clearing, they were fed produce, including sweet potatoes, from gardens. Pigs have been raised domestically in New Guinea for at least hundreds of years. Women conducted the labor-intensive and costly work of keeping pigs. In fact, owning pigs was considered symbolic of wealth and influence. Networks of trade developed, with Malaysian traders taking slaves and other salable goods, like bird-of-paradise feathers, from New Guinea. Evidence of this trade is the appearance of images of bird-of-paradise feathers on bronze kettledrums of eastern Indonesia.[29]

In Papua, the Mendi, like other groups, did not live in villages but rather in homesteads. The family did not live together; the men lived apart from the women and young children. In his article "Meeting the Mendi," D'Arcy Ryan describes a typical setting for the focus of clan activities: not a village with a center but rather a grass dance ground surrounded by tall trees and thick hedges, with narrow paths leading away from the open ground to individual houses and gardens. At one end of the dance ground, several large low huts stood, with sword-grass-thatched roofs and eaves almost touching the ground. Only adult men and youths lived in these "lineage houses"; the women, children, and pigs lived in houses spread throughout the clan territory, often near the gardens belonging to the men. Besides the care of gardens and their young children, women were charged with care of the pigs. As mentioned above, pigs were important symbols of wealth and were needed to be slaughtered, mostly on special occasions like marriages and deaths. At the front of each "lineage house," an open space looked out on the dance ground. Behind this open space, a small opening into the house allowed men to crawl through to the sleeping area. Most of the communal social life of the clan took place in the dance ground area, but on a typical day, few people would

---

29   Waiko, *A Short History of Papua New Guinea,* 10–11.

congregate in that area as most would be busy in their gardens.[30]

In a 1969 article, Ryan elaborates specifically on Mendi social structure and customs. The Mendi had a social structure based on male lines of descent (*patrilineal,* or, *agnatic*), which reached (in theory) back four to six generations.[31] As mentioned above, along with other Melanesian societies, Papuans had no central authority. Lawrence and Meggitt mention that kinship, descent, and marital alliance were emphasized in the social structure. Descent through the father (*patrifiliation*) was the main consideration in the transmission of property, but in some groups *cognatic*—that is, descent through both parents— links were important.[32] According to Edward L. Schieffelin and Robert Crittenden, in *Like People You See in a Dream,* Papuan societies did not have rank, but influential individuals dominated in some communities. When conflicts arose, Papuans had no formal judicial system to settle disputes, so they frequently resorted to armed confrontation and intimidation. In fact, the culture encouraged forcefulness in men and a tendency toward violence as a desirable trait.[33]

Linguistic diversity within Papua is notable. There are around 750 Papuan languages, most of which belong to one parent language. This group of languages was perhaps derived from a variety of languages spoken by those who cultivated plants in the Central Highlands. Studies of the languages spoken in New Guinea show that they are not clearly related to Australian Aborigine languages. Melanesian Tok Pisin, the present-day lingua franca of Papua, became more commonly used in the early nineteenth century as trade increased.[34]

---

30   D'Arcy Ryan, "Meeting the Mendi," in *Ethnographic Presents: Pioneering Anthropologists in the Papua New Guinea Highlands,* ed. Terence E. Hays (Berkeley: University of California Press, 1992), 199–231.

31   Ryan, "Marriage in Mendi," 160.

32   Lawrence and Meggitt, *Gods Ghosts and Men in Melanesia,* 5.

33   Edward L. Schieffelin and Robert Crittenden, eds., "Colonial Papua and the Tradition of Exploration," in *Like People You See in a Dream: First Contact in Six Papuan Societies* (Stanford, CA: Stanford University Press, 1991), 18.

34   Waiko, *A Short History of Papua New Guinea,* 12–13, 23.

As Ryan discovered, the Mendi were a gift-exchange society. Papuans were preoccupied with "gift-giving that entails the establishment or maintenance of social relations," otherwise known among anthropologists as *prestation*.[35] Due to gift exchange being the key to social and economic factors, the Mendi resembled other native groups throughout Papua and Melanesia as a whole—that is, "the whole of their intricate system of interpersonal and intergroup relations revolved around, and was symbolized and maintained by, the constant formal, reciprocal, public gift-giving of valuables (mainly pigs and pearl shell) between individuals and groups."[36] This custom of formal presentation of gifts defined relationships among important individuals and groups. In short, the complicated gift-exchange system was a means of revealing which members of society held power and influence.

Even though the patrilineal model was largely adhered to, individuals did have flexibility regarding where they resided and with whom they affiliated. When a lineage group could no longer carry out its key functions because of loss of members—perhaps through disease or warfare—it might join with another lineage or a stronger group. Individuals might leave the territory of their agnatic relatives to go live with other relatives from their mother's or father's lineage (*cognatic*) or with relatives by marriage (*affinal*). This might happen if the other relatives allowed them to use some of their land for gardens. Over the course of several generations those people living with non-agnatic relatives might "creatively" make changes in their genealogies in order to strengthen their position among the non-agnates.[37]

With regard to work and the importance of wealth, Papuans had no interest in accumulating wealth for its own sake. Rather, wealth was used to enhance one's status by the staging of ceremonial feasts, which included prestations. Ceremonial exchanges and marriages were the means

35 Ian Hogbin, *Anthropology in Papua New Guinea: Readings from the Encyclopaedia of Papua and New Guinea* (Melbourne: Melbourne University Press, 1973), 239.

36 Ryan, "Meeting the Mendi," 215.

37 Ryan, "Marriage in Mendi," 161.

to affirming and sustaining alliances and significant social connections. Ceremonial feasts celebrated marriages, death compensations, and rites of passage. The feasts also served as a means of building one's standing in the clan as well as a way of intimidating rivals. These feasts not only strengthened established relationships but also created new ones as the formal gifts were passed from one to another. The wealth distributed could be pigs, valuable shells, and even produce from gardens. As Schieffelin and Crittenden mention, these commodities would be given to "settle outstanding political and social accounts"; the feasts also offered an occasion to display dance, oratory, and music. In planning the ceremonial events, Papuans could be industrious and well organized. Through the spectacular feasts they staged, they gained social prestige and political influence by giving the accumulated wealth away "to the right people and thereby creating ties of obligation and patronage."[38]

RELATIONS BETWEEN THE SEXES

Among the tribes of the Southern Highlands—including the Huli, the Mae Enga, and others—relations between men and women were fraught with tension. In his work among the Huli between 1955 and 1956, anthropologist Robert M. Glasse learned much about the relations between the sexes. Men looked upon women with suspicion, considering them evil and "impure" because they undergo menstruation and because of their powerful role of giving birth to new life.[39] As mentioned earlier, men lived apart from women, who had the care of their young children. Especially among the Huli, men believed that contact with women might affect their health adversely and cause them to age prematurely. Among the tribal groups, a menstruating woman was considered dangerous to men and had to remain in seclusion in her house while she was menstruating. At the end of her period she had to recite a spell and carry out rituals to cleanse herself magically.[40]

---

38   Schieffelin and Crittenden, "Colonial Papua and the Tradition of Exploration," 19.

39   Glasse, "The Huli of the Southern Highlands," 48.

40   Glasse, 28–29.

Adult men had the responsibility of preparing young men for adulthood, which included imparting the above-mentioned view of women. Indeed, part of preparing young men for adulthood included rituals with many precautions taken to avoid being tainted by women.[41] In his article "The Mae Enga of the Western Highlands," Mervyn J. Meggitt writes that among such groups as the Huli and Mae Enga, young men from around the age of fifteen would take part in group rituals with other bachelors of their subclan. The goal of the rituals was to try to minimize the effects of any unavoidable contacts with women of their clan, whose close contact with men affected men's strength and appearance. The bachelors would live apart from the rest of the clan and participate in group rituals. The young men would also use spells on their own and would grow a bog-iris plant, the health of which corresponded to the overall well-being of the group of young men. Among other rituals carried out by the young men were intensive washing of the body and eyes, rubbing on their bodies the iris leaves, over which a spell had been cast. The rituals also included singing spells, and conforming to regulations regarding dress, diet, and overall behavior.[42] After suitable and lengthy instruction, the bachelors would emerge from their isolated ritual training. They would parade periodically among their clans, with decorated bodies and wearing the "crescent shape ceremonial wig that symbolizes manhood," which each young man had carefully created. In their parading, they were careful to avoid even the gaze of women.[43] In short, even though women were valued, men regarded them with suspicion and anxiety because of biological processes and relegated them to a subordinate social position in the culture. Men were in charge of all rituals and, as mentioned above, expected that women take care of the gardens and the pigs, very arduous tasks, in addition to nurturing the children.

---

41 Glasse, 42–44.

42 Mervyn J. Meggitt, "The Mae Enga of the Western Highlands," in Lawrence and Meggitt, *Gods Ghosts and Men in Melanesia,* 127.

43 Glasse, "The Huli of the Southern Highlands," 43.

RITUALS RELATED TO MARRIAGE

As mentioned above, prestations—that is, the formal giving of gifts—marked every important social event. One detailed example, associated with marriage and its formalities, highlights this ritual gift-giving. In his article "Marriage in Mendi," D'Arcy Ryan provides specific details of the customs among the Mendi relating to marriage. As with other important ritualized customs that constitute key features of the Mendi economy, marriage involved exchanges of wealth as part of the ceremonies.

In theory, rules relating to whom an individual could *not* marry were lineages "into which a member of one's own lineage . . . [had] married within the previous five or six generations."[44] However, since even the older men could not necessarily remember the marriages of their ancestors beyond one or two generations, individuals actually had a wider choice than the rules seemed to allow. Personal qualities, including strength and appearance, were the primary reasons stated for a spouse being chosen. However, other factors, including parental influence, affected the choice of a spouse. Ultimately, though, "most marriages . . . [were] arranged by the couple themselves."[45] Yet even with parental pressure, a young woman or man could refuse the match.

Having lived among the Mendi, Ryan writes of his observations of formal courtship rituals. The process of courtship began after a meeting between the man and young woman. Interested young men would ask permission to visit the woman's house to sing to and talk with her in turn. Women might have multiple suitors, and the men might pursue several young women. Typically, men considered marriage in their mid-twenties, by which time they had accumulated enough to pay the bride price; the marriageable age of young women was usually between fifteen and the early twenties. The couple was expected to remain chaste, but at times sexual intercourse did take place before the

---

44   Ryan, "Marriage in Mendi," 163.

45   Ryan, 164.

marriage was formalized. However, a general belief that unlawful sex would bring about men physically "wasting away"—that is, for example, losing one's hair or drying of the skin—had the effect of restraining couples from having sex.[46]

Once the young woman had narrowed her choice to one young man a series of rituals followed, beginning with a formal meeting between the prospective groom and the woman's father or brothers, in which the prospective groom stated his desire to marry. If the woman's relatives agreed, the marriage payments were arranged and the suitor, as a first step, gave the young woman's family one pearl shell as a deposit.[47] The man also gave the bride-to-be some small betrothal gifts, like mirrors or beads.

The third step in the elaborate ritual of marriage began with a formal exchange of gifts. At the house of the groom or his representative, the bride and her selected relatives privately examined a portion of the bride's payment (pearl shell and perhaps several pigs). If her kin approved, they, in turn, formally presented two of the shells to the bride. After accepting the shells and turning to the groom's family, the bride then returned the shells to her relatives. This action signified that the bride payment was accepted. Though this ritual symbolized that her relatives represented the bride, the bride was the actual recipient of the bride price and could distribute it as she chose. In fact, she did not keep any of the wealth exchanged; the actual recipients were the bride's relatives (see below).

Additional prescribed steps followed several days later. The groom's relatives publicly presented the bride payment to the bride on her ceremonial ground, and after this they stood aside. Standing in the center of all the gifts, the bride wore a heavy blackened net as a veil and held a forked wand, a bridal symbol. With her body covered entirely in a black mixture of palm oil and soot, she gave off a black sheen. Then the bride distributed each item of the bride wealth to her relatives, saying the

---

46   Ryan, 163–165.

47   Ryan, 165.

name of each individual as she presented the gifts.[48] Ordinarily the bride wealth was presented to her father, brothers, mother, and married sisters. The bride's mother then in turn passed her share on to her own brothers, and the bride's sisters gave their portion to their husbands or sons.

In freely distributing gifts to her relatives, the bride thereby created bonds of obligation. More important, the public presentation of the gifts to her relatives signified the closeness of the woman to her own relatives, to whom she was loyal, and whom she expected to rely on in the future should difficulties arise. Interestingly, among the Mendi, the bride price was not viewed as purchasing the bride, but it rather functioned as the groom's payment to her kin for the bride's services to him in the future.[49]

Following the distribution of the bride payment, some of the bride's relatives presented the groom with a return gift of pigs; the groom was then expected to add more to the agreed-upon bride price. As the payments mounted up in value, the status and prestige of both parties were enhanced.

After the major items of the bride price were distributed, the bride went with her husband to his house, bringing with her the return gift of pigs. The consummation of the marriage did not take place immediately but instead about a month later, by which time the bride's ceremonial coating of oil and soot had worn off. Additionally, the month during which the bride and groom abstained from having sexual contact was considered a trial period, which also allowed the bride to get used to her affinal relatives and her new life. If problems occurred that suggested the marriage would not last, the couple could separate and the relatives of the bride would have to return the bride price to the groom and his relatives.

Within the month, the groom completed his payment of the bride price (often with the help of relatives). The groom also did not perform heavy physical work, kept away from certain foods, abstained from

---

48   Ryan, 166.
49   Ryan, 168.

any sexual activity, and obtained and memorized "antiwoman magic" to protect himself when, finally, he had sexual contact with his wife. These taboos, common in the Highlands of New Guinea, were consistent with behaviors based on a belief in the dangerous impurity of women, as mentioned above. Breaking the taboos was believed to have two consequences: 1) the man physically wasted away (regarded as being "eaten" by the woman); and 2) his relatives could refuse to help him with the full bride price.

At the end of the month, after the full payment of the bride price, the groom staged a feast for the bride's relatives and all who had contributed to the bride price. The groom then killed the return gift pigs and some of his own, distributing the pork to show friendship toward his new affinal relatives and to acknowledge those who helped him with the bride price. The last step before the marriage was consummated was the bride and groom performing a private ceremony in her house, in which the couple each ate half of a cooked gourd. After the groom performed the "appropriate protective magic," the marriage was consummated within three days.[50]

The Mendi marriage rituals that Ryan describes reveal that marriage was both a "personal contract between two individuals" and—equally important—an alliance between two groups of people: the bride's relatives and the groom's relatives. The mandatory gift exchanges between the two groups established and supported "a network of friendly intergroup alliances brought about, and focused upon, the marriage." These two groups, formerly unconnected, were expected to maintain friendly relations by continual reciprocal economic exchanges for the duration of the marriage.[51]

Keeping in mind Ryan's description of Mendi marriage rituals in the mid-1950s, the reader may want to consider the contrast between the ritual of betrothal at that time and the more informal description provided in Monsignor Schmidt's letter of September 17, 1960, to Mrs.

---

50   Ryan, 166–167.
51   Ryan, 174–175.

Leota Motz, editor of the *Hays* (Kansas) *Daily News*. In that letter, sent so she could publish it for the readers of the newspaper, Monsignor Schmidt describes a *much* more informal action of settling the bride price, which took place between the father of the bride and her suitor. In fact, in a number of other letters Monsignor Schmidt wrote to his sister Mary, he tells of the sought-after bride not being consulted in the arrangements and then refusing to marry the suitor, which of course, disappointed him and angered her father. She might disappear into the bush and stay away until her father got over his anger. Based on the contrasts in the two accounts of marriage arrangements, it seems that, over time, the formal rituals of the 1950s became less formal, and the bride price became all important to the father of the bride, who frequently did not first take into consideration the bride's wishes.

Appendix C.

———◆———

A Brief History of
Papua New Guinea

ACCORDING TO THE *New World Encyclopedia,* the main island of New Guinea, the second-largest island in the world, lies just north of Australia. Today, the eastern half, including approximately 600 offshore islands, makes up the Independent State of Papua New Guinea, with a total land area of approximately 178,704 square miles. The western half, Irian Jaya, comprises the twenty-sixth province of Indonesia.

The topographical features and varied landscape of Papua New Guinea reveal relatively recent geological activity. About 20,000 years ago, the New Guinea mainland was connected to northern Australia by land. However, about 8,000 years ago as the climate warmed after the last advance of ice, the sea levels began to rise. The result was that the southern low-lying plains of Papua, part of the Australian Plate, were separated from Australia by the flooding of what today is called the Torres Strait. The northward-moving Australian Plate collided with the westward-moving Pacific Plate, causing faults and folding, contributing to volcanic eruptions, but ultimately resulting in plains that are stable.

The land north of these plains is a harsh, inhospitable environment consisting of a band of limestone riddled with fissures and sinkholes and covered in rainforest. Further north lie mountains running east to west (some higher than 13,000 feet) and fertile upland basins as high as 4,500 feet. These Highlands provide much cooler temperatures, and the inhabitants construct gardens laid out in grids where sweet potato is the staple crop. Finally, toward the north coast, the foothills of the mountains reveal slash-and-burn farming, where taro and yams are grown. Further on, mosquito-filled sago swamps along the Ramu and Sepik river courses give way to a well-populated fertile north coast that drops sharply to the sea.[52]

According to J. D. Waiko in his book *A Short History of Papua New Guinea*, as early as 40,000 to 60,000 years before the present, parts of New Guinea were likely occupied by successive waves of people from Southeast Asia. These people, known generally as Melanesians, arrived during the late Pleistocene era, at a time when the oceans were lower because ice sheets at the north and south poles retreated and advanced periodically.

Archeologists speculate that when the seas were lower, peoples from Southeast Asia traveled across the ocean in rafts or canoes made of bark, able to sight land both ahead and behind. Once arrived on other islands or the mainland of what became New Guinea, they gathered uncultivated food, hunted animals with wooden sticks, and fished if they were near the coast or rivers. For shelter, they used overhanging boulders or caves since they led a seminomadic existence. They lived in scattered groups, isolated from each other.

While colder temperatures prevailed in times of advancing ice sheets, tree lines in mountainous regions of Papua were lower than they are today; thus, high-altitude grasslands expanded, possibly offering opportunities for hunting and gathering. Evidence in the Mount

---

52 *Encyclopaedia Britannica*, 15th ed., s.v. "Papua New Guinea."

Hagen area of the Western Highlands suggests that yam, banana, and taro were easily grown as far back as 7,000 years ago. In fact, gardening became more important as clearing of the forest reduced the number of bush animals that could be hunted.[53]

EUROPEAN COLONIZING AND
THE ARRIVAL OF CHRISTIAN MISSIONARIES

At the end of the fifteenth century, Europeans began exploring and colonizing lands beyond Europe. By the sixteenth century, Europeans had become interested in trade, specifically the spice trade, and were keen to find the routes to that trade in the East Indies—and to bring Christianity to "heathen" peoples in as-yet-unknown parts of the world. In 1494, Portugal and Spain made an agreement, sanctioned by the Pope, that divided the world in two. On the map of the world, a straight line was drawn from the north pole to Greenland, then through eastern Brazil to Antarctica at the South Pole. The area east of the line of demarcation was designated as the Portuguese "sphere of influence" and, west of the line, the Spanish "sphere." Thus, the competition continued between the two countries, and by 1529, the Portuguese had secured control of the spice trade completely. By 1580, the Spanish and Portuguese had conquered Central and South America, and the Portuguese had posts along the African and Indian continents.[54]

With regard to New Guinea, a Portuguese sailor, Jorge de Meneses, is believed to have sighted and named Papua around 1526–1527; he supposedly named it *Ilhas dos Papuas*, ("Islands of the Curly-Haired Men"), derived from the Malayan word *papuas*, which describes the frizzled quality of Melanesian hair.[55] The name *New Guinea* came from the Spanish explorer Inigo Ortiz de Retes, who, navigating along the

---

53 Waiko, *A Short History of Papua New Guinea,* 7.

54 Waiko, 17.

55 Franco Zocca, "Papua New Guinea: Land of the Unexpected," in *SVD Word in the World* (Holland: Steyler Verlag, 1995/1996): 33.

north coast of the main island in 1545, claimed it for the king of Spain. He named it *Nueva Guinea* because it resembled the West Coast colony of Africa, Guinea, also claimed by the Spanish. Subsequently, the island was left largely unexplored until the late nineteenth century.[56]

According to Waiko, in the early seventeenth century, Luis Vaez de Torres, a Spanish explorer, charted the southern coast of New Guinea by navigating the narrow strait (eventually named for him) between Papua and Australia. During the seventeenth and eighteenth centuries, other English and French explorers navigated through islands of the Bismarck Archipelago.

The nineteenth century brought more foreigners to eastern New Guinea, including those looking for adventure and trade. In fact, companies with headquarters in Germany, Britain, and Australia were eager to exploit resources from the main island. Interested in gaining economic benefits, Germans set up coconut and tobacco plantations on the northern coast of Papua, using local people as easily available labor. When local labor was hard to get, people from neighboring islands were at times kidnapped and forced to work on the plantations, a practice known as blackbirding. Already having begun to exploit resources on the northern coast of New Guinea in the 1870s, Germany claimed the northeast quadrant of New Guinea as a protectorate in 1884; Germany then gave charge of its administration to a chartered German company until 1899, when it took direct control of the territory. Britain, and more specifically its province in Australia, Queensland, had more strategic reasons to maintain control of its interests and to gain labor for its sugar plantations. When Queensland formally tried to annex the southern half of the island of New Guinea, Britain refused the action and demanded that the territory be added to its possessions only if Australia covered the cost of administration. Australia agreed, and formal annexation occurred in 1884.[57]

Ultimately, the governments of the various foreign colonial powers

---

56 Waiko, *A Short History of Papua New Guinea*, 20.

57 Waiko, 24, 26.

saw positive economic results due to their control of lands in New Guinea. Thus, without any consultation with the native inhabitants, parts of New Guinea were claimed as possessions by European states at different times—the western half of the island was claimed by the Dutch in 1828 as part of the Dutch East Indies; Great Britain and Imperial Germany claimed the southeast quadrant and northeast quadrant in 1884 and 1899, respectively. Further, the southeast quadrant was annexed as British New Guinea in 1884.[58]

With the arrival of European colonial powers in New Guinea, from the late nineteenth century onward, English and French Christian missionaries (in addition to European traders and adventurers) also arrived on the island's southern and southeastern coastal areas. In the mid-1870s and before, English missionaries from the London Missionary Society (LMS) and the Wesleyan Methodist Missionary Society (forerunner of the Australasian Wesleyan Methodist Missionary Society [AWMMS]) established missions in Australasia.[59] Also, English Anglican missionaries arrived to set up missions in 1891 on the northern coast of British New Guinea. Further, the French Missionaires du Sacre-Coeur (Missionaries of the Sacred Heart [MSC]) founded a Catholic mission in 1885 on Yule Island, just off the southern coast of New Guinea. French sisters from the associated congregation, Filles de Notre-Dame du Sacre-Coeur (Daughters of Our Lady of the Sacred Heart), soon joined the mission.[60]

German Christian missionaries—both Lutherans and the Catholic Fathers of the Society of the Divine Word (SVD)—established missions on the north coast of the main island and the adjacent islands. German Lutherans established the first German mission at Finschafen in 1886,[61] and the Society of the Divine Word missionaries

---

58 Waiko, 24–26.

59 Diane Langmore, *Missionary Lives: Papua, 1874–1914* (Honolulu: University of Hawaii Press, 1989), 185,191.

60 Langmore, *Missionary Lives,* 1–3.

61 Waiko, *A Short History of Papua New Guinea,* 25.

arrived at Madang to set up a mission at Tumleo Island near Aitape in 1896.[62]

AUSTRALIAN ADMINISTRATION OF PAPUA

In 1906, under the Papua Act, the Commonwealth of Australia began to administer British New Guinea as Papua. In 1921, Australia took over German New Guinea and began its administration of New Guinea through a "Mandate under Covenant of the League of Nations."[63] With Australia carrying out its League of Nations mandate to oversee and govern the colony, Australian government officers and the European and Australian missionaries were in a position to have fairly close contact with Papuans. Also, according to Schieffelin and Crittenden, government officers were expected to carry out a number of tasks in their assigned districts—namely, to keep the peace, to explore new areas and make contact with tribal groups, and to bring these groups under the influence of the colonial Papuan administration. Government patrols were used to carry out these tasks. The patrols usually comprised "one or two white officers, a number of armed Papuan police, and a line of carriers"[64] who would walk from one village to another along an established path. Thus, the representative Europeans typically encountered by the Papuans were both government officers and the missionaries. Yet, according to Diane Langmore in *Missionary Lives: Papua, 1874–1914*, the missionaries "were generally in a stronger position to exert sustained influence on the Papuans than were the government officers" because of the importance the missionaries gave to learning the local languages and because of the location of the mission stations along the coast and on the islands (not just at centralized government district stations).[65] By the 1920s, after large gold deposits

---

62   Robert E. Pung, compiler, "Divine Word Missionaries in Papua New Guinea," in *SVD Word in the World* (Holland: Steyler Verlag, 1995/1996), 11

63   *Encyclopaedia Britannica*, 15th ed., s.v. "Papua New Guinea."

64   Schieffelin and Crittenden, "Colonial Papua and the Tradition of Exploration," 13.

65   Langmore, *Missionary Lives*, xi.

were discovered in Morobe Province in eastern New Guinea, more incursions were made by gold prospectors and missionaries. By the end of the decade, the Australian government, responsible for the safety of the Europeans, increased pacification patrols as a means to protect the missionaries and those with commercial interests.

EXPLORATORY EXPEDITIONS IN PAPUA

Through the 1920s and mid-1930s, several government-sponsored exploratory expeditions and patrols were conducted into the interior of Papua, which at the time was thought to be largely uninhabited. These expeditions had the purpose "to locate undiscovered natural resources (such as gold or petroleum), to open new regions to the sphere of Western political and economic influence, and to bring Western civilization and the rule of law to people generally regarded at the time as primitive savages."[66] According to Schieffelin and Crittenden, with all the interest in and claims made by European governments through the late nineteenth and early twentieth centuries, Papua became "one of the last places on earth to be incorporated within the sphere of European colonial expansion."[67]

Ian Downs in *The Australian Trusteeship: Papua New Guinea 1945–75* states that the 1933 expedition, made up of prospectors and government personnel, was surprised when it came in "contact for the first time with elements of population groups that probably exceeded 500,000. . . . Thus, in the space of one month, in 1933, the Government of the then Mandated Territory of New Guinea had its administrative responsibility for people doubled."[68] In fact, according to Schieffelin, by the mid-1930s "the interior of the island of New Guinea—protected from penetration over the centuries by rugged and

---

66 Edward L. Schieffelin, Introduction, in Schieffelin and Crittenden, *Like People You See in a Dream,* 1-11.

67 Schieffelin and Crittenden, "Colonial Papua and the Tradition of Exploration," 14.

68 Ian Downs, *The Australian Trusteeship: Papua New Guinea 1945–75* (Canberra: Australian Government Publishing Service, 1980), 175–176.

mountainous terrain, unruly rivers, and the bellicosity of its inhabitants—remained one of the few places outsiders had never seen."[69] The subsequent 1935 Strickland-Purari Patrol, commissioned by the Papuan colonial administration, covered the Southern Highlands of Papua between the Strickland and Purari Rivers. In the course of this expedition, highlanders first saw Europeans, who themselves first encountered unknown peoples still using stone technology. In short, in the 1930s, many Highlanders had their first encounters with Europeans and saw airplanes for the first time on reconnaissance trips through the area; they also found themselves the focus of interest from competing Christian missionaries. Australian government administrators, responsible for protecting the Europeans in the mandated area, saw the rivalry among missions as exacerbating hostilities among tribes, resulting in the killing of several missionaries, prospectors, and patrol officers. As a result, by 1935, the Highlands from Kainantu to Mount Hagen were "closed" to new ventures by Europeans.[70]

The Australian government–sponsored Strickland-Purari Patrol and fieldwork carried out by anthropologists in the 1930s, late 1940s, and 1950s gathered much information on the lives of the natives of the Southern Highlands of Papua New Guinea. The native population of the Territory of Papua was "by no means a homogeneous cultural group. Rather, it was fragmented into small, autonomous, often mutually antagonistic communities, speaking many different languages and exhibiting a bewildering variety of customs and beliefs." The people carried on subsistence farming by raising taro, bananas, and other crops; they lived in villages, raised pigs on a small scale, and hunted and fished.[71] (See Appendix B for more detail.)

---

69 Schieffelin, Introduction, 2.

70 Terence E. Hays, "A Historical Background to Anthropology in the Papua New Guinea Highlands," in Hays, *Ethnographic Presents*, 11-14.

71 Schieffelin and Crittenden, "Colonial Papua and the Tradition of Exploration," 18.

WORLD WAR II AND AFTER

In the late 1930s, the rise of Nazi Germany, the start of World War II, and Japan's eventual entry into war dramatically affected parts of New Guinea and other islands of Oceania. When the Japanese invaded New Guinea in 1941 and Papua in 1942, civil administration of Papua New Guinea ceased and was replaced by the Australian New Guinea Administrative Unit (ANGAU), which administered Papua until 1945. There was no exploration of the Southern Highlands during the war, and the Highlands peoples were hardly affected by the war.

After World War II, from 1949 on, Australia, which governed Papua, sought to open areas that had not been under its control before the war to missionaries and anthropologists. In 1949, Australian patrol officers reopened the government post at Lake Kutubu, Also, in 1949, Sydney Smith and Desmond Clancy, Australian government patrol officers, arrived in the Mendi Valley, where Clancy opened a station at Mendi and initiated the construction of an airstrip while Smith went on toward Ialibu. The following year Smith, Clancy, and Ron Neville traveled to the Tari Basin and established a government post at Tari in July 1951. The first Christian missionaries to arrive in the Southern Highlands were from the Methodist Overseas Missions, led by Reverend Gordon Young, who set up a camp at Mendi in 1950.

Indeed, with the Southern Highlands being the area of New Guinea least contacted by Westerners, the people there soon found themselves the focus of anthropologists and missionaries, including the Capuchin Franciscans.[72]

---

72   Stephen Reichert, "A Short History of the Mendi Mission," accessed September 9, 2008, http://www.shjboulder.org/SHJ_Parish/png.htm.

Bibliography

Bulmer, Ralph Neville Hermon. "The Kyaka of the Western Highlands." In *Gods Ghosts and Men in Melanesia: Some Religions of Australian New Guinea and the New Hebrides*, edited by Peter Lawrence and Mervyn J. Meggitt, 132-161. Melbourne: Oxford University Press, 1965.

Burkey, Fr. Blaine M.. "Bishop to Celebrate 25th Anniversary of Ordination." *Hays Daily News*, June 3, 1971.

———. *Only the Beginnings: Commemorating the Coming of the Capuchins and Their Co-Workers to the Southern Highlands of Papua New Guinea*. Denver: St. Conrad Archives Center, 2016.

———, ed. *"Schoolmaster" Schmidt and His "Family Album."* Hays, KS: Thomas More Prep/Marian, 1986.

Capuchin Friars: Province of St. Augustine. "Our Spirit & Life." http://www.capuchin.com.

Diamond, Jared. *The World Until Yesterday: What Can We Learn from Traditional Societies?* New York: Viking, 2012.

Downs, Ian. *The Australian Trusteeship: Papua New Guinea 1945–75.* Canberra: Australian Government Publishing Service, 1980.

Encyclopaedia Britannica, 15th ed., (2007) s.v. "Papua New Guinea."

Epstein, T. Scarlett. "Economy." In *Anthropology in Papua New Guinea*, edited by Ian Hogbin. Melbourne: Melbourne University Press, 1973.

Glasse, Robert M. "The Huli of the Southern Highlands." In *Gods Ghosts and Men in Melanesia: Some Religions of Australian New Guinea and the New Hebrides*, edited by Peter Lawrence and Mervyn J. Meggitt, 27–49. Melbourne: Oxford University Press, 1965.

Glasse, Robert M. and Mervyn J. Meggitt, eds. *Pigs, Pearlshells, and Women: Marriage in the New Guinea Highlands*. Englewood Cliffs, NJ: Prentice-Hall, 1969.

Global Edge. "Papua New Guinea: History," accessed January 7, 2014. http://globaledge.msu.edu/countries/papua-new-guinea/history.

Hays, Terence E., "A Historical Background to Anthropology in the Papua New Guinea Highlands." In *Ethnographic Presents: Pioneering Anthropologists in the Papua New Guinea Highlands*, edited by Terence E. Hays, 1-36. Berkeley: University of California Press, 1992.

Hogbin, Ian, ed. *Anthropology in Papua New Guinea: Readings from the Encyclopedia of Papua and New Guinea*. Melbourne: Melbourne University Press, 1973.

Langmore, Diane. *Missionary Lives: Papua, 1874–1914*. Honolulu: University of Hawaii Press, 1989.

Lawrence, Peter and Mervyn J. Meggitt, eds. *Gods Ghosts and Men in Melanesia: Some Religions of Australian New Guinea and the New Hebrides*. Melbourne: Oxford University Press, 1965.

McLean, Ann. "In the Footprints of Reo Fortune." In *Ethnographic Presents: Pioneering Anthropologists in the Papua New Guinea Highlands*, edited by Terence E. Hays, 37-67. Berkeley: University of California, 1992.

Meggitt, Mervyn J. "The Mae Enga of the Western Highlands." In Lawrence and Meggitt, *Gods Ghosts and Men in Melanesia*, 105–131.

Pung, Robert E., compiler. "Divine Word Missionaries in Papua New Guinea." In *SVD Word in the World* (1995/96): 33-38.

Reichert, Stephen, "A Short History of the Mendi Mission," accessed September 8, 2008, http://www.shjboulder.org/SHJ_Parish/png.htm.

Ryan, D'Arcy. "Marriage in Mendi." In *Pigs, Pearlshells, and Women: Marriage in the New Guinea Highlands*, edited by R. M. Glasse and M. J. Meggitt, 159–175. Englewood Cliffs, N. J.: Prentice-Hall, 1969.

———. "Meeting the Mendi." In *Ethnographic Presents: Pioneering Anthropologists in the Papua New Guinea Highlands*, edited by Terence E. Hays, 199–231. Berkeley: University of California, 1992.

Schieffelin, Edward L. and Robert Crittenden, eds. *Like People You See in a Dream: First Contact in Six Papuan Societies*. Stanford: Stanford University Press, 1991.

Schieffelin, Edward L. and Robert Crittenden. "Colonial Papua and the Tradition of Exploration." In *Like People You See in a Dream: First Contact in Six Papuan Societies*, edited by Edward L. Schieffelin and Robert Crittenden, 13-43. Stanford: Stanford University Press, 1991.

Schmeidler, Debra, Myra Staab, Pam Schmidt, Dolores Schmeidler, Glenda Schuetz, Shirley, Lawrence Schmeidler, Fr. Michael Suchnicki, and Emery Schmidt, eds. *St. Catherine Church: 100 Years, 1892–1992.* Hays, KS: Northwest Printers, 1992. 18.

Schmeidler, Debra, ed. *A Genealogy Collection of Parishioners: St. Catherine Church; St. Severine Church*, 1998.

Stakem, O. F. M. Cap. Gary. "History of the Diocese of Mendi." Catholic Diocese of Mendi, accessed August 8, 2018, http://www.mendidiocese.com "Looking to the Future."

St. Catherine's Parish: Catherine (Katharinenstadt) Kansas, 1876–2001, 125 Years. Hays, Kansas: Northwestern Printers, 2001.

Strathern, Andrew. "Looking Backward and Forward." In *Ethnograpic Presents,.* 250–270.

Waiko, John Dademo. *A Short History of Papua New Guinea.* 2nd ed. Melbourne: Oxford, 2007.

Zocca, Franco. "Papua New Guinea: Land of the Unexpected." In *SVD Word in the World,* 33–38.

Lightning Source UK Ltd.
Milton Keynes UK
UKHW020754110121
376821UK00007B/152